The Economics of Tax and Social Security in Japan

Yoshimi Adachi

The Economics of Tax and Social Security in Japan

Springer

Yoshimi Adachi
Faculty of Economics
Konan University
Kobe, Hyogo
Japan

ISBN 978-981-10-7175-1 ISBN 978-981-10-7176-8 (eBook)
https://doi.org/10.1007/978-981-10-7176-8

Library of Congress Control Number: 2017959901

Printed on acid-free paper

This Springer imprint is published by the registered company Springer Nature Singapore Pte Ltd.
part of Springer Nature
The registered company address is: 152 Beach Road, #21-01/04 Gateway East, Singapore 189721, Singapore

Preface

The Comprehensive Reform of Social Security and Tax: Japan (hereafter The Comprehensive Reform) was implemented with the aim of stabilizing social security, securing stable financial resources, and reconstructing finances. Social security accounts for a large proportion of the expenditure items in the finances of not only Japan but also other developed countries. Alongside a population aging remarkably fast, Japan's social security expenditure for the elderly, including pensions, medical care, and long-term care, have continued to increase and the country is now facing the problem of how to reduce this expenditure.

Among the developed countries, Japan has an economy that is in a serious condition and is impinging on the state's ability to support its social security system through insurance contributions and tax revenues. Therefore, to fulfill its fiduciary duty, the government is relying on government bonds. The question then arises of how to position the tax system to secure stably financial resources to overcome such structural weaknesses. There have long been arguments over determining the main basis for taxation: whether consumption and income are preferred or a combination of both is desirable. Most current arguments favor the selection of income tax and general consumption tax. However, the trust in income tax has eroded, while the comprehensiveness of the taxation base and an accurate supplementation rate are both difficult arguments to deal with. In addition, the effects of a progressive tax rate structure on economic activities are notable.

Therefore, in The Comprehensive Reform, importance is given to securing stable financial resources, and consumption tax is cited as the main financial resource. The idea of raising the consumption tax rate to secure the financial resources required for social security has been under consideration for quite some time.In the second half of the 1970s, it was foreseen that the increase in social security expenditure due to an aging population would pose a threat to finances in the future. In 1979, the Liberal Democratic Party's (LDP's) Ohira administration aimed to introduce a general consumption tax, and then in 1987, the Nakasone administration proposed the initiation of a broad-based indirect tax, a sales tax; eventually neither was introduced. In 1988, the Takeshita administration enacted the Consumption Tax Law and introduced a 3% consumption tax from April 1989. In February 1994, the

Hosokawa administration, which took over from the LDP administration, proposed raising the tax rate to 7%, changing the name to National Welfare Tax, as a financial resource for social security, but in the face of opposition, the proposal was withdrawn. After the creation of a coalition that included the LDP, in 1994 the Murayama administration decided to raise the tax rate to 5%, which came into effect in April 1997. The Asian currency crisis began in the same year (1997) and Japan slipped into an economic recession.

The facts that the cabinet collapsed on the introduction of the consumption tax and that the hike in the tax rate overlapped with the timing of the Asian currency crisis are reasons that the Japanese people have a negative view of the consumption tax, and it is Japan's political Achilles heel. In 2008, the Hatoyama government of the Democratic Party of Japan (DPJ) came to power and pledged it would not raise the consumption tax rate. However, it was unable to secure sufficient financial resources for social security, and the DPJ administration was forced to change its policy.

In 2012, the Noda Cabinet submitted a bill to raise the tax rate to 8% in 2014 and then to 10% in 2015, and the bills were passed. Subsequently, in December 2013, once again, the administration changed hands, and an LDP–Komeito coalition government came into power.

In April 2014, the Abe administration raised the consumption tax rate to 8%. However, in November of the same year, the government announced its decision to postpose the scheduled increase to 10% in 2015 by a year and a half.

Even during this period, social security expenses continued to increase. The system of long-term care insurance was introduced from fiscal 2000. With a rapidly aging population on the one hand, the need for social security services is rising; but on the other hand, the biggest challenge facing Japan is how to secure stable financial resources to pay for social security.

Several measures are currently being undertaken through The Comprehensive Reform to address this challenge. Certainly, the consumption tax is an important financial resource for social security, but at this time it is important to consider not only the consumption tax, but also individual indirect taxes. Having said that, the consumption tax is not the only financial resource for social security. If the consumption tax is considered to be the only financial resource in The Comprehensive Reform, then the outlook becomes extremely narrow.

Important financial resources for social security are insurance contributions and self-payments (primarily, the amount paid by individuals themselves). Income taxation also plays an important role as a financial resource and it must be considered widely in the framework of The Comprehensive Reform. In fact, income taxation largely supports Japan's finances, including social security finances, as a fundamental tax.

In this book, we consider the approach to be adopted for The Comprehensive Reform in order to analyze the methods for allocating the tax burden, which is a financial resource for social security, and the enormity of the burden social security will place on households, companies, and the government. The prologue explains the point of view taken in the book, the specific analyses in each chapter, and the approach for The Comprehensive Reform in the final chapter. As the author, I will be extremely happy if this book contributes toward the progress of that reform.

*** *** ***

In terms of the conclusions I reach in this book, I am grateful for the useful comments that I received from many people, even at different stages of publishing each chapter as research theses and presenting reports at conferences. While writing this book, I received several research grants that have supported me up to the present. The grants include those from: the Japan Society for the Promotion of Science KAKENHI Grant-in-Aid for Scientific Research, Fundamental Research (C) "Verification of policies to support women's employment, childbirth, children, and childcare in a declining birth-rate society"; the Univers Foundation Research Grant, "Study on households' consumption and burden of medical care and long-term care services"; and Government Finances, Finance, and Financial Legislation Research Fund Research Grant, "Analysis of the financing of social security services in local governments".

I also received assistance for the publication of this work as an academic book from the Japan Society for the Promotion of Science fiscal 2014 and fiscal 2015 Grants-in-Aid for Scientific Research. It would not have been possible to publish the book without these grants. I would like to thank all the people concerned, including those at the grant-related organizations and those who reviewed my applications and allocated the grants. Finally, as the author I would like to use this opportunity to express my gratitude to the teaching faculty and employees at Konan University who provided me with such a satisfying education and research environment.

Kobe, Hyogo, Japan
Spring 2018

Yoshimi Adachi

The original version of the book was revised: Author corrections have been incorporated. The erratum to the book is available at https://doi.org/10.1007/978-981-10-7176-8_11

Contents

Chapter 1
Prologue: Outlook and Challenges for Social Security Finances

1 Social Security and Consumption Tax

As shown in the Fig. 1, since the basic framework of the social security system in Japan was built in the 1960s, the socioeconomic situation which is the premise for the social security system has dramatically changed. While social security benefits have risen rapidly as a result of the population aging, the persistently weak economic growth has invited the fall in the tax revenues after the mid-1980s of the bubble levels and social insurance premiums have failed to catch up with the benefits expansion with the premium-benefits gap widening. Despite the fact that government has taken initiatives to control social security benefits, the gap between benefits and premiums continues to widen.

The gap has been covered not only with tax revenues but also with massive debt issues. Over the past two decades, Japan's gross public debt has more increased to well over 200% of GDP. With gross government debt of 219% of GDP in 2016, Japan's fiscal situation puts the economy at risk. It is important thesis for the revenue measures to bring down the high level of public debt in Japan. If this situation does not change, it may become difficult to sustain the present social security system so that we could support livelihood of citizens including elderly people and contribute to the world's highest life expectancy. Therefore, we must secure stable financial resources for maintaining the social security system to improve Japan's fiscal situation which is in a more difficult situation than in foreign countries.

In Japan, the year 2014 brought about major developments for social security finances, with the implementation of The Comprehensive Reform of Social Security and Tax (hereafter The Comprehensive Reform), which had been a concern for a long time. The Comprehensive Reform of Social Security and Tax Systems was conducted from the perspective of aiming to simultaneously accomplish securing stable revenues to finance social security and implementing fiscal consolidation, and the government will comprehensively and intensively establish a sustainable social security system that has a balance between benefits and burdens.

Y. Adachi, *The Economics of Tax and Social Security in Japan*,
https://doi.org/10.1007/978-981-10-7176-8_1

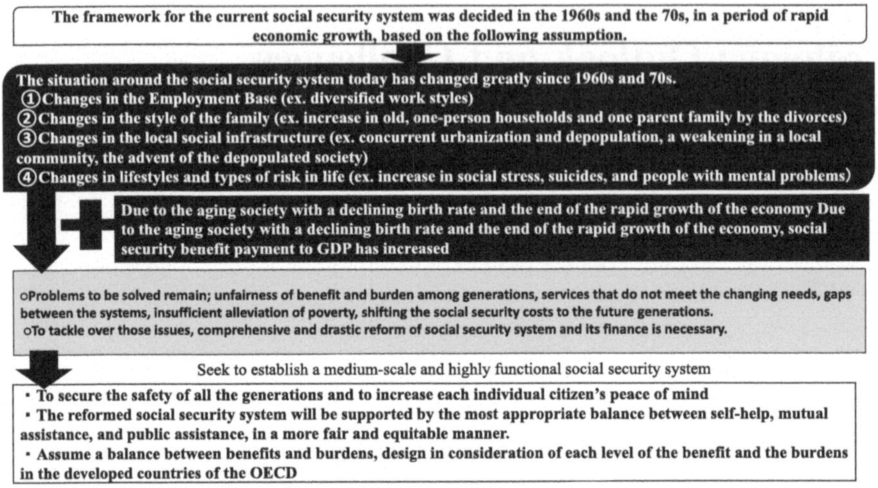

Fig. 1 The whole picture of the reform of social security *Source* Based on "Comprehensive Reform of Comprehensive Reform of Social Security and Tax," by the Department of the Ministry of Health, Labour and Welfare, Japan

Fiscal consolidation should be accompanied by introducing the earned income tax credit to assist the working poor, increasing the tax on capital income and brooding the base of the inheritance tax, and especially hiking in the consumption tax rate toward the OECD average. The biggest change that occurred was the hike in the consumption tax rate implemented on April 1, 2014. The tax rate rises to 8% during the administration of Prime Minister Abe Shinzō. In June 2016, the Abe Cabinet announced that the consumption tax rate would be raised to 10%. The consumption tax had been set to increase to 10%, up from 8%, effective April 2017. However, the prime minister decided to postpone the planned increase in the consumption tax rate given certain concerns about the economy. The prime minister on June 1, 2016 announced that a scheduled increase in the rate of the consumption tax will be postponed until October 1, 2019.

Rising the consumption tax in Japan would generate the significant revenue and play an important part for the other countries. Many advanced economies face the rising social security spending according with the aging population. Japan's social security finances have followed a consistently deteriorating path, but it can be assumed that they are approaching a major turning point. Therefore, in The Comprehensive Reform, importance is given to securing stable financial resources, and consumption tax is cited as the main financial resource. The idea of raising the consumption tax rate to secure the financial resources required for social security has long been under consideration.

In the second half of the 1970s, it was foreseen that the increase in social security expenditure due to an aging population would pose a threat to finances in the future. In January 1979, the Liberal Democratic Party's (LDP) Ohira administration aimed to introduce a "general consumption tax" to improve public finances, but abandoned the plan in the face of a severe public backlash in the October general election. Then in February 1987, the Nakasone administration proposed the initiation of a broad-based indirect tax, the "sales tax" to the Diet, but abandon it in May due to widespread public opposition.

In December 1988, the Takeshita administration enacted the Consumption Tax Law and introduced a 3% consumption tax from April 1989. In June 1989, Prime Minister Takeshita is forced to resign in the wake of an insider-trading and corruption scandal involving the human-resource company Recruit. In February 1994, the Hosokawa administration, which took over from the LDP administration, proposed raising the tax rate to 7% and changing the name of the tax to "National Welfare Tax," as a financial resource for social security; however, the plan was opposed and withdrawn the day due to a lack of coordination within the coalition government led by Prime Minister Hosokawa Morihiro. After the creation of a coalition that included the LDP, in November 1994 the Murayama administration decided to hike the consumption tax rate from 3% to 4% and add a regional consumption tax of 1%, bringing the total to 5%. The tax rate to 5% came into effect in April 1997 under Prime Minister Hashimoto Ryūtarō. The Asian currency crisis began in the same year (1997) and Japan slipped into an economic recession.

Every time the introduction of the consumption tax increase tax is considered, the cabinet collapsed. So raising the consumption tax rate has been a risky policy, and it is Japan's political "Achilles heel." In 2008, the Hatoyama government of the Democratic Party of Japan (DPJ) came to power and pledged it would not raise the consumption tax rate. However, it was unable to secure sufficient financial resources for social security, and the DPJ administration was forced to change its policy.

In September 2009, the Democratic Party of Japan, led by Hatoyama Yukio, was elected to set up an election declaration pledging no consumption tax hike for 4 years. After Naoto Kan took over the leadership of the Democratic Party, just before the House of Representatives election, the Democratic Party announced that the consumption tax would be raised to 10%, so the Democratic Party was defeated in the election in June 2010. In June 2012, the Noda Cabinet submitted a bill to raise the tax rate to 8% in 2014 and then to 10% in 2015, and the bills were passed in the upper house plenary session. Subsequently, in December 2013, once again, the administration changed hands, and an LDP-Komeito coalition government came into power. In April 2014, the Abe administration raised the consumption tax rate. From the importance of balancing economic revitalization with fiscal consolidation, securing the comprehensive sustainability of social security and tax systems, and maintaining Japan's credibility as a result of comprehensive considerations of the economic situation, etc., the Abe administration raised the consumption tax rate from 5% to 8% in April 1, 2014.

This is based on Article 18 of Supplementary Provision of the Act on Partial Revision, etc. of the Consumption Tax Act for Comprehensive Reform of Tax to Secure Stable Financial Resources for Social Security, etc. Hereinafter referred to as the "Comprehensive Tax Reform Act" and Article 19 of Supplementary Provision

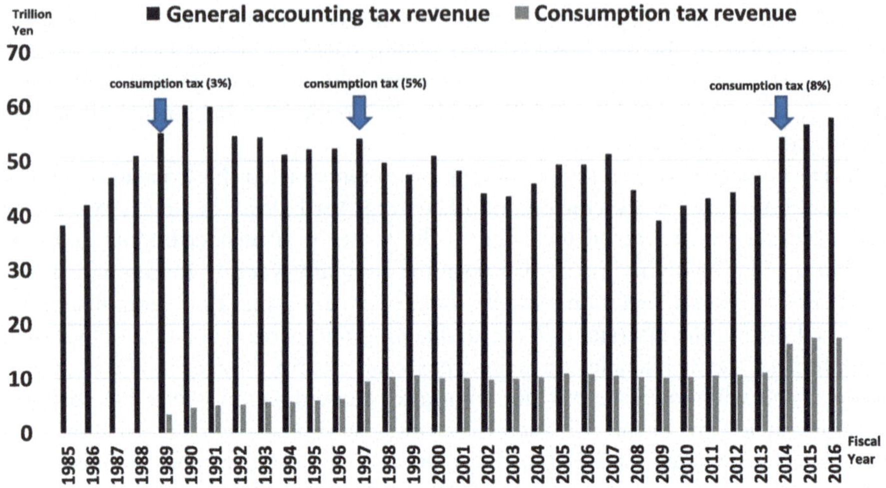

Fig. 2 Total tax revenue and consumption tax *Source* Based on "Total tax revenue and consumption tax" by the Department of the Ministry of Finance, Japan

of the Act on Partial Revision, etc. of Local Tax Act and Local Allocation Tax Act for Comprehensive Reform of Tax to Secure Stable Financial Resources for Social Security, etc." However, in November of the same year, the government announced its decision to postpose the scheduled increase to 10% in 2015 by a year and a half. Figure 2 shows the trends in total tax revenue and consumption tax.

Even during this period, social security expenses continued to increase. The system of long-term care insurance was introduced from fiscal 2000. On the one hand, with a rapidly aging population, the need for social security services is rising; but on the other, the biggest challenge facing Japan is how to secure stable financial resources to pay for social security. A recent question that has been raised is whether the hike in the consumption tax rate to 10%, which is scheduled for October 2019, will be sufficient to provide the financial resources needed for social security in the future.

However, raising the consumption tax will not mobilize sufficient financial resources for social security. In future, due to a rapidly aging population, the costs required for social security will continue to grow and, therefore, it will be necessary to continuously strive to secure the financial resources for social security.

2 Current State of Social Security Finances

In this section, we will examine the overall situation for social security finances in Japan. Figure 3 shows the trends in social security benefits and income from insurance contributions and international comparison of Burden Ratio. Social security benefits include "pensions," "medical care," and "other welfare." Income from

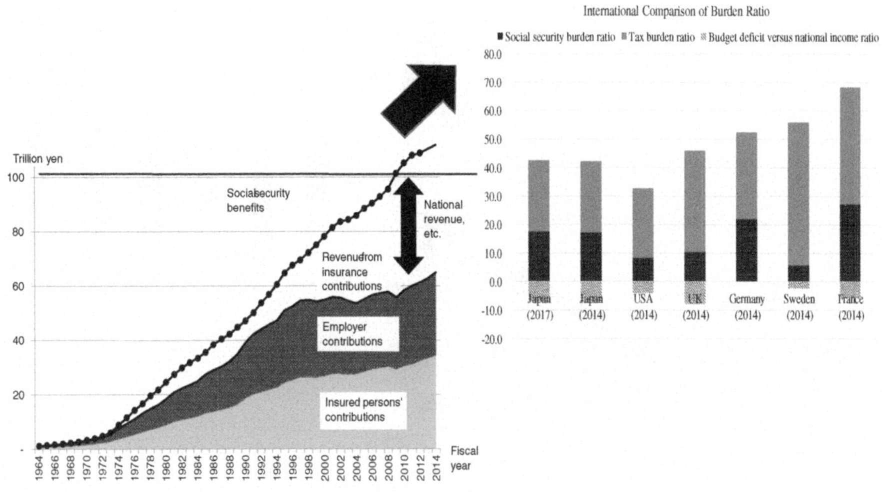

Fig. 3 Trends in social security benefits and income from insurance contribution and international comparison of Burden Ratio *Source* Based on "Social Security Costs Statistics," by the National Institute of Population and Social Security Research, Japan and in OECD "Social Expenditure Database" and other resources

insurance contributions consists of employer contributions and insured person's contributions.

Along with the advancement in the aging society, the amount of social security benefits payable has been increasing significantly, while the amount of social insurance premiums receivable has been flat, resulting in the widening of the gap between social security-related expenditure and revenue. Although the social security system in Japan is based on social insurance system, the gap between social security benefits and revenues of social insurance contributions has been subsidized by the central and local governments. The burden of the central government increases by one trillion yen level every year and most of its financial resources depend on public debts. This is the main reason of worsening fiscal deficit. If the current situation is left unaddressed, it would be difficult to maintain the existing social security system in the future.

The Japanese government continues to run a budget deficit, as its expenditure exceeds its tax revenue. The gap between the two has expanded since the 2008, due largely to a fall in tax revenue associated with the economic downturn. This gap has been financed by issuing debt of government bonds. The outstanding amount of Japan's government bonds has increased year after year, reaching 865 trillion yen at the 2017, which is 15 times as large as the annual tax revenue. This accumulated debt will impose heavy burden on future generations.

The causes behind an increase in the outstanding government bonds after the 1990, in which Japan temporarily ended reliance on special deficit-financing bonds. While in the 1990s the growth in expenditure was mainly attributable to an increase in public works-related expenditures, recent increase in expenditures has been

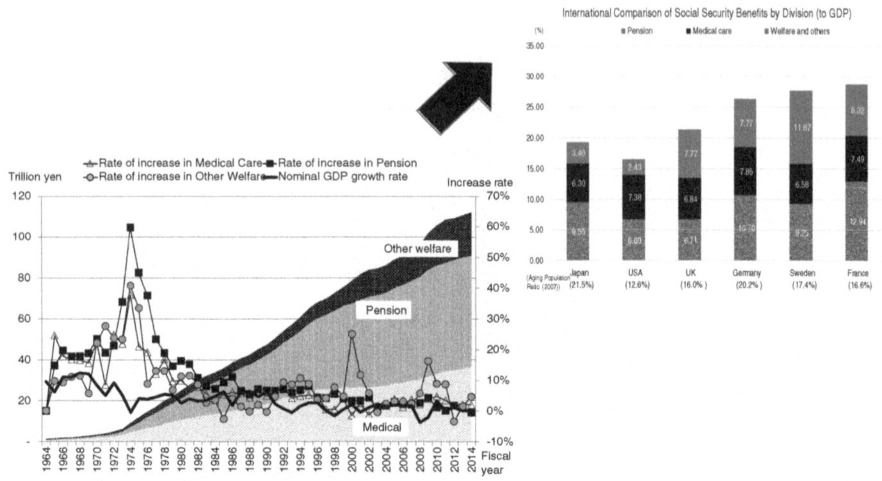

Fig. 4 Trends and rate of increase in items constituting social security benefits and international Comparison of Social Security Benefits by Division (to GDP) *Source* Based on "Social Security Costs Statistics," National Institute of Population and Social Security Research; "National Accounts Statistics" by the Cabinet Office, Government of Japan and in OECD "Social Expenditure Database" and other resources

largely driven by (i) an increase in social security-related expenditures due to population aging; and (ii) an increase in Local Allocation Tax Grants, etc, due to deterioration in local public finance. On the revenue side, the government revenue has decreased mainly because of a fall in tax revenues because of the economic downturn and tax cuts.

There are some trends in items constituting social security benefits, namely "pensions," "medical care," and "other welfare." Long-term care is included under "other welfare." Within social security benefits, "pensions" has the largest share, followed by "medical care" and "other welfare." Figure 4 shows the trends in the rate of increase in each of these items within social security benefits and International Comparison of Social Security Benefits by Division (to GDP). Fiscal year 1973, which shows a high rate of increase, corresponds to "the first year of welfare" when the aim was to supplement social security benefits. From the high growth rate of "pensions" of 60%, and of "medical care" and "other welfare" at 40%, we understand that social security benefits have increased.

Figure 4 also shows the nominal GDP growth rate. We will compare the nominal GDP growth rate and the rates of increase of items constituting social security benefits. There was a period in the 1980s when the rate of increase of "other welfare" was below the nominal GDP growth rate, but apart from this period, nominal GDP growth rate has clearly been lower than the rate of increase in social security benefits. The reason for a high rate of increase in "other welfare" in fiscal 2000 is that long-term care was introduced during that year.

What we understand from the trends in nominal GDP growth rate and the rate of increase of social security benefits is that during every period in the past, social security benefits increased at a higher rate than the nominal GDP growth rate. No country can have social security benefits that exceed its nominal GDP, and a situation in which the rate of increase in social security benefits is higher than the nominal GDP growth rate cannot continue indefinitely. Therefore, it is not possible to say that Japan can sustain the current level of benefits in its social security system. To ensure the sustainability of social security benefits, at the very least the GDP growth rate must match the rate of increase of social security benefits. In addition to raising the consumption tax rate, securing other financial resources to increase the efficiency of social security benefits is an important task.

Generally, the social security burden is comprised of self-payments and insurance contributions. Essentially, self-payments are the burden on the household when receiving medical care and long-term care services. If the self-payment ratio is high to secure financial resources, the social security benefits would be suppressed. However, it cannot be assumed that increasing the self-payment ratio and controlling the consumption of social security services is the preferred option. There is a risk that more people will suffer from serious medical conditions if their receipt of medical care services is limited by a high self-payment ratio. A high self-payment ratio also places a heavy burden on low-income earners.

Self-payments are considered as either a fixed-rate burden, fixed-amount burden, or a combination of the two. The fixed-rate burden is linked proportionally to the monetary amount received for the social security services, and the relationship between benefits and burdens is clear. Primarily, the fixed-amount burden relates to the receipt of social security services. Thus, self-payments are considered as a burden placed on the beneficiary.

The main financial resource for social security benefits is income generated from insurance contributions, which are divided into employer contributions (the portion contributed by companies) and insured person contributions (those made by the insured person). That is, half of the Social Insurance tax is deducted from employee salary and the other half is paid by the company.

In Japan, insurance contributions take the form of contributions for pension insurance, health insurance, and long-term care insurance. Of these insurances, all people is enrolled in the public pension and health insurance programs. This universal coverage in public pension and health insurance is a main characteristic of the Japanese social security system. Citizens aged 40 and over are covered by the long-term care insurance, and employees are also covered by the employment insurance and work-related accident insurance.

The social insurance systems mentioned above are financed by social insurance premiums and supplemented by the tax revenue in forms of subsidy. The social insurance premiums are shared by all insured according to their ability to pay the level of income. Thus, the function of social insurance is to share the risk. Unlike self-payments, insurance contributions are not associated with the receipt of social security services at the current point in time, but are linked to the possibility of and eligibility to receive them in future. In the case of pension insurance contributions, if a person does not pay contributions while working, he/she cannot receive pension benefits after retirement (pension age). In principle, if people do not pay contributions for both health insurance and long-term care insurance, they cannot receive medical care services or long-term care services.

For insurance, the contribution history is decisively important, and if there is no history of contributions, the person cannot avail of social security services. One of the features of social security is that the contribution history relates to the right to receive it.[1] In terms of being able to receive social security services only by subscribers who have continued paying social insurance premiums in advance, the point that the social security system is different from the tax system is that the relationship between benefits and burdens is consistent. The right to receive social security services derives from insurance contributions, and in this sense, the relationship between benefits and burdens is constructed.

What are the conditions for tax? In general, we cannot see a relationship between specific public services and benefits.[2] For example, we cannot specify which taxation financial resources are allocated to police services or to fire services. There are also no records on tax burdens that are linked to public services, as is the case with the history of insurance contributions. Even within the various taxes, under the general provisions of the budget, consumption tax is currently allocated as a welfare financial resource. Also in The Comprehensive Reform, which is currently in progress, the portion obtained from the hike in consumption tax rate has been determined to be a financial resource for social security expenses.[3]

There have been various debates on whether consumption tax is a suitable financial resource for social security. Specifically, the relationship between receipt of social security services and the burden of consumption tax has been debated. It would seem difficult to recognize a relationship in which the higher the consumption monetary amount is, and the greater the burden of consumption tax on the household, the greater the receipt of social security services. Therefore, it is difficult to find a clear relationship between benefits and burdens in the consumption tax, as is the case for self-payments and insurance contributions.

Inherently, self-payments and insurance contributions, in which the relationship between benefits and burdens is clear, are preferable from the perspective of

[1]The right to benefits is not a guarantee of an absolute amount of social security services. For example, in the public pension, a macroeconomic slide could reduce pension benefits in the future.

[2]In the case of special-purpose tax, it is strongly related to specific public services, but in Japan, the share of tax revenue for special-purpose tax is not that great, so it is not considered here.

[3]As of fiscal 2015, within the consumption tax rate of 8%, the national consumption tax rate is 6.3% and the local consumption tax rate is 1.7%. Within the tax revenues from the national consumption tax, excluding the 22.3% that represent the financial resources for local allocation tax subsidies (the allocation tax rate), 76.7% is the financial resource for social security. Further, within the local consumption tax rate of 1.7%, a 0.7% portion (this portion was raised in April 2014) is allocated to social security for local governments. Even when the hike in the tax rate to 10% scheduled for October 2019 comes into effect, it has been determined that the portion gained from this rise in tax rate will be the allocated to social security. At this time, the plan is to reduce the allocation tax rate of consumption tax to 19.5%.

benefits and burdens because they make up for the deficit in the financial resources available to social security services. As shown in Fig. 3, in recent years, revenue from insurance contributions has hit a ceiling and has ceased to increase, so there are limitations to relying on insurance contributions. The approach of increasing the self-payment ratio should be considered, but if it is increased excessively, people will avoid using or will be unable to receive the social security services they need to maintain their quality of life. Within the different types of taxes, we should consider the reasons for choosing consumption tax as the financial resource for shoring up the social security system. Certainly, there is no direct relation between the amount of consumption tax burden and the receipt of social security services. It can be assumed that social security services for medical care, long-term care, and pensions will be the components that most people have experience of receiving in the past or will probably get in the future. In considering with the people's life cycle, social security services are services that everyone receives over their lifetime, while consumption tax is the tax that everyone pays over their lifetime. In this sense, consumption tax and social security services are in a relationship of benefit and burden.[4] In this sense, we can perceive a loose relationship between the benefits and burdens of consumption tax and social security services.

In The Comprehensive Reform, one of the objectives for the hike in consumption tax is to supplement the portion of "national revenue" that relies on the issue of deficit government bonds. Compared to self-payments and insurance contributions, the relationship between consumption tax and receipt of social security services is weak, but it is also implicit that it is the "better" choice compared to that between the latter and deficit government bonds. Presently, the current generation benefits from social security services and deficit government bonds are a burden that will be placed on future generations (their children and grandchildren). Therefore it is also necessary to understand "The Comprehensive Reform" of Social Security and Tax" from this time-axis viewpoint.

3 Japan's Difficult Economic and Financial Conditions Will Likely Continue into the Future

As can be seen from Fig. 3, social security benefits are trending upward on a scale of several trillion yen each year, surpassing 100 trillion yen in recent years. In contrast, income from insurance contributions has remained unchanged below 60 trillion yen. Against this background, the slump in income from insurance contributions is considered to be attributable to factors such as the prolonged recession, changes to employment structure, declining birth rate, and income inequality.

The shortfall between social security benefits and income from insurance contributions has been greater than 40 trillion yen in recent years. To supplement for

[4]It cannot be assumed that every person pays income tax.

this deficit in financial resources for social security, financial resources other than income from insurance contributions have been introduced, such as self-payments for medical care and long-term care. However, insurance contributions and self-payments alone cannot cover social security benefits. Thus, "national revenue" was introduced. This means that the state is supplementing the financial resources for social security. The problem, as shown in Fig. 3, is that national revenue has been expanding year by year. Moreover, financial resources for "national revenue" are not only tax revenues, but include deficit-financing government bonds issued to compensate for the revenue shortfall as well.

There are several choices available by means of which financial resources for social security could be secured. As shown in the book titled "*The Economics of Tax and Social Security in Japan*", in order to secure the necessary financial resources for social security, it is important to examine ways to secure resources from taxes and social security burden. In Japan, social security benefits and contributions, healthcare expenditures, public pension expenditures, and long-term care insurance expenditures , are increasing in line with the rapid aging of the population.

It is projected that the size of the social security costs will increase rapidly because of the aging population. In particular, the benefits of health and long-term care will face higher growth than the projected GDP growth, toward 2025 when all of the first baby boomers will be 75 years old and over. Therefore, by the beginning of the 2020s (i.e., when part of the first baby boomers starts to be 75 years old and over.), we need to establish a well-balanced social security system, which strikes the balance between contributions and benefits.

The current social security benefits are mainly for the elderly, and it is not sound financial management by the government to introduce deficit government bonds to mobilize the financial resources needed for these costs. The costs of one year's social security benefits for the present living generation will be paid for by their children's and grandchildren's generation in the form of deficit government bonds that must be repaid over the course of decades. The introduction of "national revenue" causes a discrepancy in the benefits and burdens received and borne by the current generation and by their children and grandchildren's generations. Future generations such as children and grandchildren will continue paying debt treasury bonds over decades due to social security benefits of the current elderly generation. To provide a stable and efficient social security system that will be sustainable in the future, Japan must eliminate intergenerational inequality and secure a balance between social security benefits and contributions.

In The Comprehensive Reform, it was determined that tax revenues from the hike in consumption tax rate would be allocated to financial resources for social security. Most of the tax revenue from the tax increase is to be allocated to that part of national revenue used to supplement social security benefits. In fact, The Comprehensive Reform aims to restore to a robust position the unhealthy social security finances that have been reliant on deficit government bonds by covering the gap with tax revenues. This will improve the sustainability of social security finances and normalize the relationship between benefits and burdens.

There are various indicators of the state of Japan's finances, but primary balance is the best orthodox indicator. Today, revenues and expenditure in Japan's finances can be shown as follows.

$$\text{Revenues} = \text{public bonds revenue} + \text{tax revenue, etc.} \quad (1)$$

$$\text{Expenditures} = \text{public bonds expenditure} + \text{general expenditure, etc.} \quad (2)$$

Figure 5 is a conceptual representation showing revenue and expenditure in Japan's finances assuming the country's general account budget. Here, revenue from public bonds is obtained from the issuance of new public bonds.[5] In "tax revenue, etc.," "etc." refers to non-tax revenue, such as from stamps and the sale of assets. Public bond expenditure is comprised of expenditure to redeem the public bonds and their interest payments. General expenditure indicates policy expenditure, such as for social security, public works, education, and defense, and the "etc." in "general expenditure, etc." indicates tax subsidies allocated to local governments.

To simplify, tax revenues, etc., are a "burden" on the current generation, and "benefits" from public services provided to the current generation are general expenditure, etc.[6] Within tax revenues, etc., most of the revenue is a financial resource for welfare purposes, apart from the part that is a financial resource for tax subsidies allocated to local governments. Therefore, it constitutes a part of the financial resources for expenditure relating to social security.

Based on the above definition, the primary balance is shown as follows.

$$\begin{aligned}\text{Primary balance} = {} & \text{tax revenue, etc. (burden)} \\ & - \text{general expenditure, etc. (benefits)}\end{aligned} \quad (3)$$

Primary balance can be either a surplus or a deficit. In the case of a primary balance surplus, the current generation's "burden" exceeds its "benefits." Conversely, in the case of a primary balance deficit, "benefits" surpass "burden." Figure 5 shows a primary balance deficit. If using the relation that revenue=expenditure, the following relations are established.

$$\begin{aligned}\text{Primary balance surplus} \Leftrightarrow {} & \text{public bonds revenue} < \text{public bonds} \\ & \text{expenditure}(=\text{expenditure to redeem public bonds} \\ & + \text{interest payments})\end{aligned} \quad (4)$$

[5]As refunding bonds are issued from special accounting of the Government Debt Consolidation Fund, they are abstracted here.

[6]Strictly speaking, since public expenditure is expected to benefit future generations, such as from pubic work projects, it is included in general expenditure. Therefore, while it cannot be said that general expenditure is completely for the benefit of the current generation, here, for the sake of brevity, the discussion is simplified.

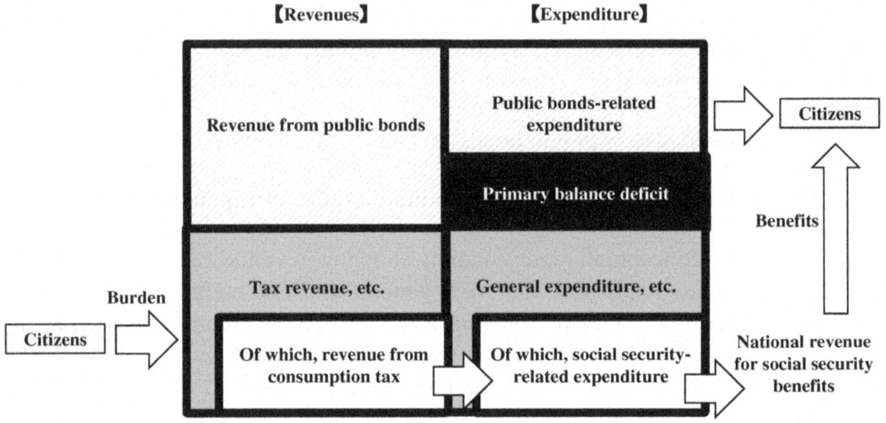

Fig. 5 General Account Expenditures and Tax Revenues

$$\text{Primary balance deficit} \Leftrightarrow \text{public bonds revenue} < \text{public bonds expenditure} (= \text{expenditure to redeem public bonds} + \text{interest payments}) \quad (5)$$

Public bonds expenditure includes expenditure to redeem public bonds and interest payments. In the case of a primary balance surplus, if public bonds revenue = expenditure to redeem public bonds, the government public bonds balance will be constant over time. Unfortunately, Japan's finances are constantly in a state of primary balance deficit. Normally, a relation of public bonds revenue > expenditure to redeem public bonds is established, and the government's public bonds balance increases.

For the primary balance, it is necessary to think not only nationally, but also locally. There is the concept of the "national and local long-term debt balance" as the government's debt redemption expenses and the tax financial resources cover interest payments. According to the Ministry of Finance, the national and local long-term debt balance at the end of fiscal 1998 was 553 trillion yen, but had risen to 692 trillion yen by the end of fiscal 2003 and 770 trillion yen by the end of fiscal 2008, and finally surpassed 1000 trillion yen at the end of fiscal 2014. When primary balance is achieved, bonds outstanding increaseby the amount equivalent to interest payment.This is because new bond issues can only be allotted to debt redemption andinterest payment. In this case, if, for example, the nominal GDP growth rate equals the nominal interest rate, bonds outstanding increase at the same rate as the nominal GDP. As a result, the bonds outstanding to nominal GDP ratio remains stable.

To control the cumulative increase in the long-term debt balance, it is vital to reduce the primary balance deficit and change it to a surplus.

The ratio of the national and local primary balance to nominal GDP has been in deficit since the 2000s. As the primary balance is in deficit, the long-term debt balance is accumulating. To curb the accumulation of long-term debt balance, it is essential to convert primary balance from a state of deficit to achieve a surplus.

The Japanese government is aiming to achieve a national and local primary balance surplus by fiscal 2020. The government has set up the following fiscal consolidation targets: 1. To halve the primary deficit of the central and local governments to GDP ratio by fiscal 2015 from the ratio in fiscal 2010, 2. To achieve a primary surplus by fiscal 2020, and 3. Thereafter, seeking to steadily reduce the public debt to GDP ratio.

In Fig. 6, we conducted projections under two different macroeconomic scenarios. First, "economic revitalization cases." The following economic and fiscal policies are assumed to have sound effects: aggressive monetary policy, flexible fiscal policy, and a growth strategy that promotes private investment. In the medium to long term, the average annual growth rate is projected to reach more than 2% in real terms and more than 3% in nominal terms. The rate of change in the consumer price index (excluding the direct effects of the increase in the consumption tax rate) is projected to be stable, at around 2%, in the medium to long term. Second, "baseline cases." The domestic economy is assumed to grow approximately at the rate of current potential growth. In this case, in the medium to long term, the average annual growth rate is projected to be less than 1% in real terms and mid 1% in nominal terms.

The primary deficit of central and local governments is projected to meet the fiscal target of halving the ratio of deficit to GDP from the fiscal 2010 rate by fiscal 2015 (about 3.3% of GDP). In the "economic revitalization cases", the primary deficit is projected to remain about 9 trillion yen (1.7% of GDP) in fiscal 2018, the year to review the progress of reform measures during the Intensive Reform Period

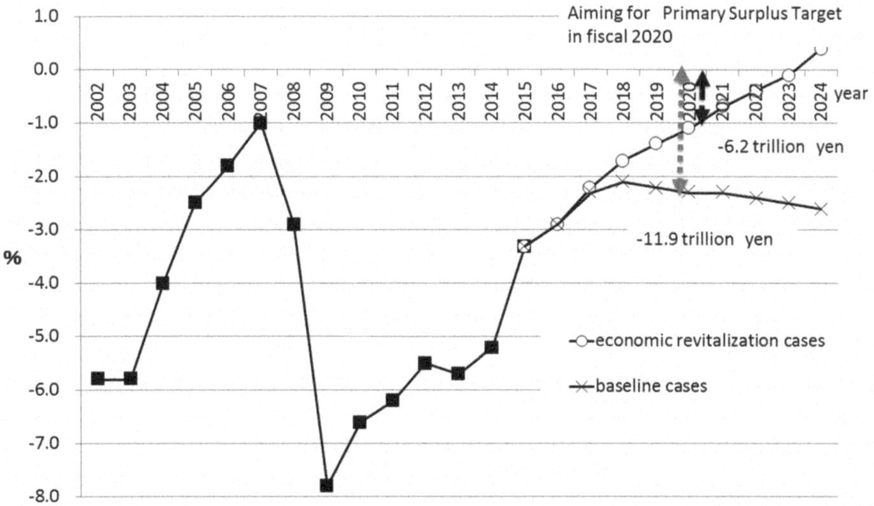

Fig. 6 Trends in the ratio of national and local primary balance to nominal GDP *Source* Based on "Provisional calculation of medium-to long-term economic finances," by the Cabinet Office, Japan

(fiscal 2016–2018) by the benchmark of about 1% of GDP, and about 6.5 trillion yen (1.1% of GDP) in fiscal 2020, the target year for reducing the deficit to zero, and it is important to continue enhancing "Integrated Economic and Fiscal Reforms."

The Comprehensive Reform is being implemented, but as can be seen from Fig. 6, it is a long way from achieving a surplus in fiscal 2020, even for the "economic revitalization cases." Both the "economic revitalization cases" and "baseline cases" incorporate the hike in the tax rate to 10%, which is scheduled for fiscal 2019. Even in the "economic revitalization cases," as of fiscal 2020, the ratio of the national and local primary balance to nominal GDP will be negative 1.6%, which is on a scale of 9.44 trillion yen. Therefore, "the Economic and Fiscal Projections for Medium- to Long-term Analysis" published by the Cabinet Office, the fiscal 2020 primary surplus target cannot be achieved even with the GDP growth of 3% in nominal and 2% in real. Therefore, the government formulated the fiscal consolidation plan called "The Plan to Advance Economic and Fiscal Revitalization(Cabinet Decision on June 30th, 2015) " which shows the clear trajectory toward achieving the fiscal consolidation target and expenditure reform measures.

On considering that 1% in the consumption tax rate is equivalent to tax revenues of 2.7 trillion yen, this in fact corresponds to revenue from a tax rate of 3.5%. Even if it is hiked to 10% in October 2019, there will once again be a shortage of financial resources to pay for social security benefits in the future. This can be shown from simple calculations.

According to information from Japan's Ministry of Health, Labour, and Welfare, a 5% hike in the consumption tax rate would increase revenue by approximately 13.5 trillion yen, and a 1% increase would be equivalent to 2.7 trillion yen and would become a viable financial resource with which to supplement social security. A 4% increase would be equivalent to 10.8 trillion yen, an increase that would stabilize social security.

A 4% increase in the tax rate equivalent to 10.8 trillion yen would likely be used to stabilize social security, but a large proportion of the financial resources needed to restore social security to a normal state would still depend on government deficit bonds. Specifically, maintaining the treasury burden rate at half of the basic pension requires around 7 trillion yen from government deficit bonds as national revenue, which will put in around 2.9 trillion yen. With regard to the state treasury's burden for the basic pension, it has been managed with unhealthy finance strategies such as that in which, over two years, financial resources were secured by issuing government bonds.

Therefore, on hiking the consumption tax rate to 10%, only 2.7 trillion yen can be used to supplement social security services. Even if the consumption tax rate is hiked, it will not improve social security services. From the perspective of citizens, it is a major factor that any hike in the consumption tax rate would not actually improve social security services.

However, The Comprehensive Reform of Social Security and Tax is very significant in terms of escaping the reliance on government deficit bonds in order to finance social security. It will be difficult to maintain social security finances without a hike in the consumption tax rate.

As seen in Fig. 3, which shows the increase in costs for social security benefits, these costs are increasing at the rate of several trillion yen a year alongside an aging population. Therefore, if the consumption tax rate is hiked, we can clearly see that soon there will once again be a shortfall in financial resources and it will be necessary to rely on government deficit bonds. The period during which social security is stabilized following a 10% hike in the consumption tax may in fact be very short.

The government likely wants to avoid having to hike the consumption tax rate again as it forces people to bear the financial burden. Thus, for precisely this reason, it cannot neglect its efforts to keep down expenditure. We must keep in mind that social security expenses are currently the largest expenditure item in Japan's finances, and they are increasing at the rate of several trillion yen a year. On considering the scale of social security expenses, the practice of restraining spending on expenses other than for social security alone cannot cover the mounting social security expenses. Alongside reducing expenditure to the minimum possible level, it is also necessary for the government to once again consider hiking the consumption tax rate and securing other financial resources.

4 With Economic Growth, Increasing the Tax Burden and Reducing Expenditure

For the government to reach its goal of achieving a surplus in the future, it will be essential to increase the burden, using measures including hiking the consumption tax rate, reducing expenditure, in addition to realize economic growth. Therefore, the answer to the question of which of the following should be implemented—increasing the burden, reducing expenditure, or realizing economic growth to achieve fiscal reconstruction—is "all of them."

In order to ensure sustainable public finance and social security system, it is necessary to deepen discussion on a link between the increase in social security benefits due to population aging and their financing burden borne by the general public.Japan's tax and social security contributions ratio (in national income terms) remains lower than those of other countries. In comparison with the OECD member countries, Japan's social security expenditures fall within the mid-level, while its tax and social security contributions ratio remains at low level. Most Japanese citizens do not want the burden to increase or expenditure to reduce. There is resistance from related parties not only to increasing the burden, but also to lowering expenditure that will also reduce public services. Therefore, normally people think that it is best if financial reconstruction is achieved only through economic growth.

Certainly, if economic growth is realized, tax revenues will increase and progress will be made in fiscal reconstruction. However, it seems impossible to expect

Japan to achieve high economic growth in the future, especially to the extent that financial reconstruction will be realized without having to increasing the burden or reducing expenditure. Moreover, if the economic growth rate increases, interest rates will also rise. An increase in interest rates will increase the government's interest payments and causes its finances to deteriorate. Further, as the economic growth rate rises, the pressure on the government to increase expenditure grows stronger.

Amid the dramatic changes in the social and economic circumstances, we are now facing the challenge as to how we should maintain and enhance our social security system while promoting the economic growth. At the same time, we should also strive to consolidate our national finance, which is currently at the worst level among major developed countries, by securing stable financial resources for social security. Thus, the government is pushing ahead the reform with the aim of simultaneously achieving two priority goals: enhancement and stabilization of social security and fiscal consolidation.

In the comprehensive system reform currently underway, the government plans to revamp the tax system thoroughly, including increasing the consumption tax rate, with the aim of achieving both enhancement and stabilization of social security and fiscal consolidation simultaneously. An increase in tax revenue resulting from the consumption tax hike of 10% will be appropriated in full as the financial resources for social security for the benefit of all citizens.

Under the annual general budget provisions, the national consumption tax revenue had been currently allocated only to the costs for the elderly (basic pension, medical care, and nursing care). The comprehensive reform expands the range of purposes to which the national consumption tax revenue is allocated to cover the costs for social security (pension, medical care, nursing care, and responding to declining birthrate) and makes this policy clear by law.

Therefore, increasing the burden is considered to include not only hiking the consumption tax rate, but also raising other taxes, insurance contributions, and self-payments. Measures such as increasing self-payments for medical service costs and the self-payment ratio for long-term care services for high-income earners are reforms that should be considered for implementation alongside the hike in consumption tax rates.

Further, reforms seem inevitable in the near future, as the present framework of The Comprehensive Reform cannot resolve the difficult conditions for social security finances. At that time, showing the results of a policy evaluation on social security finances and households' tax and social security burden will be essential to consider approaches in the future in the period after The Comprehensive Reform.

Even if social security finances are in a difficult condition, it is not possible to request that an unlimited burden be placed on households. If the burden structure is not clarified, or more specifically the responsibility that will be imposed on households, and the impact on the activities of households and companies—both private sector economic agents—is not considered, it will be difficult to conduct a policy evaluation of the tax and social security burden. Based on this background and on awareness of this problem, the objective of this book is to ascertain the current state of households' tax and social security burden and conduct a policy evaluation to consider approaches for the period after The Comprehensive Reform.

Economic growth in Japan slowed down following the collapse of the economic bubble in 1991 and the Lehman bankruptcy in 2008. Within the mature Japanese economy, it is extremely important to increase the sustainability of the social security system by ascertaining the effects the burden of tax and insurance contributions have on households and companies and to conduct a policy evaluation.

5 The Perspective of This Book

This book analyzes the effects of the tax and social security burden on the finances of private sector economic agents, namely households and companies, and on government (national and local) finances, and conducts a policy evaluation of the tax and social security burden. The perspectives for analysis in this book are as follows: (1) the impact on household and corporate behavior, (2) the effect of income redistribution and burden structure, (3) the impact of insurance contributions on tax revenues and income, and (4) the relationship between benefits and burdens, and regional disparity. Figure 7 shows the relationship between the subjects, viewpoints, and the objectives of analysis in this book.

The Prologue summarizes the current state of government finances and the background to The Comprehensive Reform. Chapters 2–9 describe the analysis conducted based on real data. In Chap. 2, on the basis of household income and consumption data, a lifecycle model is used to analyze the structure of the burden of tax and insurance contributions. The analysis is performed based on the tax and

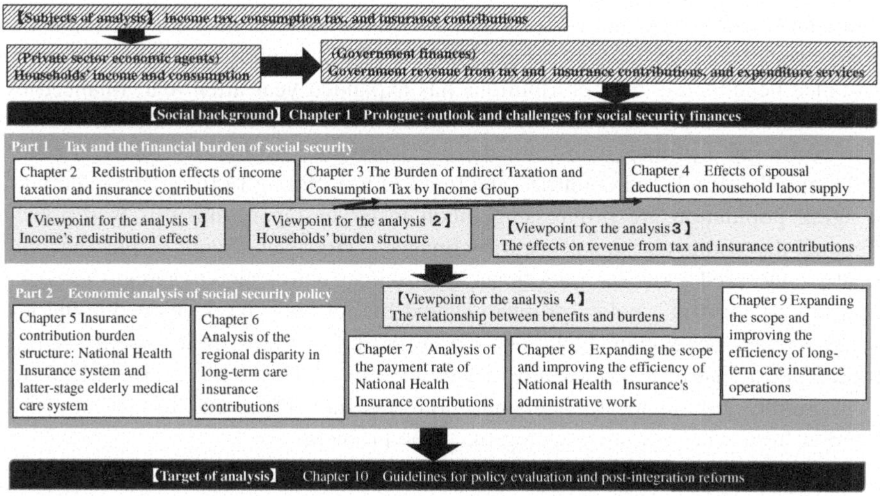

Fig. 7 Relationship between the themes in each chapter of this book

social security redistribution structure, lifetime burden rate, and the marginal effective tax rate from the lifecycle viewpoint.

Further, in Chap. 3, while considering the impact on the income taxation (personal deductions) and social insurance premiums, the economic burden and redistribution effect of tax on households is evaluated. Chapter 4 examines the effect of indirect tax on households by income class. This chapter shows the effects of income deductions for income taxation, consumption tax and individual indirect tax, and insurance contributions.

Next, the focus is on the National Health Insurance system in local finances, the latter-stage elderly medical care system, and medical care and long-term care services within long-term care. In Chaps. 5 and 6, the relationship between benefits and burdens is clarified from the burden structure and regional disparity in households' insurance contributions.

In addition, in Chap. 7, an analysis is conducted on the factors determining the payment rate and the incentive structure concerning revenue from insurance contributions in the National Health Insurance system in local finances. The reason for focusing on the National Health Insurance system is that compared to the tax and other social security systems, its payment rate is particularly low.

In Chaps. 8 and 9, the focus is on the National Health Insurance system under the jurisdiction of municipalities and the costs of long-term care administrative work. Further, the existence of economies of scale is verified and whether or not expanding scale in terms of number of insured persons is effective for improving efficiency in each of the operations.

Chapter 10 summarizes the conclusion based on the analyses, conducts a policy evaluation of the tax and social security burden, and considers the approaches for the period after The Comprehensive Reform.

With the rapid progress of aging population, Japan's social security cost, including (among others) pension, medical care, and long-term care, has grown significantly, faster than the corresponding social security contributions has. While Japan's social security system is based on a social insurance, the gap between the insurance benefits and the contributions has expanded year after year, financed by the burden borne by central and local governments.This burden has increased every year, becoming a primary cause for the fiscal deficit.

Among the developed countries, the trend of a declining birth rate coupled with an aging population are progressing much faster in Japan, and this is seriously affecting the country's social security finances. However, Japan is not the only country concerned about securing financial resources with which to support its social security system; it is a policy problem shared by not only the developed countries, but also many developing countries. To solve the problem of its social security finances, Japan has resolved to immediately implement. The Comprehensive Reform; it is currently putting the recommended reforms into effect, and this is attracting attention from other countries facing the same problem.

Part I
Tax and the Financial Burden of Social Security

Chapter 2
Redistribution Effects of Income Taxation and Insurance Contributions

1 Introduction

French economist Thomas Piketty's best-selling book has raised awareness of inequality. In Japan, income inequality has been increasing since the mid-1980s. Since the later 1980s, people face urban–rural disparities during the period of rapid economic growth, a wealth gap between haves and have-nots during the economic bubble, and the adverse effects of structural reforms were implemented by the Koizumi administration. The biggest factor in widening income inequality among the working-age population is the expanding low-income class due to increasing temporary employment. With companies focused on cutting costs, more temporary workers are hired given their relatively lower wage levels. Increasing numbers of the elderly with a wide income gap and no-employed people are also contributing to widening inequality. Middle-class income levels are decreasing, raising the risk of slipping into poverty. Japan's relative poverty rates rose since the 1980s, that is, from 12.0% in 1985 over 16% in 2000s. The percentage of households on welfare percentage of public assistance recipients has grown in single-mother households and the other households. One in six children live at less than half average living standard. The poverty rate of children in single-mother households is over 50%, the highest among OECD in 2010.

If the market determines income distribution, income inequality will increase; therefore, the government's income redistribution function plays an important role to correcting this problem. The government's direct methods of redistributing income are the tax system and the social security system. Before such a redistribution can take place, it is necessary to conduct a quantitative evaluation of the extent of its effects on income inequality.

The redistribution effects of income tax come from the various types of deductions and the tax rate itself, and the greater the deductions the higher the increase in households' after-tax income. However, if the tax rate is increased, households' after-tax income is reduced.

Y. Adachi, *The Economics of Tax and Social Security in Japan*,
https://doi.org/10.1007/978-981-10-7176-8_2

There are two types of deductions, tax deductions and income deductions, and both have different effects on income redistribution. Tax deductions are made from the calculated tax amount, and income deductions from the income amount. The decision depends on whether or not each type of deduction can be used, based on a household's attributes such as number of dependents and income. Therefore, the redistributive effects of income tax depend on the characteristics of the household in question.

The effects of income deductions on income redistribution vary based on the marginal tax rate faced by the household. Even if the income deduction is a fixed amount, if the marginal tax rate the household faces is lowered (or raised), then the household's after-tax income will be reduced (or increased). On the other hand, the tax rate's income redistribution effect depends on the extent of an excessive progressive tax rate. If the tax rate is highly (or less) progressive, the effect of income redistribution becomes larger (or smaller).

The redistribution effects of income deductions and the tax rate affect revenues from income tax. The stronger the income redistribution function, the greater the decrease in revenue from income. A tax revenue loss due to deductions not only leaks out from the revenue in a government's budget, it is not recorded as expenditure.

In addition to income taxation, insurance contributions also have redistribution effects that change households' disposable income. For example, income taxation is imposed on the basis of a household's income in a single year, and insurance contributions are made according to the household's employment situation.

Contributions and benefits from the social security system occur over the household's lifetime. In particular, in the public pension system, if a person does not pay pension insurance contributions when working, he/she cannot collect pension income after retirement. Moreover, a feature of the public pension system is that income inequality during the working period is carried forward into the retirement period. Pension benefits increase a household's disposable income during the retirement period, so it would not be sufficient to analyze only the pension insurance contributions made during the working period.

When evaluating the redistribution effects of income taxation and insurance contributions, measuring redistribution effects by using a household's income at a certain point in time is insufficient, as it does not consider time. Instead, when evaluating the redistribution effects of income taxation and insurance contributions over time, rather than at a single point in time, it is necessary to use a time axis that takes a household's lifecycle into account. Based on this point, research measuring redistribution effects has been advanced using households' microdata.

In this chapter, time axis and the household lifecycle are combined and the redistribution effects of income taxation and insurance contributions are evaluated. When evaluating income taxation and insurance contributions on the time axis, it is particularly important that the evaluation be based on the effects of revisions to the system. Therefore, as a preliminary consideration, a representative household model will be used to capture the changes to income taxation and insurance contributions over the years.

2 Previous Research on the Redistribution Effects of Income Taxation and Insurance Contributions

The analysis of most tax and transfer policy issues requires knowledge about how much is paid in taxes and received in benefits, by whom and in what circumstances. Moreover, in assessing existing tax-benefit policies and proposing reforms, it is useful to compare levels and structures of taxes and benefit. The complexity of relevant rules governing tax liability and benefit entitlement and a lack of comprehensive and comparable data at the micro-level has led to major efforts being directed toward finding methods to construct simple summary indicators such as implicit effective tax rates based on revenue statistics and national accounts data. While these measures can provide important insights regarding aggregate payments, they cannot answer questions about their detailed incidence. There have been several previous studies on the redistribution effects of the tax system and insurance contributions, but in relation to this chapter, we will focus only on studies that dealt with household microdata.

Abe (2000), Oishi (2006), and Fukawa (2006) used individual questionnaire data from the Ministry of Health, Labour and Welfare's "Income Redistribution Survey" to evaluate the redistribution effect. Abe (2000) showed that insurance contributions exacerbate the extent of inequality among the current working group, and the regressivity of medical insurance contributions and pension insurance contributions was high in that group's elderly generation. Oishi (2006) found that intra-generation income inequality is spreading in the working generation after redistribution from tax and insurance contributions, while Fukawa (2006) concluded that the expansion in income inequality between all households widened in the 1990s and the regressivity of insurance contributions by low-income households was due to the functional decline of the income redistribution policy. Tanaka et al. (2013) analyzed the "National Survey of Family Income and Expenditure" carried out by the Ministry of Internal Affairs and Communications, and found that income taxation was lower for the elderly, aged 65 years or over, than for those aged below 65 years.

Oshio and Urakawa (2008) used individual questionnaire data from the Ministry of Health, Labour and Welfare's "Comprehensive Survey of Living Conditions" and showed that income inequality has been contracting from 2000 onwards, and that the effects of income redistribution policy are limited to the elderly group. Oshio (2009) considered the lifetime income and the lifetime burden amount as lifetime bases with constant rates of interests, and clarified that, as is also the case at a single point in time, there is regressivity for the social security burden of the low-income group. Kitamura and Miyazaki (2012) and Ohno et al. (2013) used the "National Survey of Family Income and Expenditure," "Comprehensive Survey of Living Conditions," and the "Family Income and Expenditure Survey" by Ministry of Internal Affairs and Communications, and evaluated lifetime-based tax and insurance contributions, deriving results similar to those of the previous studies referred above.

Takayama and Shiroshi (2010) used anonymous data from the "National Survey of Family Income and Expenditure," and showed the regressivity of consumption tax by income group, generation, and family structure. Tanaka (2010) clarified the regressivity of consumption tax on the basis of the "Comprehensive Survey of Living Conditions" and the "Survey on Income Redistribution."

The above-described previous research used microdata from the "Survey on Income Redistribution," "Comprehensive Survey of Living Conditions," and "National Survey of Family Income and Expenditure" to clarify the redistribution effects of the tax system and insurance contributions. The "Survey on Income Redistribution" and "Comprehensive Survey of Living Conditions" are reported every three years, and the "National Survey of Family Income and Expenditure" every four years.

The analytical methods used by the above-mentioned researchers were as follows: the researchers evaluated the redistribution effects in using microdata from multiple years at a point in time. Moreover, by classifying according to household attributes, income groups, intergenerational, and family structure, they attempted to separate all of the redistribution effects.

Thus, while there are evaluation methods on the basis of income and consumption at points in time, there are also methods to evaluate in the lifetime. The concept of the lifetime base in previous research involved linking household data on people of different ages living at a point in time, processing the data so that it showed the lifetime of a household, and measuring the redistribution effects based on this data. That is, many analysis of the effects of the tax and benefit system is based on snapshot information about a single cross-section of people.

However, such an approach does not process the lifetime base data while considering the passage of time. It gives only a partial picture because it cannot account for the fact that circumstances change over life. Income mobility is higher for them, with career breaks, time off paid work, and short working hours. These episodes may have important long-term consequences for the employment and earnings capacity, suggesting that considering a long accounting period while controlling for the dynamics of employment and wages is especially relevant in distributional analysis. Households at a particular point in time have diverse heterogeneity and would have encountered in the past the tax system and the social security system, and will encounter these systems in the future.

Therefore, in this chapter, by considering the passage of time, households' microdata will be extended on the time axis, and income will be evaluated from present discount value from the viewpoint of the lifecycle in order to measure the redistribution effects of income taxation and insurance contributions. It investigates how our impression of redistribution undertaken by the tax and social security system changes when viewed from a lifetime perspective. We examine the properties of the current tax and social security system as well as historical and hypothetical reforms from both a lifetime and a snapshot perspective. We find that much of what the tax and social security system achieves is effectively to redistribute across periods of life and, as a result, it is much less effective.

Previous studies that used the lifecycle concept, which considers the passage of time in order to evaluate the tax system and the social security system, include Hashimoto et al. (1991), Maekawa (2004), Nakajima and Uemura (2006), and Hashimoto (2009). A feature of these studies is that they assumed a representative household for a single generation. This analytical method is suitable for intergenerational evaluations. However, it cannot evaluate intragenerational income inequality caused by factors such as the family structure and employment conditions. The effects of income taxation and insurance contributions on income inequality are not only intergenerational but also intragenerational; therefore, it is important to conduct evaluations from the perspective of intergenerational and intragenerational household heterogeneity.

In this chapter, taking a comprehensive approach comprised of the analytical methods used in previous research studies, intergenerational and intragenerational income inequality are measured while considering the passage of time, and income taxation and insurance contributions are evaluated.[1]

3 Households' Burden Rate from the Representative Household Model

When evaluating the tax system and the social security system, apart from an analysis using real data, it is also possible to use virtual data to conduct an analysis. It is quite relevant to conduct an analysis using virtual data because this type of data sometimes highlights the features of a system.

First, virtual representative household models are assumed, and revisions to the system are evaluated from information obtained on the households' burden rate when these models are applied to income taxation and insurance contributions. The representative household models are kept as simple as possible. Further, it is seen how the results of the analysis change when the assumptions based on the representative household model are slightly altered. Therefore, the household burden rate in each year is defined as in formula (1).

$$\text{Household burden rate} = \frac{\begin{array}{c}\text{income tax burden amount} + \text{individual resident tax burden amount}\\ + \text{insurance contribution burden amount}\end{array}}{\text{household income}} \tag{1}$$

We will consider the following eight cases as the representative household models. To analyze changes to the tax burden rate alongside changes in household attributes, the head of household's income is maintained at a constant. Specifically, the actual income of the head of household in 2004 shall be 5 million yen. The

[1]The model used in this chapter is from Uemura (2015b), who analyzed public pension deductions.

reason for selecting a level of 5 million yen is that this amount is considered to represent the average income for this income group in households with two or more workers.[2]

- Case 1: (head of household, 5 million yen, spouse unemployed)
- Case 2: (head of household 5 million yen, spouse unemployed, 1 child)
- Case 3: (head of household 5 million yen, spouse unemployed, 1 child, 1 senior citizen)
- Case 4: (head of household 5 million yen, spouse unemployed, 2 children)

Here, it is assumed that children and senior citizens are eligible for dependent deductions and elderly dependent deductions. Moreover, the consumer price index is used (according to the "Consumer Price Index Annual Report" by the Ministry of Internal Affairs and Communications), with 2004 set as 1; price adjustments are carried out, and their actualization is measured for household income at different points in time.

- Case 5: (head of household 5 million yen, spouse 2 million yen)
- Case 6: (head of household 5 million yen, spouse 2 million yen, 1 child)
- Case 7: (head of household 5 million yen, spouse 2 million yen, 1 child, 1 senior citizen)
- Case 8: (head of household 5 million yen, spouse 2 million yen, 2 children)

Next, it is assumed that the spouse is working, earned an annual income of 2 million yen in 2014, and was not eligible for spousal deduction. Here, the impact of a working spouse on the household burden rate will be analyzed.

With regard to the above representative household models, income tax from 1958 to 2012 and the individual resident tax system are applied to the household's income, and the household burden rate is measured in terms of income taxation and insurance contributions as a percentage of income.[3] Figure 1 shows the trends in the household burden rate.

---

[2]According to the Ministry of Internal Affairs and Communications' "Family Income and Expenditure Survey Report in the 2013," among worker households with two or more people "annual income" is 4.59 million yen for people aged under 30 years, 5.89 million yen for people in their 30s, and 6.33 million yen for people in their 40s.

[3]For reforms to the tax system and the social security system, I referred to *Financial Statistics: Tax Edition* by the Policy Research Institute of the Ministry of Finance, Japan. A tax reduction on the fixed rate of income tax was also considered.

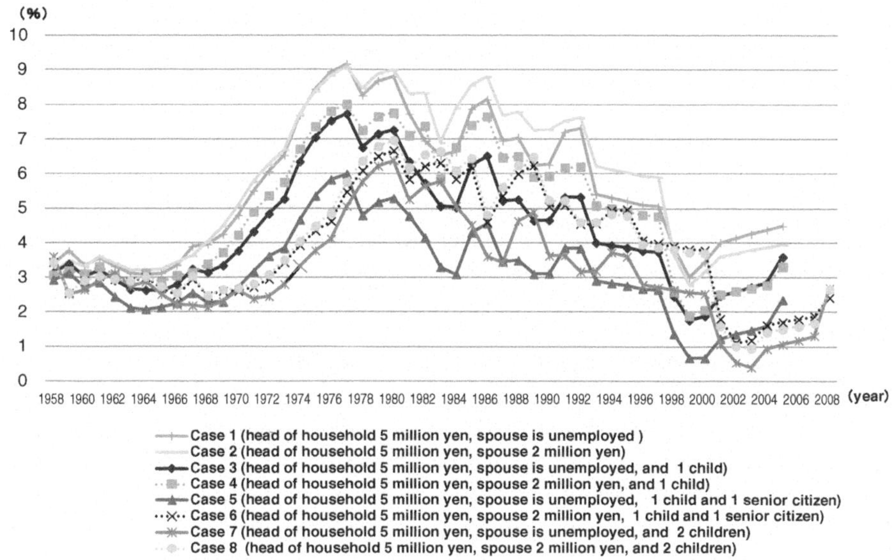

Fig. 1 Trends in the household burden rate from a representative household model

First, for the same real household income of 5 million yen, the tax burden rate on the households on a lifetime basis by using the micro-household data has been increasing to the first half of the 1970s. During the 1980s and 1990s, it is increasing and decreasing repeatedly, with the tax burden rate reaching its lowest level in 2005. Following this trend in the tax burden rate, we see that the middle-income group's household burden rate became heavier up to the first half of the 1980s, and the subsequent revisions to the tax system caused a tax reduction for the middle-income group.

Even within 1980s–2000s period, in 1989 when consumption tax was introduced, the middle-income group's income tax burden was conspicuously heavy. After the collapse of the bubble economy in the second half of the 1990s, once again, the income tax rate imposed a heavy burden on the middle-income group, and tax reductions, mainly for the middle-income group, were implemented continuously up to the first half of the 2000s, causing the household burden rate to decline.

Further, we will verify the changes to the household burden rate that result from an employed spouse. Comparing the case of an unemployed spouse (case 1) with the case of an employed spouse earning 2 million yen a year (case 2), we see that the household burden rate is higher when the spouse is unemployed (case 1) than when the spouse is employed (case 2). The difference in the household burden rate, whether or not the spouse is employed, has been expanding since 1980.

The revisions to the tax system for spousal deductions and special spousal deduction seem to have had a major effect on the spouse's employment choice. The tax burden rate trended to a higher level when the spouse was unemployed (case 1)

and remained at a low level when the spouse was employed (case 2), which is possibly a factor underlying the decline in the number of households in which only one spouse works, and an increase in the number of households in which both spouses work.

Next, the impact of number of dependents and their structure on the household burden rate will be investigated. With the income of the head of household and spousal employment conditions as constants, a common point when the spouse is unemployed or employed is that the greater the number of dependents, the lower the household burden rate. This is because the greater the number of household members who are eligible for a dependent deduction, the larger the amount of deduction.

Even if the number of dependents is the same, the tax burden rate on the households differs depending on structure such as the age of the dependent child and parent. Because the amount of deduction varies depending on whether the dependents are children or parents and depending on the age of supporters. For example, when the number of dependents is the same, namely two people, the household burden rate varies depending on whether the structure is 1 child and 1 senior citizen (cases 5 and 6) or 2 children (cases 7 and 8). Until the mid-1970s, the household burden rate for the latter case of 2 children was higher than the former case of 1 child and 1 senior citizen, but this trend has been reversed since the mid-2000s.

Over the analysis period as a whole, deduction amounts for general dependents and elderly dependents fluctuated, while the ages of family members eligible for dependent deductions also changed. From the 1980s to the 1990s, the dependents' deduction amount for those aged 70 years and above was high, so if there are elderly people who support within households, the deduction amount was large. From the 1990s to the 2000s and beyond, as children's child-rearing support policy is enriched, the deduction amount for households with children became larger.

How the dependents' deduction amount for the attributes and ages of dependents eligible for deduction is set will be from considering to what extent are expenses necessary for the family dependents. This represents one of the objectives and approaches for income taxation. The content of the revisions to the system will change depending on the kind of approach or idea society has at that time with regard to income redistribution from income taxation and insurance contributions. Therefore, when evaluating the system, it will be necessary to understand the social background.

Based on the analysis of the representative household models described above, in this chapter, actual household microdata will be used for analysis. This analysis, from the perspective of a household's lifecycle, which takes into consideration the passage of time, is conducted using microdata that can express households' heterogeneity. The previous research conducted in this area is explained in the next section, while this chapter adopts an approach that combines the merits of that research.

4 Analytical Method Using a Lifecycle Model

4.1 Household Lifecycle Model

In this section, we will consider the effects that income taxation and the social security system have on the budget constraints in a household's lifecycle, while also considering the passage of time. Figure 2 represents a conceptual diagram. The subjects of analysis are households that have a head, a spouse, and other household members, represented by subscript i. It is to estimate the imputed values of taxes and social insurance premiums by applying the information of household type and income to real tax and social security system by each family unit, and to verify the validity of the imputed value by comparing it to reported value.

The working period is the time from when the head of the household reaches the legal working age ($a = a_m$) until the year before they reach pension age ($a = a_n - 1$), the age when the person starts receiving a pension ($a = a_n$). During the working period, household i receives income W_a^H from the head of household's labor. Similarly, if there is a spouse in the household, income W_a^S is the spouse's labor. In this chapter, the age of starting work a_m is set at 20. The retirement age is determined by gender and by age in accordance with a_n, which is the year when the person starts to receive a pension in accordance with the public pension system.

From the start-of-work age until retirement age, the head of household's income W_a^H and spousal income W_a^S are subject to income tax (N_a^H and N_a^S) and resident tax (L_a^H and L_a^S), while they also pay insurance contributions (P_a^H and P_a^S) for pensions, medical care, and long-term care. For convenience, it is assumed that the head of household's income W_a^H is greater than spouse's income W_a^S, and that income taxation deduction is applied to the head of household's income.

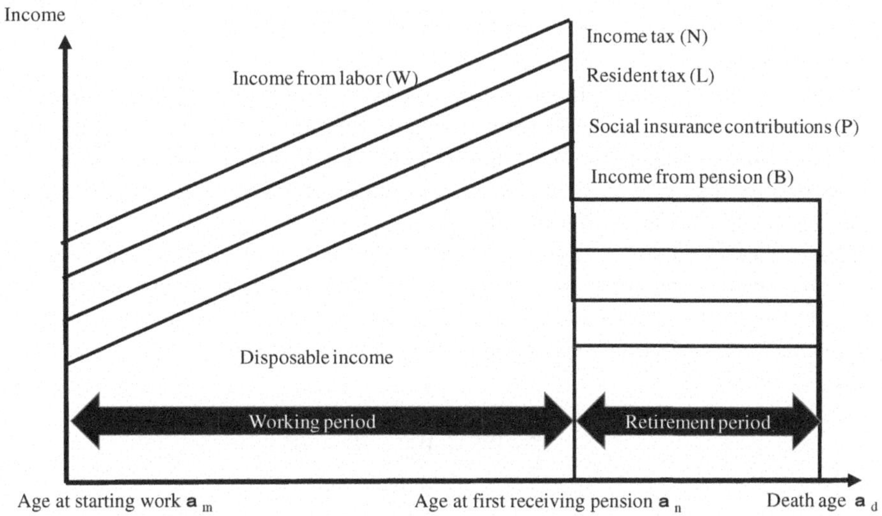

Fig. 2 A conceptual diagram of budget constraints in a household's lifecycle

In household i, the head of household receives pension benefits B_a^H during his or her retirement period, which is from the age when he or she starts receiving pension benefits ($a = a_n$) until the age he or she dies ($a = a_d$). If there is a spouse in household i, the spouse receives the same pension benefits $B_{a,}^S$ but the age at which a person starts receiving a pension and the age at death differ according to gender. It is assumed that the age at death will differ based on the average life expectancies of men and women. Pension benefits are subject to income tax and resident tax.

It is assumed that household i does not receive inheritance assets from other households and at the time of start-of-work age a_m, its savings are zero. Further, the income and savings of other household members, excluding the head of household and the spouse, are set as zero.

As with the head of household and spouse, other household members, namely cohabiting children and grandparents, grow older with the passage of time. It is considered that children become independent from household i when they reach the average marriage age. When cohabiting grandparents and other household members reach age of death, they cease to be members of the household. The average marriage age varies according to gender. It is considered that when both the head of the household and the spouse reach age of death, the household in question ceases to exist.

Based on the above assumptions, the budget constraints formula in the lifecycle of household i is formulated as formula (2) from the present discount value.

$$\sum_{a=a_m}^{a_d} \frac{C_a}{P_t} = \sum_{a=a_m}^{a_d} \frac{W_a^H + W_a^S + B_a^H + B_a^S - N_a^H - N_a^S - L_a^H - L_a^S - P_a^H - P_a^S}{Q_t} \tag{2}$$

At every age, the nominal consumption amount of household i is set as C, and the price level as Q. Subscript t shows the year. At this time, if the birth year of the head of household in household i is b, then the relation is $t = b + a$. For example, if in 2004 ($t = 2004$), the head of the household is 35 years old ($\underline{a} = 35$), then this head of the household was born in 1969 ($b = 1964 = t - a$).

In the formula (2), the right side shows the present discount value of household i's disposable income, and household i obtains lifetime utility by using the disposable income to engage in consumption C on the left side. Therefore, the size of the disposable income's present discounted value determines household i's consumption C and affects its lifetime utility.

Thus, in this chapter, analysis is conducted using an inequality scale on the effects that income taxation and insurance contributions have on the present discounted value of the disposable income. To separate the effects of income taxation and insurance contributions on income, Y is defined by four patterns, as shown below.

$$Y_A = \sum_{a=20}^{a_d} \frac{W_a^H + W_a^S + B_a^H + B_a^S}{Q_t} \tag{3}$$

$$Y_B = \sum_{a=20}^{a_d} \frac{W_a^H + W_a^S + B_a^H + B_a^S - N_a^H - N_a^S - L_a^H - L_a^S}{Q_t} \tag{4}$$

$$Y_C = \sum_{a=20}^{a_d} \frac{W_a^H + W_a^S + B_a^H + B_a^S - P_a^H - P_a^S}{Q_t} \tag{5}$$

$$Y_D = \sum_{a=20}^{a_d} \frac{W_a^H + W_a^S + B_a^H + B_a^S - N_a^H - N_a^S - L_a^H - L_a^S - P_a^H - P_a^S}{Q_t} \tag{6}$$

That is, Y_A is income from labor to which pension benefit is added, Y_B is Y_A income from which income tax and resident tax have been deducted, Y_C is Y_A income from which insurance contributions have been deducted, and Y_D is the present discounted value of disposable income on the right side of formula (2).

4.2 The Theil Index

The redistributive effects of income taxation and insurance contributions will be evaluated using the Theil scale; this is an inequality scale from Y_A to $Y_{D,}$ which are the four patterns of the present discounted value of income obtained from the lifecycle model, as previously described. The Theil scale is used as it can be broken down into various categories. It is formulated as shown below.

The Theil scale T of a household's income distribution $Y = (Y_1, Y_2, \ldots, Y_n)$ of total number n is defined as follows.

$$T = \log n - \sum_{i=1}^{n} s_i \log \frac{1}{s_i} = \sum_{i=1}^{n} s_i \log n s_i, \quad s_i = \frac{Y_i}{\sum_{i=1}^{n} Y_i} \tag{7}$$

We study the decomposition of the Theil index by population subgroups. Theil index can be seen as a weighted average of inequality within subgroups, or the inequality between those subgroups examined via regression-based methods. So, s_i is the income distribution converted to share. Under this condition, the income series for this group is represented by the vector $= s_i 1, \ldots, s_i n_{pi} = 1, \ldots, n$. The total income for each group is $\sum_{i=1}^{n} s_i = 1$. Here, the Theil scale T (s) using s_i is shown as follows. μ is the mean income of the group being denoted and the Theil index can be formulated.

$$T(s) = \sum_{i=1}^{n} \frac{s_i}{n\mu} \log \frac{s_i}{\mu}, \quad \mu = \frac{\sum_{i=1}^{n} s_i}{n} \tag{8}$$

Next, income distribution converted to share is broken down into categories. The Theil scale can be broken down into various categories, but as an example, here income groups are categorized into three, showing the patterns broken down into the 1st quantile s_L, the 2nd quantile s_M, and the 3rd quantile s_H.[4] The share of each category can be classified as follows.

$$s_L = s_L(s_1, s_2, \ldots, s_j), \quad s_M = s_M(s_{j+1}, s_{j+2}, \ldots, s_k), \quad s_H = s_H(s_{k+1}, s_{l+2}, \ldots, s_n) \tag{9}$$

Here, income distribution s, arranged in order of ascending income, is j as the number of data for the 1st quantile share s_L, of $k - j$ as the number of data for the 2nd quantile share s_M, and $n - k$ as the number of data for the 3rd quantile share s_H. The average value of each category is as follows.

$$\mu_L = \frac{\sum_{i=1}^{j} s_i}{j}, \quad \mu_M = \frac{\sum_{i=j+1}^{k} s_i}{k-j}, \quad \mu_H = \frac{\sum_{i=k+1}^{n} s_i}{n-k} \tag{10}$$

Using ratio s and the average value of each category, the Theil scale of each category is calculated.

$$T(s_L) = \sum_{i=1}^{n} \frac{s_i}{j\mu_L} \log \frac{s_i}{\mu_L}, \quad T(s_M) = \sum_{i=j+1}^{k} \frac{s_i}{(k-j)\mu_M} \log \frac{s_i}{\mu_M}, \quad T(s_H) = \sum_{i=k+1}^{n} \frac{s_i}{(n-k)\mu_H} \log \frac{s_i}{\mu_H} \tag{11}$$

The Theil scales of each category are combined to express total Theil scale $T(s)$. $T(s_L, s_M, s_H)$ is the Theil scale between categories. We will analyze how the degree of the inequality of income distribution of the entire population is explained by two factors: the inequality within each group of persons and the differences between the three groups of population. The three groups being disjoint, the inequality of incomes explained by the Theil index can be decomposed as follows.

$$T(s) = V_L T(s_L) + V_M T(s_M) + V_H T(s_H) + T(s_L, s_M, s_H) \tag{12}$$

$$T(s_L, s_M, s_H) = \log n + V_L \log \mu_L + V_M \log \mu_M + V_H \log \mu_H \tag{13}$$

Here, each category's weight V is expressed as follows.

$$V_L = j\mu_L, V_M = (k-j)\mu_M, \quad V_H = (n-k)\mu_H, \quad V_L + V_M + V_H = 1 \tag{14}$$

---

[4]In this chapter, the data were broken down into five income group quantiles and into generation groups (based on the age of the head of household).

Therefore, the formula (12) Theil scale shows the sum of the intra-category contribution of the in-category Theil scale multiplied by weight, and the inter-category contribution of the Theil scale between categories.

5 Methodology for Processing and Analyzing Data

While evaluating the redistributive effects of income from income taxation and insurance contributions from the formula (12) Theil scale, it is necessary to have Y_A to Y_D as the four present discounted values of income in the lifecycle. For the base data, approximately 44,000 records of anonymous data on "households with two or more people" from the "National Survey of Family Income and Expenditure" (hereafter, anonymous data), carried out by the Ministry of Internal Affairs and Communications (2004), will be used.[5] However, as of 2004, households where the head or spouse did not receive wage income, such as self-employed households or households with only retired senior citizens were excluded from the analysis. Therefore, only 22,640 records were used for analysis.

From the anonymous data from 2004, data was obtained about the head of household and spouse for "gender," "age group with five-year intervals," "work income," "family relations," "employed or unemployed," "company size," "industry code," and "occupation code," and for other household members, "age group with five-year intervals" ("each year" only when aged below 15 years). Names within the quotation marks are data names.

Age of the head of household and spouse in 2004 was set as the median value for the five-year group categories. For other members of the family structure aged 15 years and above in 2004, the median value was set for the five-year group categories as their ages in 2004. When going back one year into the past, the age of the household head, spouse, and other household members decreased by one year. After one year, the age of the head of household, spouse, and other members of the household increased by one year, and time is assumed to pass in this way.

Using anonymous data as a basis, other statistical data were used to calculate household income from labor from the start-of-work age to retirement age; pension income was calculated based on this, and income tax and resident tax were measured from these incomes. Based on these values, the household's income from the start-of-work age until the age of death was obtained, and the Theil scale was calculated from the present discounted value of the respective incomes.

The specific working procedure will be explained. Figure 3 shows a conceptual diagram of this procedure.

---

[5]There were two types of anonymous data in the Ministry of Internal Affairs and Communications' "National Survey of Family Income and Expenditure" (2004): on "single-person households" and "households with two or more people." In this chapter, data on households with two or more people are used. The dataset used for analysis in this chapter was created and processed independently based on the statistical method of, and anonymous date received from, the National Statistics Center.

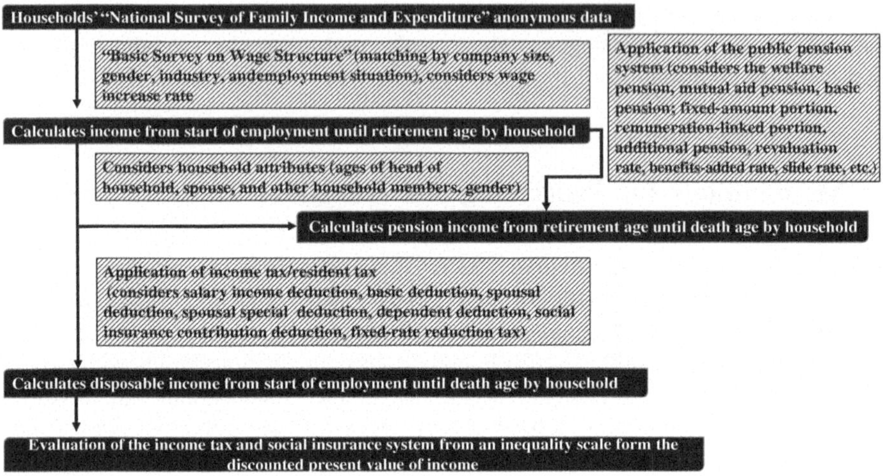

Fig. 3 Conceptual diagram of the working procedure

6 Measurement Methods Used in Analysis

6.1 Measurement of Income from Labor

Based on anonymous data from 2004 for the head of household and spousal "work income," income W_a^H from labor by the head of household in the past and future, and income W_a^S from labor by the spouse, are measured. On comparing the "work income" of the head of household and spouse in the data, when the spouse's "work income" was larger, the spouse became the head of the household.

Here, assuming that the employment conditions in 2004 will continue into the future, income from labor in the past and future was estimated based on the "gender" of the household head and spouse, "age group with five-year interval," "employed or unemployed," "company category," "company size," "industry code," and "occupation code."

If the head of the household or spouse works for a private sector company, data on the "previously determined cash salary amount" and "annual bonus and other special salary amount," based on gender, industry, company size, age, and educational qualifications, from the 2004 Ministry of Health' Labour and Welfare's "Basic Survey on Wage Structure (Wage Census)," were used. Specifically, data on five-year increments were considered as median value for the age group, linear interpolation was carried out to turn them into one-year increments, and the annual income from labor for each age was estimated. For this, the bonus multiplication factor for the salary obtained from the "previously determined cash salary amount" and the "annual bonus and other special salary amount" was calculated based on gender, industry, company size, and age.

After calculating the above, the rate of increase in annual income due to age was measured, this rate of increase was applied to the 2004 anonymous data for the head of household's spousal "work income," and income from labor in the past and future was estimated. Based on the anonymous data on "gender," "employed or unemployed," "company category," "company size," "industry code," "occupation code" and "age," this was matched to the "Wage Census" data based on gender, industry, company size, and age. Further, the previously mentioned bonus multiplication factor was used to obtain a bonus income of the past and future.

As the 2004 data were real values, they were modified to nominal values from the nominal wage growth rate.[6] By totaling the above for each age, the head of household's nominal income from labor W_a^H and income from spouse's labor W_a^S in the past and the future were measured.

If the head of the household or spouse was a national government employee, data on the "average monthly salary amount" by administrative position, educational qualification, and age was obtained from the 2004 National Personnel Authority's "Survey Report on the Actual Conditions of Salaries, etc., of National Government Employees." If they were local government officials, data on "the average monthly salary amount" of local public bodies (nationwide), general administrative position, educational qualification, and age from the 2004 Ministry of Internal Affairs and Communications' "Survey of Actual Conditions of Local Government Employee Salaries" were used. The rate of increase of annual income was calculated in the same way as for private sector companies.

However, as the bonus multiplication factor for government employees was difficult to obtain data, the bonus multiplication factor (average) used by private sector companies was applied, and the head of household's past and future nominal income from labor W_a^H and spouse's income from labor W_a^S were calculated. From the above information, the head of household's income from labor W_a^H, right from the starting-work age until retirement age, and the spouse's income from labor W_a^S in the past and future were obtained.

6.2 Measurement of Pension Income

Next, a household's pension income was measured. In the lifecycle model, pension income is extremely important, as it constitutes a large part of the present discounted value of income.

As shown in Fig. 4, following reforms to public pension, the age from when a person starts to receive a pension rose from 60 to 65 years; however, the age when a person starts to receive a pension will differ depending on the year of birth and gender. In this chapter, the head of household or spouse who has reached pensionable age is

[6]Data on the nominal wage growth rates in the past and future were acquired from the 2009 Ministry of Health, Labour and Welfare, "Financial Inspection-Related Data" and its 2012 "5th Special Subcommittee of Social Security Council Pension Committee on the Economic Assumptions and the Approaches for Fund Management for Pension Finances, Material 3-3."

	Japan	U.K.	Germany	Ferance	U.S.A
Plan system	two–tiers Employee's pension insurance / Mutual Aid Pension National Pension(Basic Pension)	two–tiers State second Pension / Occpational Pension Basic state pension	one–tier Self–emplyed worker's pension by occupation / General pension insurance / Miners' pension insurance	one–tier Self–autonomy plan by occupation / General plan / Sepecial plan	one–tier Self–autonomy planOld–age, Survivors, and Disability Insurance
Subjct Person for compulsory participation	All resients	non–working / Employees and self–employed workers	non–working,self–employed workers / Employees and part of self–employed workers	non–working / self–employed workers / Employees	non–working / Employees and self–employed workers
Premium rate	(General employees) Emplyee's pension 17.47% National Pension for the category–1 insured pension	(General employees) 25.8% Employee 12.0% Employer 13.8%	(General employees) 18.9% (Equally shared by an employee and an emplyer)	(General employees) 17.25% Employee: 7.05% Employer: 10.20%	12.40%
Pensionable age (end of 2014)	National Pension(Basic Pension) Age65 Employee's pension Male Age61 Females Age60	Males: Age65 Females: Age62 and 5 months	Age 65 and 3 months	Age 61 and 2 months	Age 66
Period of coverage required for entitlement to an old–age benefit	25 years(The period will be shortened from 25 year to 10 years in accprdance with the effective data of drastic tax reform law)	None	5 years	None	40quarters of plan participation(equivalent to 10 years)

Fig. 4 Comparison of pension system

assumed to continue to receive a pension income from retirement until death. The ages at death were set as 78 years for men and 85 years for women.[7]

The National Pension System was introduced in 1959 and is mandatory for all residents between 20 and 59 years of age. Contributions to the National Pension System are deducted from contributions for the employment-related portion of the public pension. For the self-employed, the contribution amounts to 16,490/month (for the fiscal year 2017). Monthly pension benefits after 40 years of working life and from age 65 onwards, the official retirement age for the National Pension System. Shorter contribution periods result in lower benefits.

The second part of public pension provision is earnings-related. Private sector employees are covered by Employee Pension Insurance, which was introduced in1944. Public sector employees are covered by the Mutual Aid Association. The contribution rate to Employee Pension Insurance is a part of wages, which is equally split between employers and employees. A part of this contribution is deducted for the National Pension System. Employees aged 60 and over with 25 years of contributions are entitled to benefits from the Employee Pension Insurance scheme. Retirement age will rise to 65 for men by 2025 and by 2030 for women. The Mutual Aid Association, which covers employees working in central and local governments as well as private school employees, operates mainly along the same lines.

We can receive the Basic Pension at the age of 65 if you have been covered under the National Pension and Employees' Pension Insurance systems. To be qualified, your total coverage periods need to be 10 years or more. In each respective public pension system, fixed-amount unit price, fixed-amount portion's multiplier, benefits multiplier, price-slide rate, and the modified fixed-rate were considered, and the head of household's pension benefits ${B_a}^H$ and the spouse's pension benefits ${B_a}^S$ were measured. For the multiplier, based on the date of birth, proportional division calculations were performed and matched to the head of household's and the spouse's years of birth.

Therefore, pension income was categorized into the National Pension (Basic Pension), the Employee's Pension Insurance, the Mutual Aid Pension, and the Occupational addition, depending on the head of household or spousal employment. The fixed-amount portion and the remuneration-proportional portion were calculated by the following formulas.

$$\begin{aligned}\text{Fixed-amount portion} &= \text{fixed-amount unit price} \times \text{fixed- amount portion multiplier} \\ &\quad \times \text{insured person's number of months} \times \text{price-slide rate} \times \text{modified fixed-rate}\end{aligned} \tag{15}$$

[7]According to the Ministry of Health, Labour and Welfare's (2004) "Overview of Simplified Life Expectancy Table 2. Trends in the Average Life Expectancy," the average life expectancy of men is 78.64 years and that of women is 85.59 years.

$$
\begin{aligned}
&\text{Remuneration-proportional portion} = (\text{standard monthly remuneration}\\
&\quad \text{in the period before March 2003} \times \text{benefits multiplier} \times \text{insured person's}\\
&\quad \text{number of months in the period before March 2003} + \text{standard}\\
&\quad \text{remuneration amount in the period from April 2003 onwards} \times \text{benefits}\\
&\quad \text{multiplier} \times \text{insured person's number of months in the period from}\\
&\quad \text{April 2004 onwards}) \times \text{price-slide rate} \times \text{modifiedfixed-rate}
\end{aligned}
\tag{16}
$$

The respective standard monthly remuneration or standard remuneration amount were calculated from the head of household's income from labor W_a^H and the spouse's income from labor W_a^S, both in the past and future. For this, through a proportional division calculation, bonus was not included in the standard monthly remuneration before March 2003, but was included in the standard remuneration amount from March 2003 onwards. Upper limits were set for the fixed-amount pension benefits, standard monthly remuneration, and standard remuneration amount.

If the head of the household or the spouse were short-term workers, they receive only the fixed-amount portion of pension benefits. The additional pension for the spouse and children, and the occupational area-related portion of a national government employee's mutual aid pension and the local government employee's mutual aid pension were also included.

6.3 *Measurement of Income Taxation and Insurance Contributions*

From the start-of-work age until retirement age, the head of household's income from labor W_a^H and spouse's income from labor W_a^S, and from the age when he/she receives a pension until his/her death age, we derived the head of household's pension benefits B_a^H and the spouse's pension benefits B_a^S. These amounts were subject to income tax and resident tax.

With regard to income tax and resident tax, each type of deduction, including on income from salary, basic deduction, spousal deduction, spousal special deduction, dependent deduction, insurance contribution deduction, and public pension deduction were considered, and based on the excess progressive tax rate structures table, the tax burden amounts were measured.[8] For future income tax and resident

[8]Income tax and resident tax were included in the system from 1958 onward with reference to the Ministry of Finance's "Government Finances and Financial Statistics Monthly Report: Special Tax Edition," and the Office of Financial History, Ministry of Finance (1977, 1990). A declining fixed rate tax was also considered, while the standard tax rate was adopted for resident tax, which is taxed on the previous year's income.

tax, the system was fixed at 2013 rates. In the event that both the head of household and the spouse received income, income deduction was applied only to the head of household's income.

Data on the number of dependents was necessary for calculating income deduction. Based on the income tax and resident tax systems, in households with children and/or senior citizens of an age eligible for dependent deduction, the latter were considered dependents. Further, dependent children were considered to be no longer dependent once they had reached the average marriage age—set as 29 years for men and 27 years for women. The average maternal age at childbirth was set at 28 years for the first child and 30 years for the second child, and these children became dependents.[9]

As for insurance contributions, excluding short-term workers, in the case of private sector company employees and national and local government employees, insurance contributions levied on income were calculated using the Ministry of Finance's simplified calculation method.[10] Insurance contributions derived from these calculations were applied to income tax and resident tax insurance contribution deductions. Future insurance contributions were fixed and measured, the same as for income tax and resident tax.

For short-term workers, national pension insurance contributions, fixed-amount burden from National Health Insurance contributions and long-term care insurance contributions were applied. For contributions made to the National Pension system, the Japan Pension Service's "Transitions in National Pension Insurance Contributions" in the Table 1 was used.[11], the nominal settled amount per capita from 1994 to 2011 was calculated as in the Ministry of Health, Labour and Welfare's, "Nationwide Elderly Medical Care and Heads of the Division (Department) Responsible for National Health Insurance and Latter-Stage Elderly Medical Care Wide-Area Association Secretary General's Committee." For contributions before this period, the nominal per capita settled amounts were calculated by multiplying the contributions by the ratio of the previous fiscal year's pension insurance contributions to the National Health Insurance. Long-term care insurance contributions consist of government burden

[9]According to the Ministry of Health, Labour and Welfare's (2004) "Population Dynamics Statistics," the average marriage age is 29.6 years for men and 27.8 years for women. Also, from the "Statistics on Births" from the Ministry of Health, Labour and Welfare (2010), "the average period from the average age of the first marriage of the wife until the average age at the time of the first birth: Showa 50 to Heisei 21," the average maternal age at the time of the first child's birth was 28.9 years, and 30.9 years at the time of the second child's birth.

[10]For the simplified method of calculating insurance contributions, please refer to the Ministry of Finance, Policy Research Institute, *Government Finances and Financial Statistics Monthly Report: Special Tax Edition.*

[11]Insured persons must pay contributions every month. Those months are recognized as insured periods. National Pension is operated under the principle of "fixed contribution" and "fixed benefit". Yet, in order to ensure the financial balance in the future, contribution of National Pension is regularly revised at least once every 5 years. The value of the monthly amount of insurance contributions differed for people aged less than 35 years and aged 35 years and above from April 1961 to June 1960, so the same applies in this chapter.

Table 1 Transitions in national pension insurance contributions

Month paying insurance premium		Fixed amount(yen) under 35years old	over 35years old	Half exemption(yen) since April, 2002	1/4 payment(yen) since July,2016~	3/4 payment(yen) since July,2016~
April, 2005 -	December, 1966	100	150			
January, 1967 -	December, 1968	200	250			
January, 1969 -	June, 1970	250	300			
July, 1970 -	June, 1972	450				
July, 1972 -	December, 1973	550				
April, 1974 -	December, 1974	900				
April, 1975 -	March, 1976	1,100				
April, 1976 -	March, 1977	1,400				
April, 1977 -	March, 1978	2,200				
April, 1978 -	March, 1979	2,730				
April, 1979 -	March, 1980	3,300				
April, 1980 -	March, 1981	3,770				
April, 1981 -	March, 1982	4,500				
April, 1982 -	March, 1983	5,220				
April, 1983 -	March, 1984	5,830				
April, 1984 -	March, 1985	6,220				
April, 1985 -	March, 1986	6,740				
April, 1986 -	March, 1987	7,100				
April, 1987 -	March, 1988	7,400				
April, 1988 -	March, 1989	7,700				
April, 1989 -	March, 1990	8,000				
April, 1990 -	March, 1991	8,400				
April, 1991 -	March, 1992	9,000				
April, 1992 -	March, 1993	9,700				
April, 1993 -	March, 1994	10,500				
April, 1994 -	March, 1995	11,100				
April, 1995 -	March, 1996	11,700				
April, 1996 -	March, 1997	12,300				
April, 1997 -	March, 1998	12,800				
April, 1998 -	March, 1999	13,300				
April, 1999 -	March, 2005	13,300		6,650		
April, 2005 -	March, 2006	13,580		6,790		
April, 2006 -	March, 2007	13,860		6,930	3,470	10,400
April, 2007 -	March, 2008	14,100		7,050	3,530	10,580
April, 2008 -	March, 2009	14,410		7,210	3,600	10,810
April, 2009 -	March, 2010	14,660		7,330	3,670	11,000
April, 2010 -	March, 2011	15,100		7,550	3,780	11,330
April, 2011 -	March, 2012	15,020		7,550	3,760	11,270
April, 2012 -	March, 2013	14,980		7,490	3,750	11,240
April, 2013 -	March, 2014	15,040		7,520	3,760	11,280
April, 2014 -	March, 2015	15,250		7,630	3,810	11,440
April, 2015 -	March, 2016	15,590		7,800	3,900	11,690
April, 2016 -	March, 2017	16,260		8,130	4,070	12,200
April, 2017 -	March, 2018	16,490		8,250	4,120	12,370

share, prefectures burden share, municipalities burden share, first insured person premiums (65 years old or older), and second insured persons premiums(40–64 years old). For long-term care insurance contributions, based on the Social Insurance Medical Fee Payment Fund-initiated "Fiscal 2011 Long-Term Care Insurance Special Accounts Supplementary Statement," the second insured burden payments were divided by the number of second insured persons to calculate the long-term care per capita fixed payment. Insurance premiums for second insured persons are borne by employers and the National Treasury in the same was as for medical insurance. Lump-sum payment collected nationwide is delivered to the social insurance medical fee payment fund. For future insurance contributions, these values were extended, taking into account the nominal wage growth rate.

From the above, we obtained the head of household and spouse income tax (N_a^H and N_a^S), resident tax (L_a^H and L_a^S), and insurance contributions (P_a^H and P_a^S) from the past to the future.

6.4 Theil Scale and Measurement of the Redistribution Effect

Using the values for head of household *i*'s income from labor W_a^H, spousal income from labor W_a^S, head of household's pension benefits B_a^H, spousal pension benefits B_a^S, head of household and spousal income tax (N_a^H and N_a^S), resident tax (L_a^H and L_a^S), and insurance contributions (P_a^H and P_a^S), we measured Y_A to Y_D—the four previously defined present discounted values of income.

For price-level *Q*, which is necessary in order to calculate the present discounted value, the consumer price index from the Ministry of Internal Affairs and Communications, "Consumer Price Index Annual Report" was used, with 2004 set as 1. For price-level *Q* in the future, price growth rates in the future were based on the Ministry of Health, Labour and Welfare's "Fiscal 2009 Financial Inspection of the Public Pension System based on the Financial Inspection and Financial Recalculations."

Theil scale *T* corresponding to the present discounted value of income from Y_A to Y_D was measured as $T(Y_A)$, $T(Y_B)$, $T(Y_C)$, and $T(Y_D)$, respectively. As described below, Theil scale *T* was broken down by income group and by generation. Further, with Theil scale $T(Y_A)$ in relation to income Y_A as the standard, the respective redistribution effects *R* were obtained as follows.

$$R(Y_A, Y_B) = \frac{T(Y_A - Y_B)}{T(Y_A)}, \quad R(Y_A, Y_C) = \frac{T(Y_A - Y_C)}{T(Y_A)}, \quad R(Y_A, Y_D) = \frac{T(Y_A - Y_D)}{T(Y_A)} \tag{17}$$

Here, $R(Y_A, Y_B)$ is the redistribution effect from income taxation, and $R(Y_A, Y_C)$ is the redistribution effect from insurance contributions. In addition, $R(Y_A, Y_D)$ is the combined redistribution effect from income taxation and insurance contributions.

7 Results of Analysis

Table 2 shows the results of analysis by income groups, Table 3 by generation group, and Table 4 by income group and by generation group, for the Theil scale (*T*) and redistribution effect (*R*). For income taxation levied in a single year, the results were divided for the entire period by decade (1960s, 1970s, 1980s, 1990s, and 2000s); and for insurance contributions, the results are shown for the entire period.

First, total redistribution effects from income taxation and insurance contributions were obtained from Tables 2 and 3, which show "the overall Theil scale.". On comparing "the overall Theil scale" $T(Y_A)$ (=0.0878) for income Y_A obtained from income from labor and pension, and "the overall Theil scale" $T(Y_D)$ (=0.0780) of income Y_D from disposable income, we understand that income taxation and

Table 2 Theil scale by income group and redistribution effects

All periods		Income Y_A		Income Y_B	
	Classification	Theil scale $T(Y_A)$	Weight	Theil scale $T(Y_B)$	Redistribution effect of income taxation $R(Y_A, Y_B)$
Income Theil scale within groups	1st quantile	0.0742	0.0973	0.0676	0.0970
	2nd quantile	0.0157	0.1632	0.0115	0.3636
	3rd quantile	0.0134	0.2001	0.0096	0.3980
	4th quantile	0.0120	0.2329	0.0091	0.3090
	5th quantile	0.0308	0.3065	0.0245	0.2577
Income Theil scale between groups		0.0631		0.0546	0.1554
Overall Theil scale		0.0878		0.0748	0.1742

		Income Y_C		Income Y_D	
	Classification	Theil scale T (Y_C)	Redistribution effect of insurance contributions $R(Y_A, Y_C)$	Theil scale $T(Y_D)$	Redistribution effect $R(Y_A, Y_D)$
Income Theil scale within groups	1st quantile	0.0850	−0.1272	0.0780	−0.0486
	2nd quantile	0.0161	−0.0274	0.0116	0.3575
	3rd quantile	0.0138	−0.0296	0.0096	0.3944
	4th quantile	0.0121	−0.0107	0.0090	0.3321
	5th quantile	0.0317	−0.0261	0.0248	0.2429
Income Theil scale between groups		0.0658	−0.0414	0.0568	0.1102
Overall Theil scale		0.0919	−0.0450	0.0780	0.1249

1960s		Income Y_B		Income Y_D	
	Classification	Theil scale $T(Y_B)$	Redistribution effect of income taxation $R(Y_A, Y_B)$	Theil scale $T(Y_D)$	Redistribution effect $R(Y_A, Y_D)$
Income Theil scale within groups	1st quantile	0.0502	0.4780	0.0633	0.1731
	2nd quantile	0.0058	1.6977	0.0059	1.6432
	3rd quantile	0.0058	1.3094	0.0057	1.3524
	4th quantile	0.0064	0.8574	0.0064	0.8661
	5th quantile	0.0211	0.4644	0.0221	0.3944

(continued)

Table 2 (continued)

1960s		Income Y_B		Income Y_D	
	Classification	Theil scale $T(Y_B)$	Redistribution effect of income taxation $R(Y_A, Y_B)$	Theil scale $T(Y_D)$	Redistribution effect $R(Y_A, Y_D)$
Income Theil scale between groups		0.0406	0.5549	0.0434	0.4541
Overall Theil scale		0.0559	0.5692	0.0604	0.4526
1970s		Income Y_B		Income Y_D	
	Classification	Theil scale $T(Y_B)$	Redistribution effect of income taxation $R(Y_A, Y_B)$	Theil scale $T(Y_D)$	Redistribution effect $R(Y_A, Y_D)$
Income Theil scale within groups	1st quantile	0.0636	0.1669	0.0762	−0.0263
	2nd quantile	0.0097	0.6210	0.0101	0.5579
	3rd quantile	0.0081	0.6590	0.0084	0.6017
	4th quantile	0.0079	0.5088	0.0082	0.4650
	5th quantile	0.0228	0.3514	0.0240	0.2832
Income Theil scale between groups		0.0510	0.2362	0.0537	0.1736
Overall Theil scale		0.0695	0.2631	0.0740	0.1868
1980s		Income Y_B		Income Y_D	
	Classification	Theil scale $T(Y_B)$	Redistribution effect of income taxation $R(Y_A, Y_B)$	Theil scale $T(Y_D)$	Redistribution effect $R(Y_A, Y_D)$
Income Theil scale within groups	1st quantile	0.0670	0.1070	0.0774	−0.0416
	2nd quantile	0.0110	0.4248	0.0111	0.4095
	3rd quantile	0.0090	0.4939	0.0092	0.4618
	4th quantile	0.0085	0.4091	0.0087	0.3747
	5th quantile	0.0230	0.3391	0.0248	0.2419
Income Theil scale between groups		0.0526	0.1979	0.0554	0.1386
Overall Theil scale		0.0720	0.2192	0.0764	0.1491

(continued)

Table 2 (continued)

1990s		Income Y_B		Income Y_D	
	Classification	Theil scale $T(Y_B)$	Redistribution effect of income taxation $R(Y_A, Y_B)$	Theil scale $T(Y_D)$	Redistribution effect $R(Y_A, Y_D)$
Income Theil scale within groups	1st quantile	0.0675	0.0997	0.0779	−0.0473
	2nd quantile	0.0113	0.3869	0.0115	0.3710
	3rd quantile	0.0093	0.4406	0.0095	0.4094
	4th quantile	0.0087	0.3791	0.0089	0.3472
	5th quantile	0.0230	0.3414	0.0247	0.2469
Income Theil scale between groups		0.0530	0.1890	0.0558	0.1301
Overall Theil scale		0.0726	0.2095	0.0770	0.1404
2000s		Income Y_B		Income Y_D	
	Classification	Theil scale $T(Y_B)$	Redistribution effect of income taxation $R(Y_A, Y_B)$	Theil scale $T(Y_D)$	Redistribution effect $R(Y_A, Y_D)$
Income Theil scale within groups	1st quantile	0.0678	0.0938	0.0782	−0.0512
	2nd quantile	0.0116	0.3504	0.0117	0.3435
	3rd quantile	0.0097	0.3843	0.0097	0.3795
	4th quantile	0.0092	0.2999	0.0091	0.3218
	5th quantile	0.0245	0.2587	0.0248	0.2439
Income Theil scale between groups		0.0545	0.1575	0.0567	0.1124
Overall Theil scale		0.0747	0.1747	0.0780	0.1254

Note Overall Theil scale = $\sum$ intra-income group Theil scale × weight + inter-income group Theil scale

insurance contribution have a positive redistribution effect $R(Y_A, Y_D)$ (=0.1249), which causes income inequality to contract.

On breaking down this redistribution effect $R(Y_A, Y_D)$, we find that while the redistribution effect from income taxation $R(Y_A, Y_B)$ (=0.1742) is positive, the redistribution effect from insurance contributions $R(Y_A, Y_C)$ (=▲0.0450) is negative (entire period for both). Therefore, income taxation causes income inequality to shrink, but insurance contributions cause income inequality to expand.[12]

[12]In Chap. 1, it was noted that deductions on insurance contributions have a negative income redistribution effect. Please refer to Chap. 1.

Table 3 Theil scale by generation group and redistribution effects

All periods		Income Y_A		Income Y_B	
	Classification	Theil scale $T(Y_A)$	Weight	Theil scale $T(Y_B)$	Redistribution effect of income taxation $R(Y_A, Y_B)$
Theil scale within generations	20–29 years	0.0962	0.0570	0.0793	0.2124
	30–39 years	0.0794	0.2736	0.0669	0.1865
	40–49 years	0.0864	0.3424	0.0739	0.1678
	50–59 years	0.0911	0.3270	0.0782	0.1660
Theil scale between generations		0.0012		0.0010	0.1677
Overall Theil scale		0.0878		0.0748	0.1742

		Income Y_C		Income Y_D	
	Classification	Theil scale $T(Y_C)$	Redistribution effect of insurance contributions $R(Y_A, Y_C)$	Theil scale $T(Y_D)$	Redistribution effect $R(Y_A, Y_D)$
Theil scale within generations	20–29 years	0.1015	−0.0524	0.0834	0.1522
	30–39 years	0.0836	−0.0494	0.0701	0.1325
	40–49 years	0.0904	−0.0450	0.0772	0.1192
	50–59 years	0.0955	−0.0460	0.0818	0.1144
Theil scale between generations		0.0011	0.1308	0.0009	0.3389
Overall Theil scale		0.0919	−0.0450	0.0780	0.1249

1960s		Income Y_B		Income Y_D	
	Classification	Theil scale $T(Y_B)$	Redistribution effect of income taxation $R(Y_A, Y_B)$	Theil scale $T(Y_D)$	Redistribution effect $R(Y_A, Y_D)$
Theil scale within generations	20–29 years	0.0586	0.6399	0.0636	0.5111
	30–39 years	0.0493	0.6126	0.0532	0.4921
	40–49 years	0.0553	0.5625	0.0596	0.4484
	50–59 years	0.0600	0.5190	0.0649	0.4035

(continued)

Table 3 (continued)

1960s		Income Y_B		Income Y_D	
	Classification	Theil scale $T(Y_B)$	Redistribution effect of income taxation $R(Y_A, Y_B)$	Theil scale $T(Y_D)$	Redistribution effect $R(Y_A, Y_D)$
Theil scale between generations		0.0004	1.8092	0.0004	1.8256
Overall Theil scale		0.0559	0.5692	0.0604	0.4526
1970s		Income Y_B		Income Y_D	
	Classification	Theil scale $T(Y_B)$	Redistribution effect of income taxation $R(Y_A, Y_B)$	Theil scale $T(Y_D)$	Redistribution effect $R(Y_A, Y_D)$
Theil scale within generations	20–29 years	0.0724	0.3280	0.0724	0.3280
	30–39 years	0.0616	0.2893	0.0616	0.2893
	40–49 years	0.0687	0.2569	0.0687	0.2569
	50–59 years	0.0740	0.2312	0.0740	0.2312
Theil scale between generations		0.0007	0.6806	0.0007	0.6806
Overall Theil scale		0.0695	0.2631	0.0695	0.2631
1980s		Income Y_B		Income Y_D	
	Classification	Theil scale $T(Y_B)$	Redistribution effect of income taxation $R(Y_A, Y_B)$	Theil scale $T(Y_D)$	Redistribution effect $R(Y_A, Y_D)$
Theil scale within generations	20–29 years	0.0743	0.2940	0.0799	0.2029
	30–39 years	0.0637	0.2470	0.0680	0.1676
	40–49 years	0.0713	0.2115	0.0757	0.1414
	50–59 years	0.0763	0.1945	0.0809	0.1271

(continued)

Table 3 (continued)

1980s		Income Y_B		Income Y_D	
	Classification	Theil scale $T(Y_B)$	Redistribution effect of income taxation $R(Y_A, Y_B)$	Theil scale $T(Y_D)$	Redistribution effect $R(Y_A, Y_D)$
Theil scale between generations		0.0009	0.2687	0.0008	0.4493
Overall Theil scale		0.0720	0.2192	0.0764	0.1491
1990s		**Income Y_B**		**Income Y_D**	
	Classification	Theil scale $T(Y_B)$	Redistribution effect of income taxation $R(Y_A, Y_B)$	Theil scale $T(Y_D)$	Redistribution effect $R(Y_A, Y_D)$
Theil scale within generations	20–29 years	0.0759	0.2675	0.0816	0.1789
	30–39 years	0.0645	0.2323	0.0688	0.1544
	40–49 years	0.0717	0.2047	0.0760	0.1356
	50–59 years	0.0767	0.1885	0.0813	0.1217
Theil scale between generations		0.0010	0.2340	0.0008	0.4082
Overall Theil scale		0.0726	0.2095	0.0770	0.1404
2000s		**Income Y_B**		**Income Y_D**	
	Classification	Theil scale $T(Y_B)$	Redistribution effect of income taxation $R(Y_A, Y_B)$	Theil scale $T(Y_D)$	Redistribution effect $R(Y_A, Y_D)$
Theil scale within generations	Theil between generations and groups	0.0792	0.2145	0.0833	0.1543
	30–39 years	0.0669	0.1881	0.0700	0.1340
	40–49 years	0.0739	0.1688	0.0771	0.1201
	50–59 years	0.0782	0.1661	0.0818	0.1144
Theil scale between generations		0.0010	0.1431	0.0009	0.3092
Overall Theil scale		0.0747	0.1747	0.0780	0.1254

Note Overall Theil scale = $\sum$ intrageneration Theil scale × weight + intergenerational Theil scale

Table 4 Theil scale by income group, generation group, and redistribution effects (reference)

All periods		Income Y_A		Income Y_B	
	Classification	Theil scale $T(Y_A)$	Weight	Theil scale $T(Y_B)$	Redistribution effect of income taxation $R(Y_A, Y_B)$
Income Theil scale within groups	*1st quantile*				
	20–29 years	0.0549	0.0172	0.0481	0.1411
	30–39 years	0.0116	0.0196	0.0080	0.4498
	40–49 years	0.0090	0.0109	0.0057	0.5746
	50–59 years	0.0070	0.0061	0.0055	0.2746
	2nd quantile				
	20–29 years	0.0267	0.0031	0.0129	1.0761
	30–39 years	0.0650	0.0265	0.0608	0.0702
	40–49 years	0.0082	0.0675	0.0063	0.3055
	50–59 years	0.0066	0.0776	0.0047	0.3950
	3rd quantile				
	20–29 years	0.0057	0.0584	0.0043	0.3264
	30–39 years	0.0229	0.0435	0.0180	0.2711
	40–49 years	0.0670	0.0220	0.0646	0.0371
	50–59 years	0.0048	0.0394	0.0045	0.0714
	4th quantile				
	20–29 years	0.0043	0.0637	0.0039	0.1057
	30–39 years	0.0042	0.0936	0.0036	0.1683
	40–49 years	0.0254	0.1238	0.0205	0.2360
	50–59 years	0.0591	0.0316	0.0571	0.0361
	5th quantile				
	20–29 years	0.0061	0.0366	0.0057	0.0635
	30–39 years	0.0052	0.0479	0.0048	0.0941
	40–49 years	0.0040	0.0748	0.0037	0.0829
	50–59 years	0.0241	0.1361	0.0193	0.2455
Income Theil scale between groups		0.0709		0.0602	0.1773
Overall Theil scale		0.0878		0.0748	0.1742

(continued)

Table 4 (continued)

		Income Y_C		Income Y_D	
	Classification	Theil scale $T(Y_C)$	Redistribution effect of insurance contributions $R(Y_A, Y_C)$	Theil scale $T(Y_D)$	Redistribution effect $R(Y_A, Y_D)$
Income Theil scale within groups	*1st quantile*				
	20–29 years	0.0602	−0.0868	0.0528	0.0398
	30–39 years	0.0129	−0.0991	0.0089	0.3118
	40–49 years	0.0100	−0.1065	0.0063	0.4289
	50–59 years	0.0076	−0.0815	0.0056	0.2380
	2nd quantile				
	20–29 years	0.0293	−0.0892	0.0143	0.8718
	30–39 years	0.0737	−0.1174	0.0691	−0.0587
	40–49 years	0.0089	−0.0747	0.0067	0.2311
	50–59 years	0.0072	−0.0803	0.0050	0.3204
	3rd quantile				
	20–29 years	0.0061	−0.0698	0.0044	0.2864
	30–39 years	0.0241	−0.0495	0.0186	0.2308
	40–49 years	0.0807	−0.1707	0.0781	−0.1432
	50–59 years	0.0048	−0.0001	0.0044	0.0991
	4th quantile				
	20–29 years	0.0044	−0.0271	0.0039	0.1042
	30–39 years	0.0043	−0.0381	0.0036	0.1624
	40–49 years	0.0263	−0.0370	0.0210	0.2054
	50–59 years	0.0721	−0.1801	0.0699	−0.1540
	5th quantile				
	20–29 years	0.0062	−0.0221	0.0058	0.0513
	30–39 years	0.0053	−0.0188	0.0048	0.0913
	40–49 years	0.0041	−0.0144	0.0037	0.0885
	50–59 years	0.0249	−0.0319	0.0197	0.2200
Income Theil scale between groups		0.0736	−0.0365	0.0623	0.1384
Overall Theil scale		0.0919	−0.0450	0.0780	0.1249

(continued)

Table 4 (continued)

1960s		Income Y_B		Income Y_D	
	Classification	Theil scale $T(Y_B)$	Redistribution effect of income taxation $R(Y_A, Y_B)$	Theil scale $T(Y_D)$	Redistribution effect $R(Y_A, Y_D)$
Income Theil scale within groups	*1st quantile*				
	20–29 years	0.0336	0.6350	0.0397	0.3837
	30–39 years	0.0050	1.3306	0.0053	1.2048
	40–49 years	0.0052	0.7129	0.0056	0.6091
	50–59 years	0.0065	0.0719	0.0070	0.0002
	2nd quantile				
	20–29 years	0.0067	2.9801	0.0069	2.8972
	30–39 years	0.0470	0.3848	0.0579	0.1239
	40–49 years	0.0041	1.0054	0.0041	0.9978
	50–59 years	0.0039	0.6796	0.0037	0.7749
	3rd quantile				
	20–29 years	0.0051	0.1055	0.0051	0.1156
	30–39 years	0.0178	0.2840	0.0190	0.2064
	40–49 years	0.0533	0.2556	0.0693	−0.0341
	50–59 years	0.0044	0.1000	0.0042	0.1550
	4th quantile				
	20–29 years	0.0045	−0.0312	0.0042	0.0271
	30–39 years	0.0041	0.0136	0.0039	0.0632
	40–49 years	0.0200	0.2662	0.0211	0.2015
	50–59 years	0.0493	0.2006	0.0637	−0.0711
	5th quantile				
	20–29 years	0.0059	0.0240	0.0059	0.0192
	30–39 years	0.0057	−0.0856	0.0055	−0.0541
	40–49 years	0.0046	−0.1236	0.0045	−0.0948
	50–59 years	0.0191	0.2604	0.0199	0.2098
Income Theil scale between groups		0.0423		0.0452	
Overall Theil scale		0.0559		0.0604	

(continued)

Table 4 (continued)

1970s		Income Y_B		Income Y_D	
	Classification	Theil scale $T(Y_B)$	Redistribution effect of income taxation $R(Y_A, Y_B)$	Theil scale $T(Y_D)$	Redistribution effect $R(Y_A, Y_D)$
Income Theil scale within groups	*1st quantile*				
	20–29 years	0.0447	0.2278	0.0505	0.0877
	30–39 years	0.0068	0.7145	0.0074	0.5667
	40–49 years	0.0049	0.8155	0.0055	0.6454
	50–59 years	0.0054	0.2896	0.0059	0.1830
	2nd quantile				
	20–29 years	0.0088	2.0247	0.0090	1.9541
	30–39 years	0.0579	0.1232	0.0682	−0.0468
	40–49 years	0.0056	0.4700	0.0060	0.3805
	50–59 years	0.0042	0.5681	0.0044	0.4940
	3rd quantile				
	20–29 years	0.0040	0.3981	0.0042	0.3392
	30–39 years	0.0171	0.3340	0.0183	0.2503
	40–49 years	0.0621	0.0773	0.0775	−0.1359
	50–59 years	0.0044	0.1000	0.0043	0.1197
	4th quantile				
	20–29 years	0.0038	0.1327	0.0039	0.1175
	30–39 years	0.0035	0.2035	0.0035	0.1793
	40–49 years	0.0198	0.2812	0.0210	0.2088
	50–59 years	0.0556	0.0642	0.0696	−0.1500
	5th quantile				
	20–29 years	0.0058	0.0523	0.0059	0.0310
	30–39 years	0.0049	0.0534	0.0050	0.0487
	40–49 years	0.0039	0.0350	0.0039	0.0317
	50–59 years	0.0192	0.2509	0.0202	0.1929
Income Theil scale between groups		0.0554	0.2805	0.0583	0.2162
Overall Theil scale		0.0695	0.2631	0.0740	0.1868

(continued)

Table 4 (continued)

1980s		Income Y_B		Income Y_D	
	Classification	Theil scale $T(Y_B)$	Redistribution effect of income taxation $R(Y_A, Y_B)$	Theil scale $T(Y_D)$	Redistribution effect $R(Y_A, Y_D)$
Income Theil scale within groups	*1st quantile*				
	20–29 years	0.0471	0.1673	0.0517	0.0623
	30–39 years	0.0072	0.6234	0.0079	0.4696
	40–49 years	0.0049	0.8412	0.0056	0.6058
	50–59 years	0.0054	0.2832	0.0062	0.1232
	2nd quantile				
	20–29 years	0.0094	1.8296	0.0099	1.7005
	30–39 years	0.0602	0.0794	0.0686	−0.0520
	40–49 years	0.0061	0.3530	0.0065	0.2627
	50–59 years	0.0044	0.5174	0.0047	0.4059
	3rd quantile				
	20–29 years	0.0038	0.4841	0.0042	0.3508
	30–39 years	0.0170	0.3447	0.0189	0.2084
	40–49 years	0.0642	0.0423	0.0778	−0.1400
	50–59 years	0.0044	0.0975	0.0044	0.1001
	4th quantile				
	20–29 years	0.0038	0.1261	0.0040	0.0726
	30–39 years	0.0034	0.2110	0.0036	0.1481
	40–49 years	0.0194	0.3058	0.0214	0.1860
	50–59 years	0.0568	0.0416	0.0697	−0.1511
	5th quantile				
	20–29 years	0.0057	0.0651	0.0059	0.0270
	30–39 years	0.0048	0.0892	0.0050	0.0451
	40–49 years	0.0038	0.0793	0.0039	0.0386
	50–59 years	0.0188	0.2831	0.0203	0.1864
Income Theil scale between groups		0.0578	0.2256	0.0605	0.1710
Overall Theil scale		0.0720	0.2192	0.0764	0.1491

(continued)

Table 4 (continued)

1990s		Income Y_B		Income Y_D	
	Classification	Theil scale $T(Y_B)$	Redistribution effect of income taxation $R(Y_A, Y_B)$	Theil scale $T(Y_D)$	Redistribution effect $R(Y_A, Y_D)$
Income Theil scale within groups	*1st quantile*				
	20–29 years	0.0494	0.1119	0.0542	0.0139
	30–39 years	0.0083	0.3972	0.0092	0.2597
	40–49 years	0.0057	0.5875	0.0063	0.4324
	50–59 years	0.0055	0.2746	0.0057	0.2342
	2nd quantile				
	20–29 years	0.0126	1.1188	0.0139	0.9164
	30–39 years	0.0620	0.0492	0.0704	−0.0762
	40–49 years	0.0066	0.2407	0.0071	0.1621
	50–59 years	0.0049	0.3389	0.0053	0.2535
	3rd quantile				
	20–29 years	0.0042	0.3455	0.0044	0.2923
	30–39 years	0.0177	0.2899	0.0183	0.2492
	40–49 years	0.0651	0.0281	0.0788	−0.1499
	50–59 years	0.0045	0.0730	0.0044	0.0976
	4th quantile				
	20–29 years	0.0039	0.0976	0.0040	0.0895
	30–39 years	0.0036	0.1542	0.0037	0.1392
	40–49 years	0.0203	0.2488	0.0208	0.2180
	50–59 years	0.0572	0.0332	0.0701	−0.1560
	5th quantile				
	20–29 years	0.0057	0.0646	0.0058	0.0516
	30–39 years	0.0047	0.0980	0.0048	0.0942
	40–49 years	0.0037	0.0846	0.0037	0.0890
	50–59 years	0.0193	0.2441	0.0198	0.2185
Income Theil scale between groups		0.0608	0.1655	0.0629	0.1273
Overall theil scale		0.0754	0.1637	0.0787	0.1150

(continued)

Table 4 (continued)

2000s		Income Y_B		Income Y_D	
	Classification	Theil Sscale $T(Y_B)$	Redistribution effect of income taxation $R(Y_A, Y_B)$	Theil scale $T(Y_D)$	Redistribution effect $R(Y_A, Y_D)$
Income Theil scale within groups	*1st quantile*				
	20–29 years	0.0482	0.1392	0.0529	0.0382
	30–39 years	0.0080	0.4482	0.0089	0.3095
	40–49 years	0.0057	0.5860	0.0062	0.4369
	50–59 years	0.0054	0.2855	0.0056	0.2470
	2nd quantile				
	20–29 years	0.0129	1.0674	0.0143	0.8630
	30–39 years	0.0609	0.0672	0.0693	−0.0611
	40–49 years	0.0063	0.2999	0.0067	0.2249
	50–59 years	0.0047	0.3932	0.0050	0.3165
	3rd quantile				
	20–29 years	0.0042	0.3340	0.0044	0.2916
	30–39 years	0.0178	0.2819	0.0184	0.2408
	40–49 years	0.0646	0.0359	0.0782	−0.1441
	50–59 years	0.0045	0.0736	0.0044	0.1012
	4th quantile				
	20–29 years	0.0039	0.1061	0.0039	0.1038
	30–39 years	0.0036	0.1683	0.0036	0.1612
	40–49 years	0.0204	0.2405	0.0210	0.2098
	50–59 years	0.0571	0.0361	0.0699	−0.1540
	5th quantile				
	20–29 years	0.0057	0.0637	0.0058	0.0514
	30–39 years	0.0048	0.0943	0.0048	0.0915
	40–49 years	0.0037	0.0832	0.0037	0.0888
	50–59 years	0.0193	0.2456	0.0197	0.2201
Income Theil scale between groups		0.0602	0.1777	0.0622	0.1390
Overall Theil scale		0.0747	0.1747	0.0780	0.1254

Note Overall Theil scale = $\sum$ intra-income group Theil scale × weight + inter-income group Theil scale

Second, from Table 2, we can verify the Theil scale by income group and redistribution effects. Differentiation of income groups is as follows: income Y_A, the present discounted value of total income from the head of household and spouse (including income both from labor and pensions), was divided equally into five quantiles, from low-income households in the 1st quantile, through the 2nd, 3rd, 4th, and 5th quantiles, implying that these are the income groups in the lifecycle.

From an overview of the internal disparity in income groups and the disparity between income groups according to income Y_A Theil scale $T(Y_A)$ we see that, basically in every case, the income group's internal disparity was smaller than the disparity between income groups (0.0631). However, the 1st quantile's internal disparity (0.0742) was so large that it exceeded the disparity between groups; it was followed by the 5th quantile's internal disparity (0.0308), which was also large. From this, we understand that income inequality is large at the top and bottom levels of income distribution.

Income taxation's redistribution effect $R(Y_A, Y_B)$ is positive and, in particular, its effects in the 3rd quantile (0.3980) were large, followed by the 2nd quantile (0.3636), with the 1st quantile (0.0970) having the smallest redistribution effects. Moreover, it shows that in recent decades, the redistribution effect of income taxation has declined. In other words, it would seem that the revisions to the income tax system that have been made in the past have weakened its redistribution effects. On the other hand, the redistribution effect of insurance contributions $R(Y_A, Y_C)$ has a strong negative redistribution effect of causing inequality to increase, and among the quantiles, the extent of its negative redistribution effect is greater in the 1st quantile (▲0.1272). Notably, insurance contributions tend to be regressive for low-income earners.

Third, Table 3 shows the Theil scale by generation group and the redistribution effects. The differentiation of the generations was as follows: with the head of household's age in 2004 taken as the standard, they were divided into four groups of 20–29 years (20s), 30–39 years (30s), 40–49 years (40s), and 50–59 years (50s).

From the income, Y_A Theil scale $T(Y_A)$, the intrageneration disparity was greater than intergenerational disparity (0.0012). In particular, income inequality within the group in their 20s (0.0962) and in their 50s (0.0911) has been expanding. The expansion in income inequality among the older group is explained by population aging, but it is necessary to focus on the expansion in income inequality during the younger age period. Looking at the intrageneration Theil scale by decade, for the 20s group, we see that the Theil scale was highest in the 2000s, and income inequality is expanding for the young generation. The redistribution effect for income taxation $R(Y_A, Y_B)$ is positive and its effects are particularly significant for the 20s group. The redistribution effect for insurance contributions $R(Y_A, Y_C)$ is negative and its negative effect tends to be stronger on the group in their 20s with low-income levels.

Finally, for reference purposes, Table 4 shows the results of the analysis of the Theil scale by income group and by generation group and the redistribution effects.

8 Conclusion

In this chapter, household microdata was used to construct a lifecycle model and the redistribution effects of income taxation and insurance contributions were measured. The results of the analysis show that while income taxation corrects (reduces) income inequality, insurance contributions expand income inequality. Further, income inequality is greater in the upper and lower levels of income distribution; the redistribution effects of income taxation have been gradually declining; and insurance contributions have tended to regress for low-income earners; and income inequality expands for people who are young.

Notably, income inequality has been spreading in Japan in recent years. Further, tax revenue from income tax is slumping due to continued tax cuts, despite its being the fundamental levy in national taxes. It is important to strengthening the income redistribution function of income taxation and improve the ability to procure tax revenues if we are to restore income tax to its position as the fundamental tax. As income inequality increases indefinitely when the market takes over income distribution, only the government's income redistribution function can be expected to correct income inequality.

Today, population aging is the underlying factor behind the expansion of income inequality; however, overall, we find that the problem of the expansion of income inequality among the young is a problem with more policy implications. However, if income inequality among the young is carried forward into the future, further expansion of the problem could destabilize society. Moreover, when considering that insurance contributions tend to have a regressive and negative redistribution effect, it is important to strengthen the redistribution effect of income taxation.

Specifically, making tax deductions for each income deduction and changing the income levels subject to taxation are approaches that could be considered. In particular, reducing public pension deduction will tax high-income senior citizens and it is a reform that will be necessary if we are to correct income inequality. Strengthening the income redistribution function of income taxation and the ability to procure tax revenues by changing the tax brackets will likely be an important reform in the future. Even if the highest tax rate is hiked, it will still be necessary to strengthen the income redistribution function of income tax, but even more important is the negative income redistribution effect resulting from income deductions. Replacing income deductions with tax deductions will strengthen the income redistribution function. Alternatively, setting an upper limit for deduction in insurance contributions that cause a major loss of tax revenues can be considered. However, the problem is how to make it consistent with the social security system.

9 Addendum: Marginal Effective Tax Rate and the Lifetime Burden Rate

By looking at monetary aggregates without considering the institutional rules as they apply to each taxpayer and benefit recipient, they also cannot capture the extents to which taxes and benefits affect incentives of people in different incomes. This chapter aims to fill these gaps by providing detailed measures of both average and marginal effective tax rates facing households in Japan.

Effective tax rates capture the net tax burden resulting from the interaction of different types of taxes and contributions on one hand and benefit payments on the other. Average effective tax rates express the resulting net payments as a fraction of the income on which they are levied. They are therefore useful in assessing the size of transfers given the incomes and circumstances observed at a given point in time.

Marginal effective tax rates, on the other hand, measure the degree to which any additional income would be “taxed away”. Marginal effective tax rates are therefore useful measures for evaluating the financial incentives to engage in activities meant to generate or increase income.

Macro-based summary indicators of effective tax burdens do not capture differences in effective tax rates facing different sub-groups of the population. They also cannot provide information on the level or distribution of the marginal effective tax rates thought to influence household behaviour. The tax-benefit microsimulation model, to compute distributions of average and marginal effective tax rates across the household population in Japan.

Using different definitions of “net taxes”, the tax, base and the unit of analysis, I present a range of measures showing the contribution of the tax-benefit system to household incomes, the average effective tax rates applicable to income from labour, and marginal effective tax rates faced by working people. Effective tax rates are broken down to separately show the influence of each type of tax-benefit instrument. The results show that measures of effective tax rates vary considerably depending on incomes, labour market situations, and family circumstances. Using single averages or macro-based indicators will therefore provide an inappropriate picture of tax burdens faced by large parts of the population.

In this chapter, the focus was on the impact income taxation and insurance contributions have on a household’s disposable income; these effects on a household’s income distribution were verified by income group and by generation group. Income taxation and insurance contributions can be evaluated from the perspective of fairness and efficiency. In this chapter, the evaluation of the redistribution effect was from the viewpoint of fairness, but it is also possible that the greater the redistribution effect from the pursuit of fairness, the larger becomes the excess burden, leading to loss of efficiency.

There in this addendum, we evaluate from the perspective of efficiency. Specifically, based on this chapter’s lifecycle model, the lifetime income amount by household and the lifetime burden amount by household are provisionally calculated, and the marginal effective tax rate of income tax and the lifetime burden rate in the lifecycle are calculated.

The reason for focusing on the marginal effective tax rate and the lifetime burden rate in this addendum is as follows. The marginal effective tax rate is considered to have a negative effect on a household's economic behavior, particularly labor supply. That is, if the marginal effective tax rate is raised, the household's labor supply efficiency is lost. In addition, marginal economic behavior is affected by this marginal effective tax rate. Through the public pension system and income taxation insurance contribution deductions, the marginal effective tax rate also affects after-tax income following retirement.

Conversely, the lifetime burden rate is the public burden of lifetime tax and social security relative to lifetime income in the lifecycle. If the national burden rate is the public burden rate in a macro single year, the lifetime burden rate here is the public burden in a household's lifecycle. This is a feature of the lifetime burden rate when considering generations and time.

The lifecycle model's conceptual diagram, data processing method, work procedure, measurement of income from labor, measurement of pension income, and the measurement of income taxation and insurance contributions are all the same as previously in this chapter. Here, the marginal effective tax rate τ and lifetime burden rate T are derived from the following formulas. Both are evaluated from the present discounted value.

$$\begin{aligned} \tau_t &= \frac{\partial \sum_{a=a_m}^{a_d} \left(N_a^H + N_a^S + L_a^H + L_a^S + P_a^H + P_a^S\right)/Q_t}{\partial W_t^H} \\ T &= \frac{\sum_{a=a_m}^{a_d} \left(N_a^H + N_a^S + L_a^H + L_a^S + P_a^H + P_a^S\right)/Q_t}{\sum_{a=a_m}^{a_d} \left(W_a^H + W_a^S + B_a^H + B_a^S\right)/Q_t} \end{aligned} \tag{18}$$

In the above, the marginal effective tax rate τ_t is assumed to be the increase in income on the one-year unit of year t, and is obtained by provisionally calculating the extent of the occurrence of the lifetime public burden (numerator) with regards to this one unit of income (denominator). The year t was set as 1980, 1990, 2000, and 2010. Further, the lifetime burden rate T is calculated by dividing the present discounted value (numerator) of the tax burden and insurance contribution burden obtained from the lifecycle model by lifetime income (denominator) in the lifecycle. Figure 5 shows the trends in the marginal effective tax rate and the lifetime burden rate, and Fig. 6 shows the trend in the marginal effective tax rate by income.

First, from Fig. 5 onwards, we will examine the relationship between the marginal effective tax rate and the lifetime burden rate (vertical axis) based on lifetime income (horizontal axis). In accordance with the income taxation and insurance contribution systems, the marginal effective tax rate and the lifetime burden rate increase in general as lifetime income increases. However, compared to the marginal effective tax rate and the lifetime burden rate, the marginal effective tax rate seems to trend above the lifetime burden rate. In particular, in households with high lifetime income, we see that the marginal effective tax rate tends to be higher.

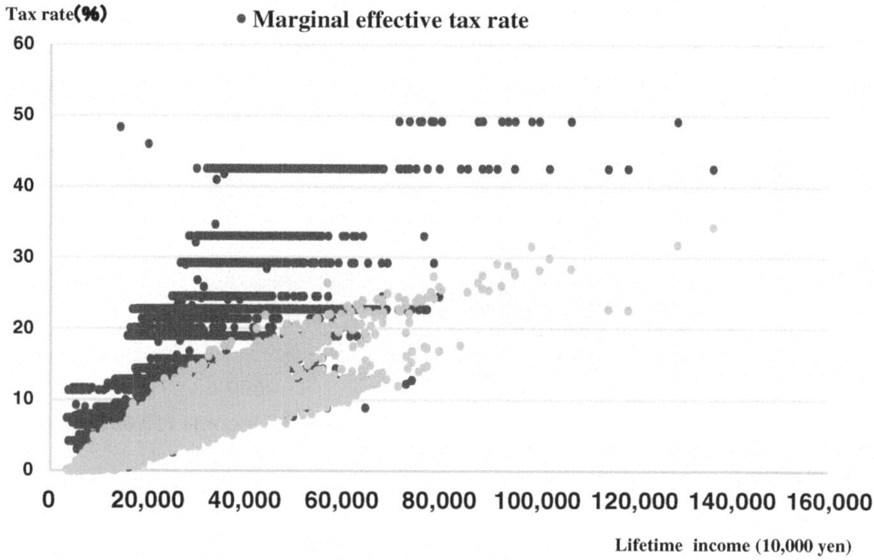

Fig. 5 Marginal effective tax rate and lifetime burden rate

The divergence between the marginal effective tax rate and the lifetime burden rate is notably large in the middle-income and high-income groups, while it is not so large in the low-income group. This means that divergence suggests the possibility that income taxation is inefficient with regard to a household's labor supply. It is also important to observe the effects of system reforms for income taxation and the social security system in a time series.

We will verify the yearly changes (five-year intervals) in the marginal effective tax rate by income group. Below, income groups are divided into five quantiles, namely 1st income group (lowest group) to 5th income group (highest group). Figure 5 depicts the marginal effective tax rate (vertical axis) for each respective income group's annual income (horizontal axis).

The low-income group's marginal effective tax rate is naturally lower than that of the high-income group. The low-income group's marginal effective tax rate was relatively low in 1990 compared to 1980. It rose slightly in 2000 and was at its highest in 2010. A similar trend can be seen for the 2nd to 4th income groups, with the marginal effective tax rate rising from 1980 to 2010. The rate for the highest income group, the 5th income group, repeatedly increased and decreased, and its marginal effective tax rate in 1990 was higher compared to in 1980, but it declined in 2000 before rising in 2010.

From the above, we understand that the marginal effective tax rate has been rising in recent years for practically all the income groups. Even among them, the middle-income group's marginal effective tax rate has traced a rising path, and there is concern that this is obstructing the efficiency of the household's labor supply. The middle-income is subjected to considerably larger marginal tax burdens than their

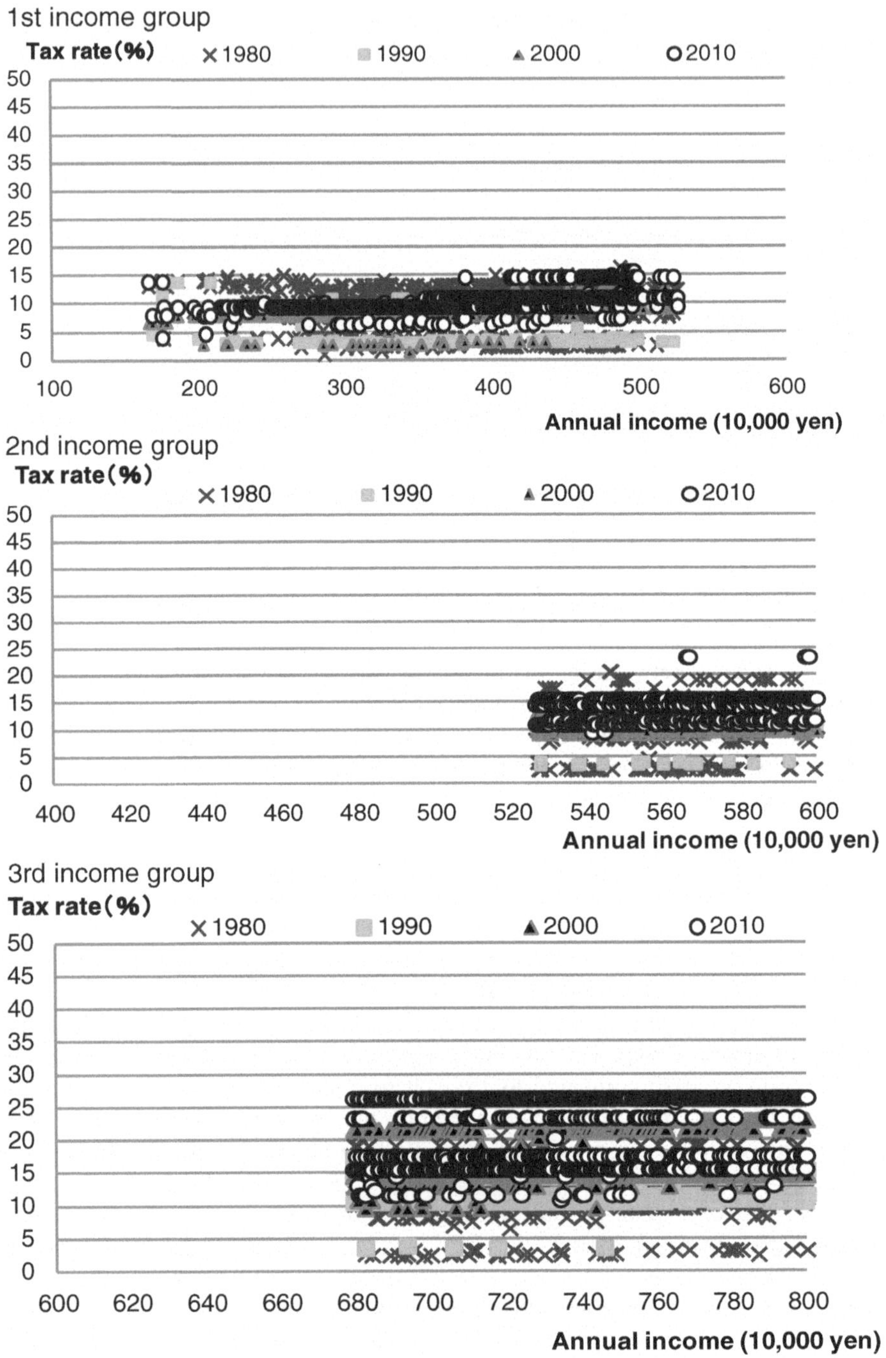

Fig. 6 Trends in the marginal effective tax rate

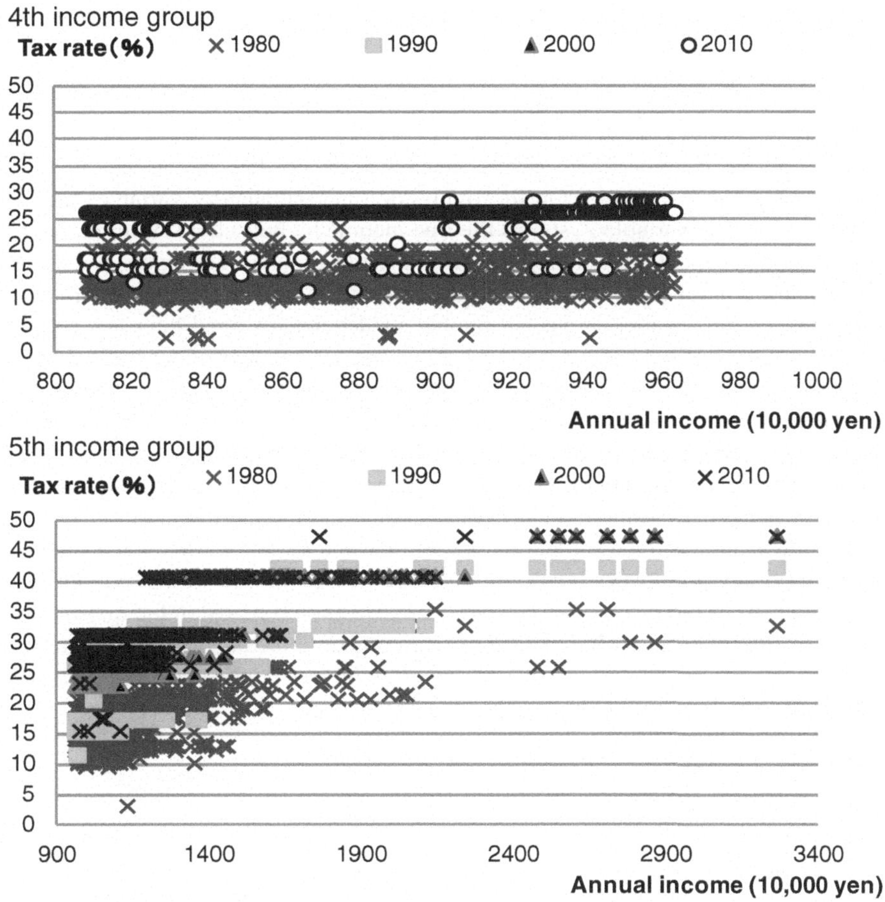

Fig. 6 (continued)

low-income and high-income counterparts. Lowering the marginal effective tax rate requires revising the tax rate structure. However, Japan's income taxation has been biased toward revising the system of deductions rather than the tax rate structure. Investigations have begun on approaches for the marginal effective tax rate and labor supply, particularly for women's working conditions, and it is considered that it will continue to be an important issue of debate in the future.

On the other hand, it is believed that a household's lifetime burden rate is determined by its characteristics. So which types of households have high and low lifetime burden rates? Moreover, to what extent are these factors influential? Next, we will estimate the extent to which the number of household members used when calculating spousal deduction, general dependent deduction, and elderly dependent deduction, affect the lifetime burden rate. The estimation model is shown in Formula (19) below.

$$T_i = a_0 + a_1 Z_i + a_2 \mathrm{DUM}_i + a_3 H_\mathrm{i} + \mu_i \quad (19)$$

In the above formula, the variable explained on the left side is the lifetime burden rate T_i by household. On the right side, the explanatory variables are Z_i, DUM_i and Hi. The variable Z_i shows lifetime income by household. With regard to (spouse's employment conditions), DUM_i is the full-time worker (spouse) dummy and part-time worker (spouse) dummy. Further, (deduction factor) H_i is the number of dependents aged under 16 years, number of dependents aged between 16 and 18 years, number of dependents aged 19–22 years, and number of dependents aged 70 years and above. The subscript i represents households. Table 5 shows the descriptive statistics of the variables and Table 6 the estimation results. The estimations were conducted separately for all households: households eligible for a spouse deduction, those eligible for general dependent deduction, and households eligible for elderly dependent deduction.

From the results of the estimations shown in Table 6, we see that when lifetime income by household grows larger, the increase in the lifetime burden rate reflects the mechanism of the income tax system. Here, we should focus on the question of to what extent, after controlling for the lifetime income factor, the lifetime burden rate is affected by the presence of persons eligible for spouse deduction, general dependent deduction, and elderly dependent deduction.

Table 5 Descriptive statistics

For the thesis					
Variable name	No. of samples	Average	Dispersion	Minimum value	Maximum value
Lifetime burden rate (%)	27,134	5.76	4.07	0.00	34.40
Lifetime income (10,000 yen)	27,134	20,643.34	11,958.82	0.00	13,6018.30
Full-time work (spouse)	27,134	0.26	0.44	0	1
Part-time work (spouse)	27,134	0.22	0.41	0	1
No. of dependents aged under 16 years	27,134	0.76	0.97	0	5
No. of dependents aged 16–18 years	27,134	0.23	0.53	0	3
No. of dependents aged 19–22 years	27,134	0.17	0.44	0	3
No. of dependents aged 70 years and above	27,134	0.12	0.38	0	3

Table 6 Factor analysis of the lifetime burden rate by household

For the thesis												
Lifetime burden rate by household	All households			Eligible for spousal deduction			Eligible for general dependent deduction			Eligible for elderly dependent deduction		
	Coefficient	*t*-value	*P* > |t|	Coefficient	*t*-value	*P* > |t|	Coefficient	*t*-value	*P* > |t|	Coefficient	*t*-value	*P* > |t|
Lifetime income by household	3.22.E−04	445.35	***	3.18.E−04	379.92	***	0.023	296.25	***	2.69.E−04	121.42	***
Full-time work (spouse)	−1.469	−72.82	***				−2.366	−37.56	***	−1.026	−19.06	***
Part-time work (spouse)	−1.202	−56.02	***				−1.198	−18.96	***	−0.970	−14.88	***
No. of dependents aged under 16 years	−0.588	−63.67	***	−0.525	−49.33	***				−0.499	−16.40	***
No. of dependents aged 16–18 years	−0.752	−46.72	***	−0.864	−46.22	***				−0.626	−16.45	***
No. of dependents aged 19–22 years	−0.508	−25.80	***	−0.574	−25.00	***				−0.425	−8.67	***
No. of dependents aged 70 years and above	−1.021	−45.64	***	−1.241	−46.54	***	−1.171	−17.04	***			
Cons	0.596	30.62	***	0.010	0.48	***	−0.002	−0.04		0.085	1.49	
AdjR-squared	0.887			0.857			0.836			0.839		
F-test	*F*(8, 27,126) =30,502.73***			*F*(5, 25,366) = 30,487.48***			*F*(4, 17.414) = 22,118.58***			*F*(6, 2938) = 26,849.83***		

***, **, and * indicate significance levels of 1, 5, and 10%, respectively

On verifying the effects according to the spouse's employment conditions, for both full-time workers and part-time workers, the spouse deduction is a factor reducing the lifetime burden rate. Notably, compared to households in which the spouse is unemployed, households in which the spouse is employed receive a rise in income that exceeds the increase in the burden amount, causing the lifetime burden rate to decline. Further, with regard to children eligible for the general dependent deduction and to senior citizens eligible for elderly dependent deduction, if the number of such dependents increases, the lifetime burden rate decreases. An outcome of this decrease is that people eligible for spousal deduction have the largest coefficient.

Households that receive the respective deductions were analyzed as being eligible for spouse deduction, for a general dependent deduction, and for an elderly dependent deduction.[13] While examining each household's eligibility for a deduction, it was seen that in households eligible for spouse deduction, as the number of dependents increases, the lifetime burden rate becomes significantly larger, and both households are eligible for a general dependent deduction. In households eligible for elderly dependent deduction, the household tax burden rate significantly decreases in households in which the spouse is employed, compared to those in which he or she is unemployed.

[13]The estimations were made by only extracting information on the targets of the analysis. For example, in the case of spousal deduction, only information on households eligible for such a deduction were extracted.

Chapter 3
The Burden of Indirect Taxation and Consumption Tax by Income Group

1 Introduction

Since the cost of social security in Japan is rising due to an aging population and a low birth rate, an enormous quantity of long-term public bonds have been issued in order to cope with the lack of funding for social security programs. As part of its efforts to reform and secure financial resources for social security, the Japanese government implemented its Comprehensive Reform of Social Security and Tax, thus raising the consumption tax.

The Japanese government implemented The Comprehensive Reform by raising indirect taxation to reform, and secure financial resources for, social security. Indirect taxation in Japan includes excise taxes in addition to a consumption tax. As such, the rise of indirect taxes would lead to an increase in the tax burden on households, and there is concern that the burden will mostly increase among low-income groups, especially the consumption tax. The regressivity of the consumption tax has become a problem, whereby the lower the income group in Japan, the greater the burden of tax on income, and governments have historically had difficulty with raising tax rates.[1] Consequently, opposition to the consumption tax

This chapter is an updated version of Adachi et al. (2017) "Measuring the burden of indirect taxation including consumption tax in Japan by income group," *Public Finance and Management* 17(3).

[1]Revenue from the consumption tax, based on the provisions of the Local Allocation Tax Act (Act Second11 of 1951), will be assigned every fiscal year to cover the expenses required for the social security benefits of pension, medical care, and nursing care. An increase in tax revenue resulting from the consumption tax hike will be appropriated in full as the financial resources for social security for the benefit of all citizens.

Y. Adachi, *The Economics of Tax and Social Security in Japan*,
https://doi.org/10.1007/978-981-10-7176-8_3

increase was deeply rooted. Moreover, declining household incomes in recent years have spurred opposition to the increase in consumption tax.[2]

Japan introduced the consumption tax as a value-added tax in April 1989 in response to its aging society. This tax increased from 3% in 1989 to 5% in April 1997, and to 8% in April 2014. The Japanese standard VAT rate is 8.0%, which is below the OECD average. The average VAT/GST standard rate in the OECD was 19.2% as of January 1, 2016, up from 17.7% on January 1, 2009. A further rate rise to 10% is planned for October 2019. While Japan's current consumption tax rate includes both national and local consumption taxes, in this chapter, "consumption tax" refers to these taxes taken together.

Consumption taxes are noted for their regressivity. A regressive tax is a tax that takes a larger burdens percentage of income from low-income earners than from high-income earners. It is in opposition with a progressive tax, which takes a larger percentage from high-income earners. Policy makers have considered various policies, the reduction of tax rates, zero taxes on food products, and tax refunds to lower-income earners, to reduce this regressivity of consumption tax. The ruling coalition agreement for introducing a lower tax rate on food products when the consumption tax is raised in April 2017 is a compromise that appears to have prioritized political interests over both the nation's fiscal sustainability and efforts to reduce the impact of the increased tax burden on low-income people. It was proposed to keep the current 8 percent rate on food and beverages, except for alcoholic drinks and dining in restaurants, when the consumption tax rate is hiked to 10 percent may be intended to ease the regressive nature of the consumption tax, which will proportionately hit poorer households more severely than wealthy ones. Many European economies that impose a value-added tax of over 20 percent have either reduced or eliminated taxes on such necessities, and a similar system may make sense for Japan as it raises the consumption tax to 10 percent — and possibly even higher in the future. As such, the Japanese government is planning to reduce food taxes once the consumption tax increases to 10%.

However, indirect taxation in Japan includes excise taxes in addition to the consumption tax. Figure 1 shows the burden of indirect taxes as a percentage of national income for a number of developed countries. As with the European VAT and American sales and use tax, the burden of excise taxes accounts for a considerable share of national income. According to Fig. 1, in 2012, consumption tax accounted for a 3.7% share of national income (including local consumption tax). As the consumption tax rate in 2010 was 5%, calculations for a rate of 8% yield a share of around 5.92% of national income, while a 10% rate yields a share of around 7.4%. Nonetheless, the burden of consumption tax as a percentage of national income will decrease if reduced tax rates are applied to food products.

[2]National Tax Agency reports the result of the Statistical Survey of Actual status for Salary in the Private Sector every year (Private sector means that it does not include public servants salaries, and it does not include self-employed persons also). According to the latest result (2013), the average annual salary of wage workers in the private sectors has gradually declined 4,118,000 in 1996 to 3,595,000 yen in 2013.

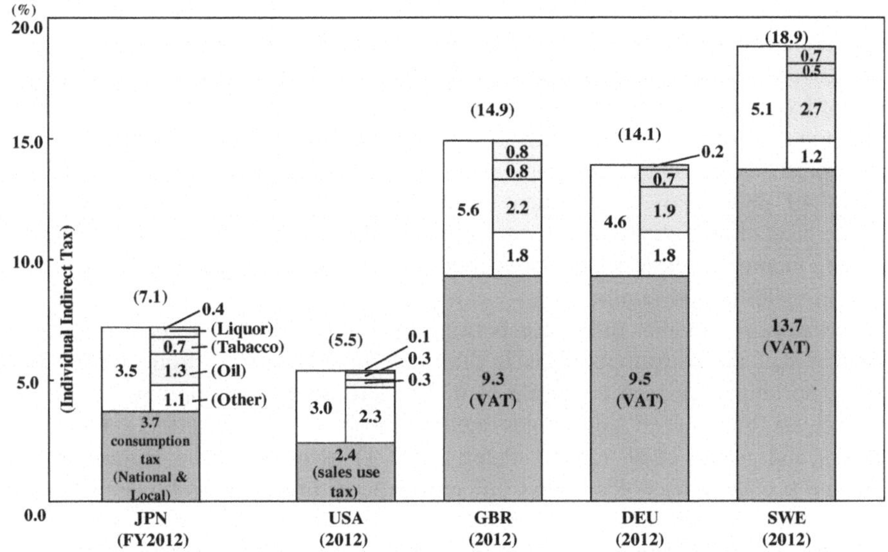

Fig. 1 International comparison of consumption tax burden as percentage of national income. *Source* Ministry of Finance, "Consumption taxes as percentage of national income" (National and local taxes), 2012; OECD, "Revenue Statistics 1965–2013" and "National Accounts"

Japanese excise taxes account for 3.5% of national income. In other words, they account for a roughly similar share of national income to that of the consumption tax with a rate of 5%. The burden of excise taxes in Britain, Germany, France, and Sweden also accounts for an approximate 5% share of national income. Accordingly, when considering the burden of indirect taxes on households, it is necessary to take into account the burden of excise taxes in addition to that of consumption ones. Any arguments on the regressivity of consumption taxes are bound to be inadequate if they fail to consider excise taxes.

2 Previous Studies

In previous studies, tax regressivity has been evaluated mainly by targeting the consumption tax using household microdata. In the early days, it was evaluated using single-year data (Davies et al. 1991; Rogers 1995; Mathur and Morris 2014); more recently, such studies have been based on trends in panel data for multiple fiscal years, whereby lifetime earnings and consumption are calculated to verify the burden of consumption tax (Poterba 1991; Lyon and Schwab 1995; DeCicca and McLeod 2008).

Chernick and Reschovsky (1997) and Lyon and Schwab (1995) stated that their studies used total consumption data from a single year as a basis for their tax incidence calculations, and estimated their income data on the basis of a sample of individuals from the PSID (The Panel Study of Income Dynamics (PSID) is a longitudinal panel survey), who were continuously heads of households over 18- and 20-year periods, respectively. By excluding female-headed households, in the case of Lyon and Schwab (1995), and maritally unstable households, in the case of Fullerton and Rogers (1991), these sample selection rules result in samples that are not representative of the US population. This is not a minor problem, because nearly 40 percent of the women in the first wave of the PSID lived in a female-headed household during one or more years of the sample period, and the average income of these women was about one-half of the income of women who were in male-headed families.

Furthermore, another difference between the consumption and excise taxes in Japan is that the consumption tax is often specified separately from the price of goods, so consumers can be aware of it. Previous studies attempting to estimate indirect tax burdens on households include those by Poterba (1991), Go et al. (2005), and André et al. (2010). Poterba (1991) investigates the regressivity of gasoline tax for households across different expenditure classes, showing that the burden of the gasoline tax as a share of total expenditure was less regressive than as a share of household income. Go et al. (2005) use a social accounting matrix to evaluate South African VAT and find that it is mildly regressive. They also consider an increase in VAT that took place when zero tax rates were applied to daily necessities as a means to ameliorate regressivity and secure government revenues. André et al. (2010) analyze the regressivity of indirect taxes (VAT and commodity taxes) by income group in five European countries (Belgium, Germany, Hungary, Ireland, and Britain). They conclude that these indirect taxes are regressive in relation to disposable income levels in each of the five countries.

Mirrlees et al. (2010, 2011) argue for consideration to be given to low-income earners in light of the acknowledged regressivity of VAT, and provide proposals for British taxation reform following the Meade report. They also conclude that a more comprehensive and uniform system of indirect taxation, as well the application of a single VAT rate to a wide range of goods, would be preferable.

Each of the studies mentioned found evidence for the regressivity of indirect taxes. While these studies analyze the burden on households of VAT, individual excise taxes, or aggregated indirect taxes, they do not specifically measure the burden of all indirect taxation, including consumption and excise taxes.

Japanese studies that calculate indirect tax burdens on households include those by Hayashi and Hashimoto (1993), and Uemura (2006).[3] Although they analyze the impacts of most typical indirect taxes on representative households, they do not measure indirect tax burden by income group. Such measurements are essential in order to assess the degree of indirect tax regressivity.

Accordingly, this chapter measures the burden of excise and consumption taxes by income group and explains the structure of indirect tax burdens inclusive of

[3]Uemura (2006) measures the tax burden on households for the commodity tax, an excise tax that existed prior to the introduction of the consumption tax.

excise taxes in Japan.[4] On this basis, we consider measures that could be taken to ameliorate the regressivity of indirect taxes including the consumption tax.

The chapter is structured as follows: Sect. 2 provides an overview of the regime of indirect taxes paid by Japanese households; Sect. 3 estimates the burden of indirect taxes according to income group; Sect. 4 evaluates the structure of the estimated indirect tax burden according to income group; Sect. 5 considers the policy responses to multiple tax rates debated in recent years, such as a lower or zero tax on food products; and conclusions and policy implications are given in Sect. 6.

3 The History of Consumption Tax in Japan

The Japanese consumption tax basically consists of a direct and an indirect tax. This is similar to the systems of VAT, GST, and other sales taxes in Western countries. In buying the goods, we pay the consumption tax, while the store operator pays duty on the goods to the government.

Originally, the consumption tax increase was introduced by the Liberal Democrat (LDP) administration under Prime Minister Nobuo Takeshita at a 3% rate in 1989, but it has been repeatedly withdrawn many times because of its regressivity. It was first proposed in 1979 under Prime Minister Masayoshi Ōhira, but at that time, the introduction of a general consumption tax (5% tax rate) was withdrawn due to strong arguments against it. In 1987, during the premiership of Prime Minister Yasuhiro Nakasone, it was submitted to the Diet as a "new indirect tax" (5% tax rate) in a legislative bill concerning sales tax that includes cuts in personal income taxation, elimination of the savings interest exemption, a reduction in the corporate taxation rate accompanied by inclusion of capital reserves in the tax base, and the introduction of a 5% broad-based value-added tax. It was neither comprehensive nor a "large indirect tax," but it was nonetheless withdrawn as a result of strong opposition from the retail industry.

In 1989, during the period in office of the Cabinet appointed by Prime Minister Noboru Takeshita in 1988, the Consumption Tax Act came into effect thanks to vigorous support from the Liberal Democratic Party. It was initially introduced as 3% and subsequently raised to 5% in 1997 under Prime Minister Ryutaro Hashimoto's administration. As social security benefits expanded as a result of the declining birth rate and aging population, it became difficult to secure the source of funds for social security expenses, and, in 2014, this tax was raised to 8% under Prime Minister Shinzo Abe's administration. When the consumption tax was proposed, it was feared that it would be set at more than 10% and it seems that within the next few years, it will reach that level.

---

[4]This paper updates the estimations of Saitoh and Uemura (2011) using new data.

However, consumption taxes are noted for their regressivity because of the greater tax burdens incurred by lower income groups. A number of policy measures aimed at reducing this regressivity have been considered in the past, including reduced tax rates and zero taxes on food products, as well as tax refunds to lower income earners. As such, the Japanese government is planning to raise food taxes once the consumption tax increases from 8 to 10%. One cautious theory warns that as Japan is on the way to recovering from deflation, increasing the consumption tax would have an adverse effect on the economy, for example by decreasing consumer demand. The general consumption tax is the best option for tax neutrality, but some people declare that it is problematic from the standpoint of fairness because lower-income earners bear a heavy burden. Noting that the economy is on a steady path of recovery, Abe and his Liberal Democratic Party emphasize that they would "accelerate" the Abenomics policies to make sure that Japan is finally out of deflation. The Abe administration explains that it will be boost the economy using Abenomics and realize an increase in wages while boosting consumption. Although the tax was originally set to be raised to 10 percent in October 2015, Abe has twice postponed the plan to try to ensure a solid economic recovery. The nation's economy is on a moderate recovery path at present, expanding for a sixth consecutive quarter in the second quarter of 2017, the longest stretch since the period between January 2005 and June 2006. Abe said at the time that to secure funding for his drive to foster human resources, intending to change how revenue from the consumption tax hike will be used. Under the previous plan, the government was to use a large portion of the nearly 5 trillion yen in increased revenue from the tax hike to repay debt and the remainder to improve the country's welfare system. In addition, Abe proposed that government will spend 2 trillion yen on a policy package focused on boosting support for childcare and higher education on the premise that the sales tax will be raised. While Japan's current consumption tax rate includes both national and local consumption taxes, in this study, "consumption tax" refers to these taxes taken together.

4 An Overview of Indirect Taxation in Japan

In Japan, the Constitution of Japan declares the principle of "taxation under the law," in Article 30, "the people shall be liable to taxation as provided by the law," and in Article 84, "no new taxes shall be imposed or existing ones modified except by law or under such conditions as the law may prescribe." These provisions clarify that taxation is a means to transfer part of the people's wealth to the state's coffers to procure funds for public services. Therefore, tax assessment and collection should be conducted according to the provisions of the law. This section provides an overview of the system of indirect taxation in Japan and analyzes national and local taxes separately. A tax is imposed also on an individual and a corporation to

		Taxation form	Designation	
National taxes		Direct taxation	Taxes on income and profits	Income tax / Corporate tax
			Taxes on property	Inheritance tax / Gift tax / Land tax
			Taxes on consumption	
		Indirect taxation	Taxes on income and profits	
			Taxes on property	Stamp duty/registration license tax
			Taxes on consumption	Liquor tax / Consumption tax / Gasoline tax / Petroleum gas tax / Aviation fuel tax / Petroleum tax / Tobacco tax / Customs duty/Local road tax / Power source development promotion tax
Local taxes	Prefectural taxes	Direct taxation	Taxes on income and profits	Prefectural inhabitant tax / Enterprise tax
			Taxes on consumption	Fixed assets tax Automobile tax Mine product tax Hunter's registration tax / Hunting tax
			Taxes on property	Real estate acquisition tax
		Indirect taxation	Taxes on income and profits	
			Taxes on consumption	Local consumption tax / Prefectural Tobacco tax / Golf course tax / Special local consumption tax/Local road transfer tax / Gasoline gift tax / Aviation fuel transfer tax
			Taxes on property	property acquisition tax
	Municipal taxes	Direct taxation	Taxes on income and profits	Municipal resident tax
			Taxes on property	Fixed property tax / Light car tax / Mine product tax / Special land holding tax
			Consumption tax	Municipal Tobacco tax
		Indirect taxation	Taxes on income and profits	part of Income tax / Corporate tax
			Taxes on property	Irrigation tax / Public facility tax / City planning tax / Residential land development tax / Business office tax
			Consumption tax	Liquor tax / Tobacco tax/Bathing tax

Fig. 2 Taxation system in Japan

income. There are an income tax and a corporation tax by a national tax. Municipal taxes are resident tax and business tax. The property tax is imposed on the real estate which an individual and a corporation. Commodities and the sales of services are taxed by the consumption tax. The tax is added onto the prices of commodities and services, and consumers buying commodities or services pay the tax. Non-taxed items are limited to which are made non-taxable in view of social policy. Non-taxed items include the sale and lending of land, the sale of securities, interest received, fees paid for government services, foreign exchange businesses, and expenditures for medical care, welfare, and a portion of educational outlays. As shown in Fig. 2, the tax system in Japan is organized into these two kinds of taxes. Local taxes represent the sum of prefectural and municipal taxes charged by local governments. National, prefectural, and municipal taxes have both a general tax and a specific tax. As such, indirect taxation forms part of both national and local taxation. For example, the consumption tax is the general tax in national taxation.

Japan's consumption tax was raised to 8% in April 2014, while the data used are from a period prior to 2011. Hence, this study examines the system of indirect taxation as of 2011 with a consumption tax rate of 5%. As the purpose of this study is to establish the burden of indirect taxation on households, Sects.4.1 and 4.2 present the indirect taxes paid by households.

4.1 National Indirect Taxation

First, the consumption tax was initially designed to be paid by households and is levied on transactions, with businesses paying at each stage of the commodity distribution process. The amount of tax payable is obtained by multiplying the tax rate by the amount of taxable sales and deducting the amount of tax paid at the time of purchase. Purchase tax deductions are carried out by using an accounting method that requires invoice amounts to be recorded.

Between April 1997 and the end of March 2014, the local consumption tax was calculated by multiplying the local rate of 25% by the amount of payable consumption tax at the national rate; that is, the tax rate of 5% included the national consumption tax rate of 4% and the local tax converted rate of 1%. As of April 2014 the consumption tax was raised to 8%, which is comprised of a 6.3% national tax and a converted local tax rate of 1.7%.[5]

Two special consumption-tax-related measures aimed at small- and medium-sized businesses have been established in Japan: an exemption of tax liability and a simplified tax system.[6] Under the tax exemption system, businesses with annual

---

[5]From October 2019, the consumption tax will be set at 10%. This will be comprised of a national consumption tax rate of 7.8% plus a 2.2% local tax rate.

[6]We calculate a rate of 1 dollar to 110 yen.

taxable sales of less than USD 92,000 are not required to pay the consumption tax. Meanwhile, the simplified tax system is aimed at businesses with annual taxable sales of less than USD 462,000, whereby the input tax may be calculated by multiplying the deemed purchase rate by the tax on sales.[7]

Under the tax liability exemption system, when a tax liability is exempted, it creates a tax profit. Within the simplified tax system, where the deemed purchase rate is higher than the actual purchase rate, tax amounts to the difference between the two tax profits. Tax profits are considered legal business earnings, just as if they were profits, which the business would have to pay taxes for without any preferential treatment.

Nonetheless, since the time at which the consumption tax was originally introduced, the scope of tax profits has been gradually reduced, owing to the multiple adjustments carried out in the intervening period.[8] In addition, Japan's consumption tax is not applied to all goods and services, with some non-taxable transactions being specified.[9]

The second is the liquor tax, which is levied at different rates, depending on the type of alcohol. For example, for every liter, a tax of USD 2.0 is payable for beer, 1.09 for sake rice wine, 1.82 for *shochu*, a type of spirit, 0.73 for wine, and 3.36 for whiskey. The tax rate on *happoshu*, a low-malt beer, varies according to the percentage of malt used, with a rate of USD 1.62 per liter of product containing between 25 and 50% malt, and 1.22 for one containing less than 25% malt.

The third is the national tobacco tax. The tobacco tax is set at USD 0.96 per box of 20 cigarettes. In addition, a special tobacco surtax of USD 0.15 is levied.

The fourth are the various energy-related indirect taxes. A gasoline tax is levied at a rate of USD 0.44, and a local gasoline tax at USD 0.05 per liter.[10] A motor vehicle tonnage tax is collected at USD 45.45 per 0.5 tons of weight for passenger vehicles, along with a promotion of power resources development tax of USD 3.64 per 1000 kW-h of electricity sold.

---

[7]The deemed purchase rates are set at 90% for Type 1 businesses (wholesalers), 80% for Type 2 (retailers), 70% for Type 3 (producers), 60% for Type 4 (other types) and 50% for Type 5 (service industry, etc.).

[8]In principle, the consumption tax was not intended to be paid by businesses, but by consumers. However, because of the circumstances surrounding its introduction, preferential measures were put in place for small- to medium-sized businesses.

[9]Non-taxable transactions include those concerning land, securities, interest on loans, postal stamps, revenue stamps, government administrative fees, services provided under the Health Insurance Act and Long-Term Care Insurance Act, services provided under the Social Welfare Services Act, midwifery services, burial or cremation charges, school fees at certain schools, school textbooks, and housing loans.

[10]Before 2007, the gasoline tax was known as the local roads tax.

4.2 Local Indirect Taxation

While many local indirect taxes were abolished with the introduction of the consumption tax in April 1989, some have remained.

The most representative local indirect taxes are the local tobacco taxes. A prefectural tobacco tax is levied at 21.48 yen, and a municipal one at 65.96 yen per box of 20 cigarettes. From April 2013, these rates were set at 17.2 and 105.24 yen, respectively.

A further local indirect tax is the automobile acquisition tax, which is levied at the point of acquisition. This tax is set at 5% of the value of private vehicles, and 3% of the value of business vehicles, and a light oil delivery tax is levied at 32.1 yen per liter. In addition, there is a golf course utilization tax with a standard rate of 800 yen per person per day, and a bathing tax of 150 yen per person per day.[11]

5 Estimation of Indirect Tax Burdens by Income Group

In this section, we describe the method used to estimate indirect tax burdens by income group. For this estimation, we used data from the Statistics Bureau of the Ministry of Internal Affairs and Communications, including the Family Income and Expenditure Survey (FIES), the National Survey of Family Income and Expenditure, the Population Census, Linked Input-Output Tables, and the White Paper on Local Public Finance, as well as the National Tax Agency's Annual Statistics Report. The estimation period covers the 12 years from 2001 to 2012.

5.1 Data Tendency

Table 1 shows the data for the rate of change in the nominal income of the tenth decile level data for 2005 and 2011. As shown in Table 1, there was a decrease in income of 6.52–8.77% in all income groups from the first to the tenth decile. Only the tenth decile was found to have a stable evolution, with a decrease of only 0.75%. Conversely, only the tenth decile of monthly living expenditure showed a tendency to increase, while the first to ninth deciles declined from 3.69 to 10.27%. From the data, it can be understood that income and consumption had declined in 2011 from its level in 2005 for most income groups.

The change in expenditures was far greater for the seventh to eighth deciles than the first to fifth deciles. This was caused by their change in income. For example,

[11]Local governments independently levy a number of indirect taxes. These taxes vary widely in type and do not bring in significant revenues, and thus are not discussed in this paper.

Table 1 Yearly income and monthly living expenditure

	Yearly income (in 10,000 yen)			Monthly living expenditure (in yen)		
	FY2005	FY2011	Change rate (%)	FY2005	FY2011	Change rate (%)
1st decile	136	127	−6.62	117,817	111,612	−5.27
2nd decile	235	217	−7.66	170,056	157,940	−7.12
3rd decile	304	284	−6.58	191,747	184,662	−3.69
4th decile	368	344	−6.52	220,072	210,099	−4.53
5th decile	436	400	−8.26	243,459	230,578	−5.29
6th decile	513	468	−8.77	269,330	248,057	−7.90
7th decile	603	554	−8.13	298,756	268,282	−10.20
8th decile	720	661	−8.19	323,774	290,509	−10.27
9th decile	886	822	−7.22	373,549	340,687	−8.80
10th decile	1335	1325	−0.75	415,033	429,801	3.56

Table 2 Proportions of household burden (%)

	FY2000	FY2005	FY2011
Gasoline tax/local gasoline tax (%)	63.017	65.262	66.388
Light oil delivery tax (%)	6.266	7.852	8.461
Promotion of power resources development tax (%)	30.823	31.043	31.862
Automobile acquisition tax (%)	49.838	49.572	61.651

the income of the seventh decile in 2005 is between the income of the seventh and eighth deciles in 2011. In particular, the income of the upper-middle-income groups decreased as a result of the Lehman shock. However, the tenth decile was not affected.

Since household income and consumption have declined since the Lehman shock in 2008, there is a high possibility that tax burden is increasing as a result of the regressivity of indirect tax, mainly in low-income groups. Therefore, this study examines how the consumption and excise tax burden ratio are changing, according to changes in household income and consumption.

The proportions of household burdens, S_n, thus estimated are shown in Table 2. "Consumption expenditure item" refers to the 10 major consumption items in FIES ($j = 1, \ldots, 10$) and income groups are divided into the same 10 brackets used in that survey ($i = 1, \ldots, 10$). Below, we explain the procedure we followed when estimating the indirect tax burden rates according to income group.

5.2 Estimation Model

Here, we describe the data and the method used to estimate indirect tax burdens by income group. For the estimation, we will use data from the Statistics Bureau of the

Ministry of Internal Affairs and Communications, including the Family Income and Expenditure Survey (FIES), the National Survey of Family Income and Expenditure, the Population Census, Linked Input-Output Tables, and the White Paper on Local Public Finance, as well as the National Tax Agency's Annual Statistics Report. The estimation period covers the 11 years from 2001 to 2011.

Next, we shall explain the method used to estimate indirect tax burdens by income group. Following the example of Hayashi and Hashimoto (1993), Murasawa et al. (2005), and Uemura (2006), we measure the effective indirect tax rate τ_{ij} against consumption expenditure item j for income group i, using Eq. (1). R_{ij} indicates the macro indirect tax revenue against consumption item j of income group i. C_{ij} indicates macro household consumption of consumption expenditure j of income group i. A is an adjustment factor.

$$\tau_{ij} = \frac{R_{ij}}{C_{ij}} A. \tag{1}$$

Following this, we measure the proportion of household indirect tax burdens. In principle, this is calculated from the Linked Input-Output Tables, released every five years.

From the data for "Producer's Price," "Nominal Values," and "Transaction Amount" in the Linked Input-Output Tables we define the household burden proportion, S_n, for indirect tax n as per Eq. (2). Household consumption expenditure is represented as C_n, total domestic demand as T_n, and increase in stocks as I_n.

$$S_n = \frac{C_n}{(T_n - I_n)}. \tag{2}$$

The excise tax is borne not only by households, but also by businesses. For example, gasoline, local road, light oil delivery, promotion of power resources development, and automobile acquisition taxes are borne by businesses as well as households. Therefore, in order to calculate the accurate household burden portion from the household and corporate burden ratio, it is important that we only measure the household burden ratio from the Linked Input-Output Table.

The Linked Input-Output Table shows the burden ratio of companies and the burden ratio of households in each manufacturing process. Consumption tax is the value added by manufacturing process, that is, raw materials, finished products, distributors, retailers, and consumers, at each point in the production chain. It can apply to both manufactured goods and services. Businesses collect the consumption tax on their sales and pay it on their purchases from other businesses. This consumption tax moves up the production chain until consumers ultimately pay the entire cost of the consumption. As described above, goods and services have a chain-like connection of ">sales," which the Linked Input-Output Table shows. Therefore, by measuring the ratio of the corporate and household burden of indirect tax using a Linked Input-Output Table, the tax revenue as household burden is derived by means of the five steps described below.

The increase in stocks, I_n, is obtained by the sum of the increase in producer's stocks of finished goods, P_n; the increase in semi-finished goods and works in progress, H_n; the increase in dealer's stocks of goods, D_n; and the increase in stocks of raw materials and supplies, R_n:

$$I_n = P_n + H_n + D_n + R_n. \tag{3}$$

The indirect effective tax rate, τ_i, is based on the macro indirect tax revenue, R_{ij}, from consumption item j paid by income group i, divided by macro household consumption, C_{ij}, of consumption item j by income group i. As the data comes from sampling surveys, the difference between the figures for aggregated tax revenues derived from the FIES and the actual macro tax revenues is problematic. Thus, we use the adjustment factor, A, as proposed by Murasawa et al. (2005).

Additionally, from the estimated indirect effective tax rate, τ_{ij}, we calculate the indirect tax contribution rates, b_{ij} and B_i, in order to identify regressivity. In summary, the steps for estimating the indirect tax burden are:

Step 1: Estimation of macro household consumption by income group;
Step 2: Sorting of macro indirect tax revenues into 10 major consumption expenditure items;
Step 3: Estimation of household burden ratio;
Step 4: Adjustment of indirect effective tax rate, τ_{ij}, of consumption expenditures by income group;
Step 5: Estimation of indirect tax burden rate by income group and consumption expenditure items, b_{ij}, and indirect tax burden rate by income group, B_i.

First, we estimate macro household consumption, C_{ij}, for consumption item j of income group i, which is the denominator for the indirect tax effective tax rate in Eq. (1). "Consumption expenditures" and "yearly income" against each of the 10 major expenditure items are obtained from the "Yearly amount of expenditures and purchase frequency of commodities per household (total households)" within FIES. Consumption expenditures for each of the 10 major consumption items correspond to each of the individual consumption expenditure items within the definition of the effective indirect tax rate. Consumption expenditures by consumption item are as follows:

"Consumption expenditures" for income group i

$$\begin{aligned} &= \text{Food} + \text{Housing} + \text{Fuel, light, and water charges} + \text{Furniture and household utensils} \\ &\quad + \text{Clothing and footwear} + \text{Medical care} + \text{Transportation and communication} \\ &\quad + \text{Education} + \text{Culture and recreation} + \text{Other consumption expenditures.} \end{aligned} \tag{4}$$

The above consumption also includes some expenditures not subject to the consumption tax. Accordingly, these are captured as follows:

$$\begin{aligned}&\text{Consumption expenditures for income group } i \text{ not subject toconsumption tax}\\&= \text{Rents for dwelling and land (housing)} + \text{Medical services (medical care)}\\&\quad + \text{School fees (education)}.\end{aligned} \quad (5)$$

The data obtained above are from calendar years, and have been converted to fiscal year data. For example, the 2001 fiscal year data were obtained by summing up three-quarters of the data from the 2001 calendar year and one-quarter from the 2002 calendar year. The reason for this is that the revenue from indirect taxes is collected per financial year, not calendar year. Data for monthly amounts is converted into annual amounts by multiplying it by 12.

Subsequently, we obtained data on the total number of ordinary households from the Population Census. This census is carried out every five years, thus for each of the years for which there is no data the total number of households is estimated by linear interpolation across the estimation period of 2001–2011. Since the number of households in the Population Census was not presented by income class, we assume that in one decile of the household survey there is one tenth of the number of households in the Population Census, as per Murasawa et al. (2005).

Consequently, we estimate macro household consumption, C_{ij}, according to consumption items in each income group by multiplying the household consumption data by item and income group in each fiscal year, as obtained from FIES, by the total number of households in each income group, obtained from the Population Census. This is the denominator of the effective indirect tax rate, τ_{ij}, in Eq. (1).

Next we estimate the macro indirect tax revenue, R_{ij}, for each consumption item by income group, which is the numerator of the indirect effective tax rate, τ_{ij}, in Eq. (1). For national taxes, we shall use general and special accounts tax revenue data from the "Tax and stamp revenues" section of the National Tax Agency Annual Statistics Report. For data on local taxes, we shall use prefectural and municipal inhabitant tax revenue data from the Ministry of Internal Affairs and Communications' "White Paper on Local Public Finance."

In order to measure the indirect tax burden according to consumption item and income group, we distribute macro indirect tax revenue data for each income group amongst the consumption expenditure items. Revenues from indirect taxation are distributed proportionally across each consumption expenditure item and consumption tax applied to most goods and services is apportioned to consumption items by income group via shares, from which untaxed consumption expenditures from FIES have been deducted. Consumption share by income group is obtained by dividing household consumption data for each consumption item at each decile by household consumption data for each consumption item.

Table 3 shows how revenues from each indirect tax are apportioned across the 10 major consumption expenditure items. The gasoline, local road, light oil delivery, promotion of power sources development, and automobile acquisition taxes are borne by both businesses and households. Thus, we extract the tax

Table 3 Indirect tax types and distribution of revenues among 10 major consumption expenditure items

Tax	Distribution amongst 10 consumption items
National taxes	
Consumption tax and local consumption tax	Proportional distribution amongst 10 major consumption expenditure items via consumption shares by income group from which untaxed consumption from FIES is deducted
Liquor tax	Food
Tobacco tax, special tobacco surtax	Other consumption expenditures
Gasoline tax	Transportation and communication, extracting household burden from Linked Input-Output Tables
Local road tax	Transportation and communication, extracting household burden from Linked Input-Output Tables
Promotion of power resources development tax	Fuel, light, and water charges, extracting household burden from Linked Input-Output Tables
Prefectural taxes	
Prefectural tobacco tax (Prefectural tobacco consumption tax)	Other consumption expenditures
Golf course utilization tax (Recreational facility utilization tax)	Culture and recreation
Special local taxes (Food and beverage consumption tax, amusement and drinking tax)	Food
Automobile acquisition tax	Transportation and communication, extracting household burden from Linked Input-Output Tables
Municipal taxes	
Municipal tobacco tax (Municipal tobacco consumption tax)	Other consumption expenditures
Bathing tax	Culture and recreation

revenues from households by measuring the proportion of the indirect tax burden borne by households from the Linked Input-Output Tables. For details on how the proportion of household burden is measured, please refer to the addendum.

We distribute indirect tax revenues across consumption expenditure items according to income group for the financial years 2001–2011. With macro consumption for each consumption item and income group, C_{ij}, as denominator and the indirect tax revenues for each item and income group as numerator, we can calculate the unadjusted effective tax rates of indirect taxes.

With macro consumption, the indirect tax effective rate denominator is estimated using FIES data, as consumption data from this survey is known to have been underestimated in comparison with macro consumption data.[12] Accordingly, dividing the effective consumption tax rate, t_N, derived from the nominal tax rate by the estimated effective consumption tax rate, t_E, gives adjustment factor A, which is multiplied by the pre-adjusted effective indirect tax rate to obtain the effective indirect tax rate, τ_{ij}. In measuring adjustment factor A, we refer to Murasawa et al. (2005).

$$\mathrm{A} = \frac{t_N}{t_E}. \tag{6}$$

If the consumption tax rate of the national tax is 4% and the conversion rate of local consumption tax is 1%, the effective tax rate on consumption tax should be $\mathrm{t_N}$ = 4.762% (= 5%/(1 + 5%)), but is never the sum of the two. Meanwhile, the estimated effective consumption tax rate, t_E, is the estimated effective rate of consumption taxes excluding indirect taxes other than those obtained up to this point (i.e., macro consumption tax revenues against consumption expenditure item j for income group i/household consumption excluding macro untaxed items of consumption expenditure item j for income group i).

Adjustment factor A has an approximate value of 0.5.[13] While the adjustment factor has been obtained by focusing on consumption tax, the disparity between FIES consumption data and macro consumption data is believed to affect all indirect taxes.

Applying adjustment factor A to Eq. (1), we estimate the effective indirect tax rate, τ_{ij}, for each consumption expenditure item by income group. Concerning consumption tax, the effective indirect tax rate for adjusted consumption tax only equals the effective consumption tax rate, t_E, obtained from the nominal tax rate.

In order to check for regressivity within indirect tax burdens by income group we shall measure the proportion of tax burden as a share of income. Previously, we measured the (adjusted) effective indirect tax rate, τ_{ij}, by consumption item and income group. Consequently, we are able to obtain the indirect tax burden rate, b_{ij}, by consumption items and income groups as per Eq. (7):

$$b_{ij} = \frac{\tau_{ij} c_{ij}}{y_i}. \tag{7}$$

FIES consumption data by item and income group are represented by c_{ij}, and yearly income by y_{ij}. The indirect tax burden rate by income group with aggregated consumption expenditure items, B_i, is obtained using the equation below:

$$B_i = \frac{\sum_i \tau_{ij} c_{ij}}{y_i}. \tag{8}$$

[12]Please refer to Iwamoto et al. (1995, 1996) for problems such as imputed rents.

[13]Estimations by Uemura (2006) and Saitoh and Uemura (2011) use an adjustment factor of 0.5.

6 The Burden of Indirect Taxation by Income Group

Figure 3 displays indirect tax burden rates by income group as calculated using the procedure described above. While results have not been obtained for every financial year between 2001 and 2012, owing to the absence of any large-scale tax reforms during the estimation period, no particularly significant differences can be seen between the analyzed years. Indirect tax burden rates by income group are shown in relation to indirect taxation overall, consumption tax, and excise tax.

As an overall trend, the indirect tax burden of low-income earners has remained relatively high. Regarding the burden of indirect taxation overall, the first decile is up to three times larger than the tenth. Accordingly, we can confirm the regressivity of indirect taxation inclusive of excise taxes.

Looking at the burden of consumption and excise taxes, the burden rate for the former is higher than that of the latter. While consumption and excise taxes account for a similar portion of national income, we have only considered the proportion of excise taxes paid by households, which is proportionally lower than the amount paid by businesses. From the figure, we see that the consumption tax burden rate drops more steeply than that for excise tax from the first to tenth decile. This indicates that the relative weight of consumption tax regressivity is larger than that

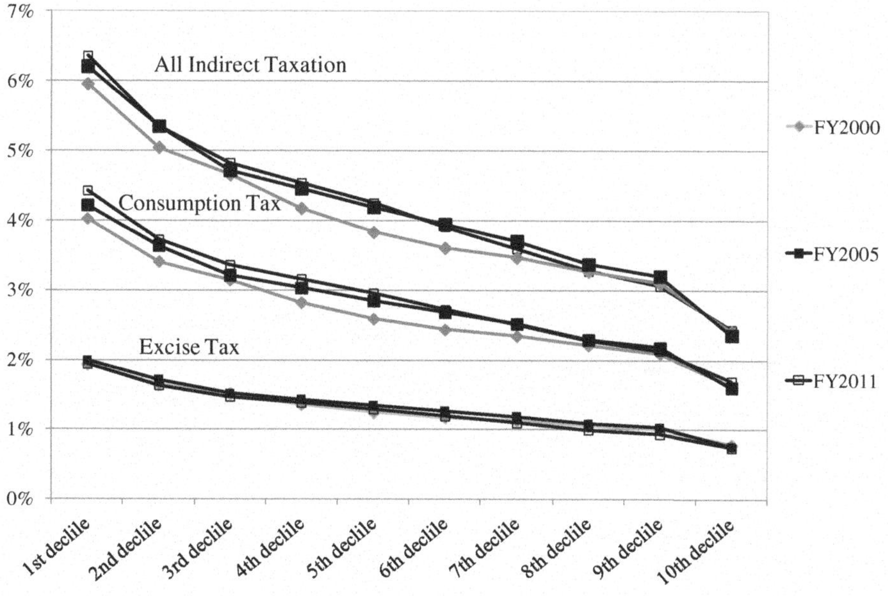

Fig. 3 Indirect tax burden rates by income group

of excise tax. As no significant differences exist between the years, the discussion below is based on data from FY2012.

Figure 4 shows the indirect tax burden rate for each consumption expenditure item and income group. From each of the tax burden rates shown, we can see which consumption items account for regressivity in consumption taxation. Figure 4 shows that the consumption tax burden rate for food, in particular, drops steeply from the first decile to the tenth, and hence regressivity is relatively high.[14] The fact that consumption taxes applied to food are particularly regressive may provide justification for measures to reduce the tax burden of low-income earners.

Figure 5 shows the burden rates of excise taxes for each consumption expenditure item. For ease of comparison, units along the vertical axes in both Figs. 4 and 5 are aligned. As with the consumption tax figures, regressivity can be noted with regard to most consumption items. Nonetheless, the burden rates for consumption tax shown in Fig. 4 are higher than those for excise taxes shown in Fig. 5.

However, "Transportation and Communication" shows a higher burden rate for excise tax than it does for consumption tax, owing to the burden of excise taxes such as the gasoline tax. In addition, while the burden rate for "Food" is higher than that of other consumption items, the main cause of this is the liquor tax.

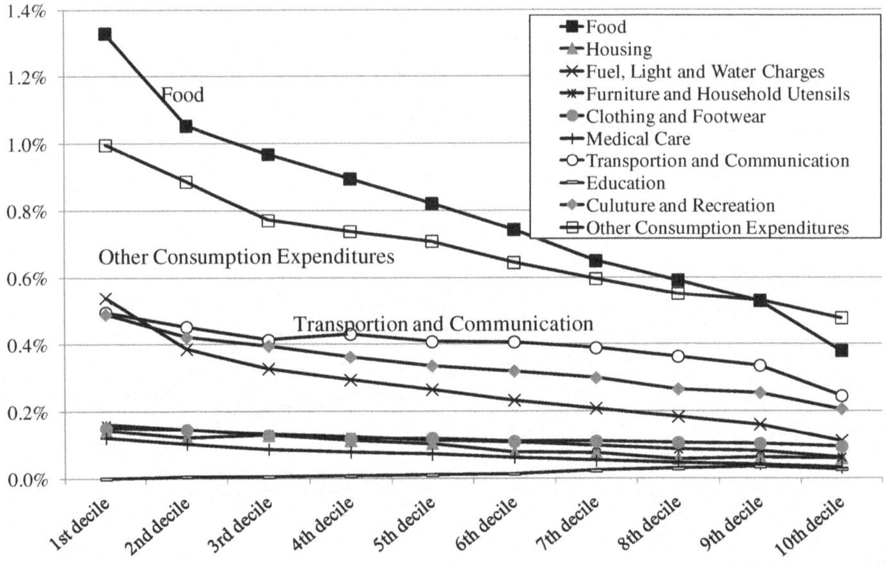

Fig. 4 Consumption tax burden rates by consumption expenditure item and income group (FY2012)

[14]Yearly income for each decile in 2012, as reported by FIES, was as follows (in millions of yen): 1.26, 2.14, 2.79, 3.37, 3.96, 4.65, 5.46, 6.54, 8.13, and 13.17, from the first to the tenth decile.

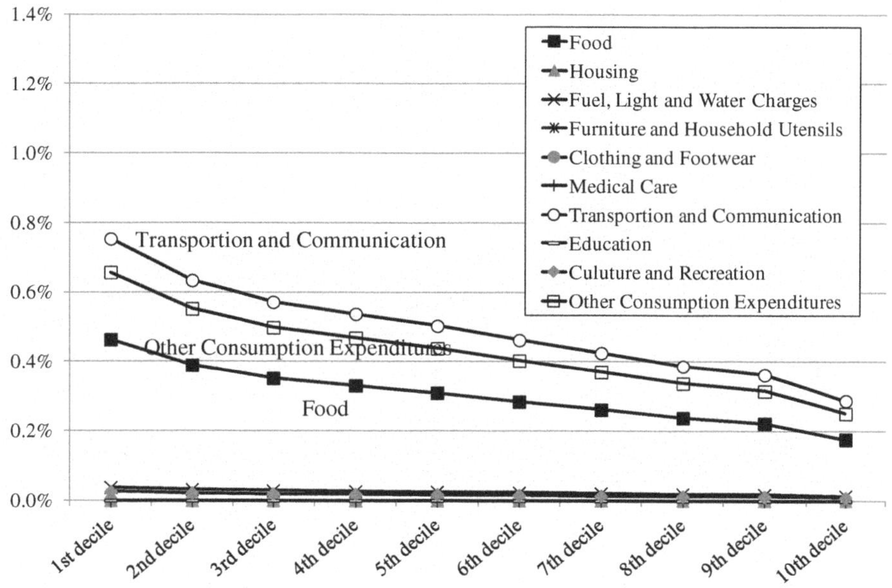

Fig. 5 Excise tax burden rates by consumption expenditure item and income group (FY2012)

The burden rate for "Other Consumption Expenditures" is largely driven by tobacco-related taxes.

7 The Effects of a Consumption Tax Increase on Indirect Tax Burden Rates

Hitherto, this paper has discussed the structure of indirect tax burden rates inclusive of consumption taxation by income groups in Japan. The consumption tax has been raised in the past in an effort to secure funding for social security programs. Accordingly, we apply an analytical framework to consider the effects of an increase in the consumption tax on the household indirect tax burden rates. We pay particular attention to the issue of regressivity associated with the consumption tax.

Figure 6 shows the results of test calculations for several policy patterns related to the consumption tax, based on the indirect tax burden rates by income group for FY2012. The graph indicates five patterns of indirect tax burdens corresponding to each of the five cases described. Case 1 is used as a benchmark whereby the consumption tax is set at 5%. Cases 2–5 all involve an increase to 10%.

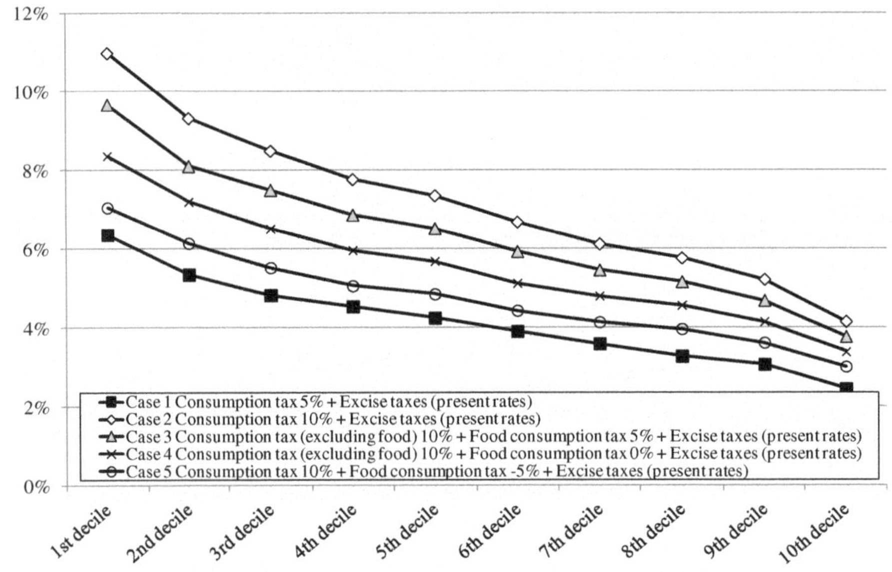

Fig. 6 Indirect tax burden rates for each income group in an increased consumption tax scenario

As consumption tax increases are criticized for their regressivity, we consider several policy patterns including a tax reduction on food, a zero tax rate on food, and a partial tax refund.[15]

As such, the following cases are considered:

Case 1: Consumption tax 5% + Excise taxes (present rates)
Case 2: Consumption tax 10% + Excise taxes (present rates)
Case 3: Consumption tax (excluding food) 10% + Food consumption tax 5% + Excise taxes (present rates)
Case 4: Consumption tax (excluding food) 10% + Food consumption tax 0% + Excise taxes (present rates)
Case 5: Consumption tax 10% + Food consumption tax −5% + Excise taxes (present rates)

Consumption tax regressivity rises relative to the tax increase. In particular, the lines in Fig. 6 decline more steeply from the first decile in Cases 2, 3, and 4 compared to the other two cases.

We consider a reduced tax rate and zero tax rate applied to food as a means of ameliorating regressivity. Case 3 leaves the consumption tax on food at 5%, while Case 4 applies a zero tax rate to food. Nonetheless, as can be seen in the indirect tax burden rate in Case 4, regressivity is not easily dealt with, even when a zero tax rate on food is applied.

[15]In Case 5, a refund of the 5% consumption tax levied on food is provided.

Thus, as a further means of mitigating regressivity, we consider Case 5, in which a negative 5% rate on food is applied, in order to measure the effects of refunding the 5% tax burden on food to households. Relative to the other cases, the descending trend from the first decile is somewhat flatter, indicating a slight reduction in regressivity. Nevertheless, in all cases the overall tax burden for each income group is higher than the benchmark Case 1.

Finally, in order to evaluate these regimes of indirect taxation as a whole, we calculate redistribution effects by finding the extent of improvement in the Gini coefficient in each case. The redistribution effect, *E*, is obtained by the following equation:

$$E(\%) = 100\frac{(G_I - G_T)}{G_T}. \tag{7}$$

Here, G_I represents the Gini coefficient for yearly income, and G_T indicates the Gini coefficient of yearly income minus indirect tax burden. Results are shown in Table 4.

The negative values for the redistribution effect, *E*, are attributable to the regressivity of indirect taxation. From Table 4, the most regressive scenario is that of Case 2, whereby the consumption tax rate is raised to 10%. Cases 3 and 4 are considered as a means of mitigating this regressivity through the effects of reduced or zero rates, but these do not result in positive improvements in the Gini coefficients.

Moreover, even providing a tax refund produced no marked improvement over the benchmark Case 1. This is because the measures of reducing tax rates, setting zero tax rates, and refunding tax lower the tax burden for low- and high-income earners alike. Thus, attempts to mitigate tax regressivity associated with a rise in the consumption tax should involve social security policies heavily targeted towards low-income earners, as opposed to the application of reduced/zero tax rates or refunds.

Table 4 Redistribution effect under different tax regimes by income group

Case 1	Consumption tax 5% + Excise taxes (present rates)	−1.52%
Case 2	Consumption tax 10% + Excise taxes (present rates)	−2.62%
Case 3	Consumption tax (excluding food) 10% + Food consumption tax 5% + Excise taxes (present rates)	−2.23%
Case 4	Case 4 Consumption tax (excluding food) 10% + Food consumption tax 0% + Excise taxes (present rates)	−1.88%
Case 5	Consumption tax 10% + Food consumption tax −5% + Excise taxes (present rates)	−1.52%

The Gini coefficient is an indicator that measures the inequality of income distribution in a society. In the case of Japan, although the rise in the Gini coefficient has been suppressed to a certain extent by the redistribution of social security, because of the decline of the redistribution function of wealth due to taxation, the rise of the Gini coefficient is accelerating with population aging.

According to a report from the Organisation for Economic Cooperation and Development (OECD), the Japan's Gini index has risen every year since the 1980s, and although it has been on a recovery trend since 2000, its poverty level is still high compared to other OECD countries. According to the Ministry of Health, Labour and Welfare, 0.5–0.6 is said to be "a level at which chronic riots are likely to occur"; the Gini coefficient before income redistribution in 2011 was 0.5536, and 0.3791 after income redistribution.

On the one hand, when compared to other OECD countries, the domestic Gini coefficient has a lower tax rate for middle-income groups by income class. On the other, the poverty rate of child-rearing households is high, and is coupled with a low redistribution effect for young people with low incomes and a lack of adequate social security benefits. When discussing an increase of consumption tax based on such a social background, we believe it to be necessary to verify income redistribution for each income class along with the Gini coefficient.

8 Conclusions

In the context of an aging population, the consumption tax was introduced in Japan as a means to secure financing for social security programs; its level has been raised on a number of occasions. While consumption taxes are regressive, excise taxes also place a burden on household finances. In this chapter, we estimated the portion of income captured by consumption and excise taxes for different income groups, considering the proportion of the tax burden associated with excise taxes. The results indicated that regressivity is present for both consumption and excise taxes. In particular, indirect taxes on food are shown to be highly regressive, giving grounds for measures aimed at reducing the tax burden on low-income earners. Accordingly, we quantified the redistributive effects of several policy patterns aimed at reducing indirect tax burdens. For taxes on food, the redistributive effects of reduced taxes, zero rates of taxation, and tax refunds were not significant. This is because these measures lower the tax burden across all income groups and do not target low-income earners only. As a result, alleviating the regressivity of indirect taxes requires social security policies that are closely targeted at low-income earners.

In this chapter, we have explained the structure of indirect tax burdens, including excise taxes, in Japan by measuring the burden of excise and consumption taxation by income group.

The results of our analysis can be summarized as follows. Firstly, low-income earners are exposed to a relatively high burden of indirect taxation. Comparing the first and tenth deciles of income earners, the first decile was found to have an overall indirect tax burden rate of around three times the size of that of the tenth decile. Thus, we can conclude that the system of indirect taxation overall, even including excise taxes, is a regressive one.

Secondly, consumption tax was found to be more regressive than excise taxation. In particular, the tax burden rate associated with food was found to be relatively regressive and most onerous for the first decile of income earners. This may require the introduction of some type of policy measure aimed at reducing the regressivity of consumption tax applied to food for low-income earners.

Thirdly, regarding excise tax burdens, for "Transportation and Communication" the excise tax burden rate is higher than the consumption tax. This is owing to the presence of excise taxes such as the gasoline tax.

Finally, we considered the effects on household indirect tax burdens occasioned by an increase in the consumption tax. Estimating the outcomes of several policy patterns, we found that regressivity increases alongside the consumption tax rate. Our measurements of redistributive effects show that, even accompanied by policies aimed at mitigating this regressivity, an increase in the consumption tax produces a negative redistribution across all income groups. This is because policies providing for reduced tax rates, zero tax rates, or tax refunds lower the tax burden for both low- and high-income earners alike.

In order to lower the tax regressivity accompanying any increase in the consumption tax, instead of measures such as lowering tax rates, setting zero tax rates, or providing tax refunds to all income earners, social security policies closely targeting low-income earners are required,.

In Japan's Comprehensive Reform, the increase in revenue afforded by raising the consumption tax is to be used for social security expenditure. Instead of using lower tax rates to redistribute income, a more effective policy would redistribute income via social security spending. Highly targeted and efficient income redistribution policies will be more important than policies seeking to lower the burden of indirect taxation.

We would like to conclude this chapter with the following considerations. There is a need to consider the external diseconomies of taxation. For example, the correction of external diseconomies is an objective of several indirect taxes, such as health promotion in the case of the tobacco tax, and environmental protection in the case of the gasoline tax. Therefore, we must take into account that the burden of indirect taxation includes the aspect of external diseconomies correction.

Furthermore, the burden of indirect taxation varies among regions. For example, the differences in lifestyle between city dwellers and rural residents affect automobile-related indirect taxes, such as the gasoline tax. While there is less need for car use in cities where public transportation is available, it is essential in the

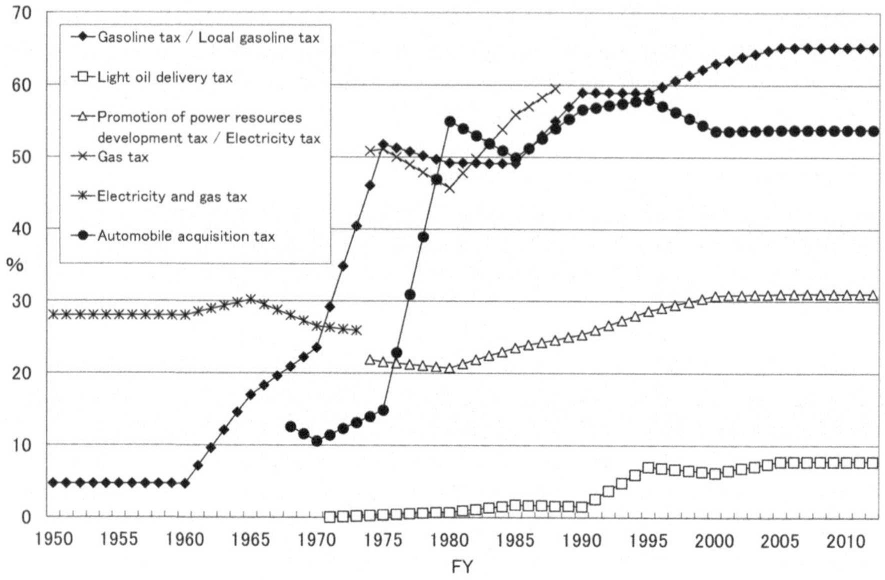

Fig. 7 Proportions of household burdens

countryside, regardless of income levels. Therefore, to understand the burden structure of indirect taxes more precisely, there is a need to also focus on regions. These points can also be considered as topics for future research.

8.1 Addendum. Measuring the Proportions of Household Indirect Tax Burdens

Here we measure the proportion of household indirect tax burdens. In principle, this is calculated from the Linked Input-Output Tables, which are released every five years. For the four-year periods in between reporting years, figures are estimated by linear interpolation. As the data from 2006 onwards was unavailable, we use the same proportions as those in 2005.

From the data for "Producer's Price," "Nominal Values," and "Transaction Amount" in the Linked Input-Output Tables we define the household burden proportion, S_n, for indirect tax n as per Eq. (8). Household consumption expenditure is represented as C_n, total domestic demand as T_n and increase in stocks as I_n.

$$S_n = \frac{C_n}{(T_n - I_n)} \tag{8}$$

The increase in stocks, I_n, is obtained by the sum of the increase in producer's stocks of finished goods, P_n, the increase in semi-finished goods and works in progress, H_n, the increase in dealer's stocks of goods, D_n, and the increase in stocks of raw materials and supplies, R_n.

$$I_n = P_n + H_n + D_n + R_n \tag{9}$$

The proportions of household burdens, S_n, thus estimated are shown in Fig. 7.

Chapter 4
Effects of Spousal Deduction on Household Labor Supply

1 Social Background to Women's Employment

There have been warnings in recent years that the decrease in labor supply resulting from the declining birth rate could lead to an economic downturn. In the background is the alarming decline in the nation's working-age population between 15 and 64 years old, which in the 2013 statistics fell 1.16 million from a year earlier to 79 million—below 80 million for the first time in 32 years. With the rapid aging of the population and low birthrate, experts warn that the number of working-age people would fall by another 10 million to below 70 million by 2030.

It makes sense to tap into Japan's under-utilized workforce to make up for the labor shortages and to support the nation's economic vitality. A contraction in labor supply leads to a reduction in salary income and affects tax revenues. As part of a growth strategy, attention is focused on promoting the activities of married women as a potential labor force. There are active discussions on the supply of married women as labor, and the approach to take for spousal deductions and dependent deductions. Prime Minister Shinzo Abe told a joint meeting of the government's Council on Economic and Fiscal Policy and another pan el on industrial com petitiveness to consider changes to the rules as a means of promoting women's greater participation in the workforce.

Japan's finances are in a difficult condition, and in order to reform deductions and the tax rate, it is important to clarify how such reforms will affect labor supply and whether tax revenue will change. The government needs to realize that it requires more comprehensive efforts than simply eliminating the spousal tax and social security benefits to boost the labor participation of women, especially working mothers. Therefore, this chapter shows quantitatively whether income tax deductions cause a loss in tax revenue via the supply of women as labor.

Changes in labor force and labor force ratio decline in both. Japan's total population stands at 127.08 million. Of this total, 16.23 million are aged 0–14, 77.85 million are in the 15–64 bracket, and 32.78 million are 65 or above (as of

Y. Adachi, *The Economics of Tax and Social Security in Japan*,
https://doi.org/10.1007/978-981-10-7176-8_4

October 1, 2014; Population Estimate by the Statistics Bureau, Ministry of Internal Affairs and Communications). In 1960, Japan's labor force ratio was 69.2%, but it declined to 59.4% in 2014 (male: 70.4%, female: 49.2%) (Ministry of Internal Affairs and Communications, 2014 Annual Report on the Labour Force Survey).

Even as Japan's workforce has begun shrinking in recent years, the number of women employed has been growing, and over the past few years women have consistently made up approximately 40% of the labor force. From 67.66 million in 2000 to 65.77 million in 2013, but in 2013, the number of women in the workforce was the highest ever at 23.29 million. This is influenced by changes in the industrial structure. For example, while employment in the construction and manufacturing industries has steeply declined, it has increased in the healthcare and welfare sectors, where female workers are more numerous.

"Dual income households" have increased in recent years, outstripping households consisting of an employed male and wife not in employment (so called "full-time housewife households") since 1997. While studying women's employment on the unit of households in the "Labor Force Special Survey" carried out by the Ministry of Internal Affairs and Communications in 1980 there were 1,114 households in which the man worked and the spouse was a full-time homemaker, and both spouses worked in only 614 households. Subsequently, reflecting the advancements in society, households in which both spouses work increased and the number of households with a full-time homemaker had dropped to 687 households by 2015, while households in which both spouses work had risen sharply to 1,114 households.

The female labor force ratio develops in the M-shaped curve: the labor force ratio of female workers declines for workers in their late 20s through their 30s and increases again after that. The reason given for this is that women often interrupt their employment for marriage, childbirth, and childcare during this period. However, the labor force participation rate for all age groups rose over the period surveyed, and the valley part of the M-shape moves upward and to the right over time. If we compare the figures for 1985 and 2014, the M-shaped curve is shallower and the bottom of the curve has moved to the right in 2014. This results from an increased rate of labor force participation by unmarried women, as well as later marriage and childbirth. However, the rate of continued employment at around the birth of the first child has hardly changed at all.

Significant Gender Gap in the Non-regular Ratio Turning next to types of employment, the ratio of non-regular employment is in a gradually increasing trend for both men and women. Part-time workers are short-term labor and work fewer than 35 hours a week. In 1965, only 1.68 million people (5.8% of the total number of employees) were part-time workers, but by 2013, this had risen to 28% (15.68 million people) of the total number of employees (55.53 million people), meaning that one in every three workers was a part-time worker. While the non-regular ratio for men is around 20%, for women it is more than 50%, revealing a considerable disparity between the two. Among women aged 55 to 64, the percentage was 65.4%, and among those aged 45 to 54 it was 58.4%. The lowest percentage was 40.9%, for the 25–34 age group, followed by 15–24 at 50.6% and 35–44 at 53.8%.[1]

However, the rapid increase in female part-time workers represents an aspect that casts a shadow over women's development in society. One underlying factor in women's forming most of the part-time labor force is that they are deeply involved in such life events as marriage and childbirth, and the responsibility of childcare. Among women who do not form part of the labor force population of 28.87 million people, there are 3.1 million who want to work. In the survey, more than 30% responded with "they can't work due to childbirth/childcare" as the reason why they were neither working nor looking for work, though they want to work.[2,3]The survey also showed that only about 40 percent of women continue working after the birth of their first child, highlighting the need to provide support for families with children both at home and work. While part-time status is seen as one reason that women find it difficult to continue work after childbirth, women with full-time jobs-particularly in metropolitan areas—often give up or postpone returning to work following child-care leave after failing to find nursery schools for their children.

Time spent on housework and childcare by men in homes with preschool children is still only about 1 hour per day, a low level in international terms. Far more Japanese women work in part-time or non-regular jobs and the increase in labor force participation has been accompanied by an increase in the share of women working part-time or in non-regular jobs. Above all, for policy makers,

---

[1]According to the Ministry of Internal Affairs and Communications, "2009 Labor Force Survey," the group aged 15 to 24 years made up 9.8%, 25 to 29 years formed 14.8%, and 30 to 34 years accounted for 24.2%.

[2]In 1970, the average life expectancy of women was 74.66 years old; this had risen to 86.83 years old in 2014, and changes to women's lifecycle during this period were observed. The rate of participation of women in the labor force rose from 45.5% (1970) to 80.3% (2015). However, Women's labor market opportunities and choices are often intertwined with marriage and children. Particularly in Japan, earlier cohorts of women typically left the labor force during their 20s and 30s, re-entering only after their children had grown older.The lifecycle profile for female shows an M-shaped curve, which indicates that many women leave the labor force when they marry or give birth to children; they tend to return to work after their children have grown. The M-shaped curve has become flatter in recent years. Alongside the postponement of marriage, the average age at the time of first marriage increased from 24.2 years old (1970) to 29.4 years old(2014), and similarly, alongside the postponement of giving birth, the average age of the mother at the time of the birth of the first child rose from 25.6 years (1970) to 30.6 years (2014). The total fertility rate in 1970 was 2.13 children, but by 2014 this had fallen to 1.42 children.

[3]According to the Ministry of Internal Affairs and Communications' (2014) "Labor Force Survey: Basic Totals," women's participation in the labor force by age group started to depict a clear M-shaped curve from around 1950. The rate in 1920 for women aged from 15 years to 19 years was 68.4%, but this participation declined as they became older, and a mountain shape could be seen for young people in 1950 and an M-shaped curve could be recognized due to the decline in the rate of participation in the labor force of women aged in their thirties by 1970. The bottom part of the M-shaped curve, of women aged 25 years to 35 years, was 42.6% in 1975, but by 2011 it had risen to 77.2%.

women's labor force participation and the quality of women's labor market opportunities are dual objectives, both important for economic growth.

In fact, in the "Basic Survey on Birth Trends" (nationwide survey on marriage and childbirth) (survey on married couples), conducted by the National Institute of Population and Social Security, the rate of employment continuation before and after marriage rose from 60.3% between 1985 and 1989 to 70.5% from 2005 to 2009. However, the percentage of married women who were working before pregnancy and continued to work after childbirth remained unchanged during both the studied time periods, at around 38 to 39%, and the rise in the percentage of women continuing to work after marriage does not lead to their continuing work after childbirth. From this, we can see that the barriers of marriage and childbirth have prevented married women who wanted to work from doing so. While the rate of female employment has been growing over the years, considering that the employment patterns of women are determined largely by a series of life events, it is difficult to say that progress is being made for married women's development in society. Therefore, while we can confirm that the rate of female employment is increasing, it is still the case that married women are required to select their form of employment according to the life events such as marriage and childbirth, and the responsibility of childcare.

What prevents women from continuing to work is not just marriage and childcare. According to the "2011 General Survey of Part-time Workers," conducted by the Ministry of Health, Labour and Welfare, in the question (by gender) on the reasons why part-time workers selected part-time work (multiple answers possible), looking only at female part-time workers, there were answers that "Because I can adjust my employment" (that is, adjustment of their annual income and working hours). Looking at the breakdown of the answer, while this answer was selected by 8.1% of unmarried women, it was significantly higher for married women, at 21.1%.[4] In the same survey, in a question for married women on their "Reasons for adjusting employment" (multiple answers possible), the replies included "I have to pay tax if I exceed the tax exemption limit (1.03 million yen) of our income tax category (63.0%)," and "My spouse will not receive his company's special spousal allowance if my income exceeds a fixed amount (20.6%)."[5] From this, it is possible to conclude that part-time workers are attempting to adjust their work hours and keep their annual income from surpassing these thresholds to retain the status advantageous for aspects such as spousal deduction and allowance.

---

[4]In its "10th Longitudinal Survey of Adults in the 21st Century," the Ministry of Health, Labour and Welfare found that after marriage, regular employment was 43.6%, while non-regular employment such as part-time employment, which before marriage was at 29.2%, decreased to 20.4%. The employment rate dropped further due to childcare, and on the birth of the first child, the number of regular employees declined to 19.8% and that of non-regular employees to 9.4%.

[5]In terms of the reasons given by married women for selecting part-time labor, the most selected answer, at 49.3%, was "If I exceed the fixed amount (1.3 million yen), and as the spouse if I am excluded from the dependent health insurance coverage, welfare pension, etc., I will have to subscribe myself".

Under the system introduced in 1961, 380,000 yen is deducted from the taxable income of the head of a household if his or her spouse earns 1.03 million yen or less a year. It has been pointed out that this leads housewives with part-time jobs to limit their work days and hours so their income will not exceed the threshold—and allow their husbands to keep the taxable income deduction. It has therefore been cited as a ceiling that limits women's roles in the labor market. The 1. 03 million-yen barrier, meanwhile, is at the point in which the spouse is obligated to pay her own health insurance and pension premiums. Once a spouse earns 1.41 million yen, her husband is no longer eligible for the special spousal deduction, the system that reduces his tax burden even after his wife's income exceeds 1.03 million yen.

The spousal tax deduction was introduced back in 1961, when Japan was in the midst of its postwar modernization drive and undergoing rapid economic growth. Deductions that covered the spouse were based on the tax law of the right to live in Article 25 of the Constitution. According to the "Report on Tax System Reforms in 1964," by the Government Tax System Investigation Committee for personal deductions, "Different tax burdens are set according to the family structure and number of family members, in compliance with the principle of the burden being placed according to their ability to pay." Wives at that time were expected to stay home, perform household chores, and raise the kids while their husbands toiled away at the office to support Japan's resurgence. As such, the tax break helped support the typical Japanese family that was subsisting on a single income. Half a century later, that model has crumbled as the norm. Today's women are increasingly looking to continue work after marriage and even after bearing children. In a situation in which household structures are diversifying and the number of households in which both spouses work is continuing to increase, it is difficult to say that the personal deduction approach is suitable for the changing social situation.

The working population is a key driver of the economy. It is shrinking as a result of the nation's declining birthrate and rapidly aging population. This has prompted the government to find new sources of labor to sustain the economy. Several policies have been implemented so far to promote women's employment. The aim is to raise GDP via the rise in household income and the increase in consumption from the demands to strengthen social infrastructure supporting women's activities and promoting the participation of women in the labor force. Trading house Goldman Sachs released a report titled "Womenomics 4.0" in which it called for closing the workforce gender gap. The report said that if the women's employment rate, which stood at 62.5% in 2013, were raised to the male ratio of 80.6% that year, it would add 7.1 million employees to the workforce. This could lift Japan's gross domestic product by 12.5%, it said.

Prime Minister Shinzo Abe first instructed the government's Tax Commission in 2014 to review the spousal deduction system. The review will be in step with the Abe administration's push for greater participation by women in the labor force to make up for the manpower shortage caused by the rapid aging of society and decline in the working-age population.

Changing the system should not end in just imposing higher taxes on households that currently benefit from the scheme. If the system is abolished or curtailed, the tax burden may increase for some 14 million people to whom the spousal deduction is now applied. There may be confusion among businesses that currently use the 1.03 million yen mark as a threshold for providing spousal and dependent allowances to their employees.

Taking the above societal trends as its starting point, this chapter focuses on the relationship between the labor supply of married women and spousal deduction. The structure of this chapter is as follows. The next section covers the tax system and the social security system, and the existing research is introduced in Sect. 3. Section 4 provides an overview of the data used for analysis and describes the hypothesis and the variables. Section 5 presents the results of the empirical analysis. Finally, in Sect. 6, the conclusion obtained in this chapter are summarized and the research issues for future are arranged.

2 A Neutral Tax and Social Security Systems

Spousal deduction, enacted in the fiscal 1961 revision to the tax system, is a personal deduction in which the head of household's taxable capacity is adjusted when the spouse's total income is below a certain amount. This was introduced to evaluate the so-called "wife's help," Wives at that time were expected to stay home, perform household chores and raise the kids while their husbands toiled away at the office to support Japan's resurgence. It was introduced to adjust taxpayers' ability to pay tax, specifically in cases when a head of household with income below a certain amount had a spouse.

In retrospect, the spousal deduction was first introduced as one of the dependent deduction. However, the spouse deduction system was created in 1961 from the viewpoint of a relationship of mutual aid between husband and wife, rather than the wife being a dependent. The spousal tax deduction cuts the taxable annual income of the household's main earner by 380,000 yen if the dependent spouse is earning 1.03 million yen or less a year. By reducing their taxable income, the main earner and the household pay less taxes overall.

However, if the spouse's total income exceeded 380,000 yen, income tax would be levied on the spouse, and the head of household's deduction amount would be reduced, causing the tax burden to increase for such a household. Also, if the wife is employed, rather than self-employed, and earning less than 1.03 million yen, that income is free of income tax, thanks to the combined effect of the 650,000 yen deduction on salaried income for single or married people, and a 380,000 yen basic deduction that is app lied uniformly to all taxpayers. What's more, many companies offer such benefits as health insurance to employees with dependent spouses, but such benefits typically stop when the spouse's income exceeds 1.03 million yen. Above all, the spousal tax deduction is a significant factor in preventing some women from work as much as they'd like.The tax benefit discourages many women from seeking jobs that would take their income above the 1.03 million yen threshold.

The average yearly income by type of employment for women workers is seen in the "Employment Status Survey (2016)," conducted by the Ministry of Internal Affairs and Communications. Income distribution of regular (full-time) employees describes a parabola, with the 2–2.99 million yen category being the highest, at 20%. In the income distribution of part-time employees, 90% are in the 1–1.99 million yen category, and only a small number have income of 2 million yen or more, based on which we can conclude that people are aiming to adjust their employment, including through spousal deduction.

In fact, according to the "2011 General Survey of Part-time Workers" conducted by the Ministry of Health, Labour and Welfare, when irregular (part-time) employees were asked for their reasons for adjusting their employment, more than 60% answered that "I have to pay tax if I exceed the tax exemption limit of 1.03 million yen for my income tax category." In the same survey, while examining spousal annual income distribution, it was shown that the annual income of female irregular employees peaks at an annual income of close to 1 million yen.

Therefore, the main point of discussion for a review of spousal deductions is that the outcome of encouraging women to adjust their employment in order to receive the tax system's preferential treatment in the form of spousal deduction is impeding the engagement of women in the labor force.

First of all, why was the spousal special deduction system established? In 1987, in consideration of households' tax burden and part-time labor, the system of spousal special deduction was created. When part-time workers' income exceeded a certain amount, spousal deductions ceased to apply, and this created a reverse phenomenon of reducing the households' total proceeds after tax. Spousal special deduction was created in response to this trend. A special tax deduction for full-time homemakers is an additional deduction for spouses. When first launched, the deduction amount corresponded to half of the spousal deduction (set at 112,500 yen in 1987 and 165,000 yen in 1988). It was revised in the following year, 1989, to increase the income requirements of the taxpayer (this was changed from a total income of less than 8 million yen to a total income of less than 10 million yen) and the deduction amount was raised (from 165,000 to 350,000 yen).

There are graded income-based barriers to women's entry into the workforce. As previously mentioned, there is the 1.03 million-yen barrier, which is the maximum amount a spouse can earn in a year if her husband is to receive a spousal deduction on his taxes. It is also the point at which many employers reduce the amount of spousal allowances given to their employees. The 1.3 million-yen barrier, meanwhile, is at the point in which the spouse is obligated to pay her own health insurance and pension premiums. Once a spouse earns 1.41 million yen, her husband is no longer eligible for the special spousal deduction, the system that reduces his tax burden even after his wife's income exceeds 1.03 million yen.

In the fiscal 2003 revisions to the system, the extra spousal special deduction measure was abolished. It had been established with the purpose of reducing the tax burden on households with a full-time homemaker. However, as the number of households in which both spouses worked exceeded the number of households with a full-time homemaker, spousal employment was seen to have transitioned from merely subsidizing the head of the household to being a full-fledged employment in itself. Thus, alongside this societal change, it was decided that "second special deduction," or spousal special deduction, which was in addition to the spousal deduction, was an excessive consideration, and so it was abolished.

With the creation of spousal special reduction in the fiscal 1987 revisions to the tax system, the "reverse phenomenon" that reduced households' after-tax income was eliminated, and this lowered the wall in the tax system of 1.3 million yen from spousal deduction. Further, in the fiscal 2003 revisions to the tax system, the extra deduction portion of the spouse special deduction was abolished, and the motivation to adjust employment in order to obtain preferential treatment in the tax system was reduced further.

Moreover, household spousal deduction is applied to the head of the household living with spouse having the annual income less than 380,000 yen. In other words, there are likely to have been examples of spousal deduction being applied even when the household head's salary income was high. In fact, in the percentage of applications of spousal deduction by income group, the percentage increases as the income group gets higher. The reason for the low application percentage in the low-income group is that many young people are not married (and many young people are in the low-income group). The current situation has also come about as a result of economic recessions; spouses in low-income households have had no choice but to work without adjusting their employment.

Therefore, the barrier to employment presented by the limitation to earnings of 1.3 million yen, created by an awareness of spousal deduction, occurs within the high-income group, in which the head of the household receives a certain level of income, and not the low-income group. In a situation whereby a spouse in the low-income group must work, especially in cases where the head of household's annual income is below a certain level, the spouse is forced to clear this barrier and work. Evidently, the effects of the tax burden generated by the review to the spousal deduction system are likely to be different depending on the household.[6] If married women are in the younger generation they will likely be affected by childcare, and if middle-aged, they will face problems such as the long-term care of parents. When considering the relationship between the employment of married women and spousal deduction, it is necessary to consider age and the family structure.

[6]The problem of double deduction exists in the spousal deduction system. If the spouse is a non-regular employee, not only is the basic deduction applied to the spouse's income, but they can also receive spousal deduction applied additionally to the basic deduction of the head of the household. Further, the total deduction amount in such cases is greater than for households with full-time homemakers or dual-income households, and this problem of double deduction has been noted.

3 Previous Research

Several studies conducted both in Japan and overseas have discussed the issue of married women's labor supply.[7] Among them, studies that used individual questionnaire data to examine the relationship between wages and married women's labor supply include that of Shimada and Sakai (1980), Higuchi and Hayami (1984), Nagase (1997), and Oishi (2003). A common approach in these studies is the use of working hours to express labor supply. Shimada and Sakai (1980) extracted individual questionnaire data on heads of household aged 55 years and above from the "Employment Status Survey," estimated the head of the household and spousal labor supply function, and derived the wage rates. Higuchi and Hayami (1984) extracted data on the employment of heads of household from the "Employment Status Survey," and showed a significantly positive relation between the wage rate of spouses aged 30–44 years and working hours. Nagase (1997) used the "1983 Occupational Movement and Career Survey" conducted by the Japan Institute of Labor Policy and Training. Comparing the wage rates and working hours of non-regular employees and regular employees including short-time workers (less than 35 hours a week) and long-time workers (over 35 hours a week) aged between 20 and 44 years and with a spouse, the study noted that the wage rate of short-time workers was significantly negative.

There are many previous studies that verify labor supply from the viewpoint of employment selection (Okamoto (1988), Takayama and Arita (1992), and Ohara (2001)). Okamoto (1988) used the "Questionnaire Survey on Household Behavior," which targets urban households. Whether or not the person was employed, the study detected that the wage rate has a statistically significant negative impact; by employment type, he showed that the wage rate of non-regular employees had a negative impact on labor supply, while regular employees' wage rate affected it positively. Takayama and Arita (1992) conducted a multinomial logit analysis for data on spouses aged less than 60 years from the "National Survey of Family Income and Expenditure," and found that in addition to regular employees, non-regular employees' wage rate has a significantly positive impact to the labor supply. Ohara (2001) used data from the "Panel Survey on Consumption Life" by the Institute for Research on Household Economics, and analyzed the effects of the head of household's wages to give the spousal labor supply. The results of the estimations could be seen that the husband's income has slightly negatively

[7]Pioneering research that has approached the theme of spousal employment behavior in terms of its effects on wages and income includes the studies by Rosen and Welch (1971), Gunderson (1977), and Keeley et al. (1978). Previously, continuous variables were adopted for labor supply, but Gunderson (1977) and Keeley et al. (1978) explained that employment selection is made based on a certain level of designated working hours. Further, they showed that for spousal employment, selections are discontinuous selections of employment and non-employment. Gronau (1973, 1977) and Heckman (1974) evaluate behavior patterns from individual units to households according to lifecycle processes from employment, housework, and leisure perspective.

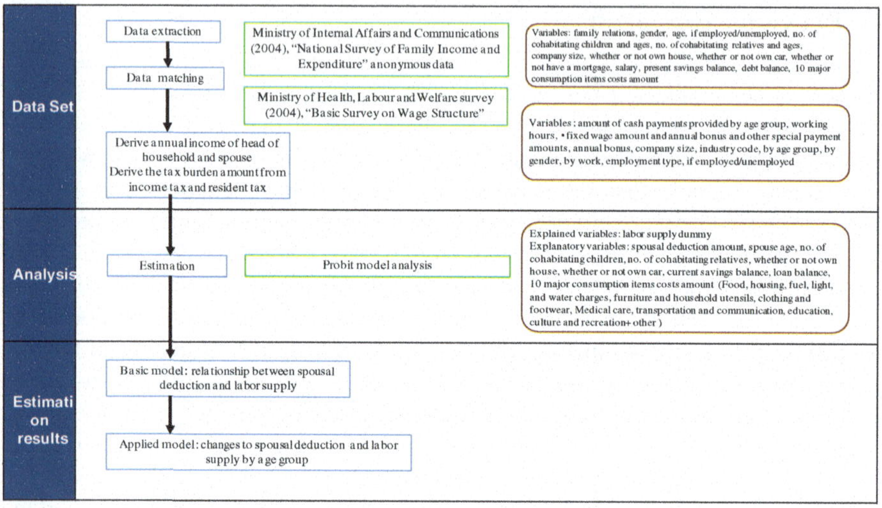

Fig. 1 Order of tasks in the analysis. *Source* Prepared by the author

significant impact to the spousal employment rate in 1993, but a significant result was not obtained in 1996.

From the above, we see that there are different results on the relationship between the wage rate and married women's labor supply, according to age group and type of employment. This tendency shows that in regular employment, a rise in the wage rate has the effect of encouraging labor supply, but it has the reverse effect in irregular employment. This suggests that although the head of household's income affects married women's labor supply to a certain extent, these effects are changing.

Further studies that have focused on the relationship between married women's labor supply and spousal deduction, which is the focus of this chapter, include Abe and Otake (1995) and Oishi (2003). Abe and Otake (1995) used data from the "General Survey on Part-time Workers" for annual part-time income, annual part-time working hours, marital relations, and academic history, to analyze the effects that spousal deduction has on the employment of unmarried and married women. The income distribution of part-time workers was disbursed. Compared with the unmarried part-time workers, the study verified that the married part-time workers adjust their income and working hours at the minimum income tax level to the household head's income.

Using individual questionnaire data from fiscal 1998 in the "Comprehensive Survey of Living Conditions" carried out by the Ministry of Health, Labour and Welfare, Oishi (2003) conducted estimations using a probit model for whether or not the person was employed or unemployed. The results of the estimations clarified that spousal deduction has the effect of suppressing employment, and Oishi concluded that non-regular employees reduce their working hours and adjust their employment because of spousal deduction.[8]

The studies described above show that the relationship between the wage rate and married women's labor supply differs depending on the age group and the type of employment; moreover, to a certain extent, the head of household's income also has an effect. Based on this situation in terms of wages and married women's labor supply, spousal deduction is said to have the effect of suppressing employment. However, the existing research used not wages before tax but wages after tax and used not the deduction amount but the tax.

Further, it is possible that the effects of spousal deduction differ depending on the household income and family structure. As no conditions are applied to the head of household's income, the higher the income group, the greater the spousal deduction will be, so it seems that the effects of spousal deduction will vary depending on the income group. Further, while it is recognized that the spousal deduction has some effect on the tax burden ratio and spousal labor supply in households, the exact nature of the impact seem to vary according to the spouse's age group and the structure of the household's dependents. In low-income households, even if they receive spousal deduction, it is possible that childcare costs and long-term care costs exceed the tax burden, so the spouse continues her employment.

In this chapter, we shall first calculate the spousal deduction amount will be calculated from annual income; this calculation will be based on the head of household and spouse's wages, and the spousal deduction's relationship with employment shall be demonstrated. Second, we shall investigate whether or not spousal deduction has different effects on married women's labor supply depending on household income and spousal age group.

4 Estimation Model and Data

4.1 Data

Figure 1 shows the specific order of the tasks in this analysis. The main data used consist of anonymous information collected on households of two or more people from the Ministry of Internal Affairs and Communications' (2004) "National Survey of Family Income and Expenditure."[9] In analyzing the effects of spousal

[8]Kawaguchi (2002) used data from the 1977 "Comprehensive Survey of Living Conditions" carried out by the Ministry of Health, Labour and Welfare, and obtained a significantly negative result for spousal employment rate relative to the husband's income.

[9]Anonymous data are collected in such a way as to make it impossible to identify specific individuals, companies, or other groups in individual questionnaire data and households' data (steps are taken to make the data anonymous). From the data on the subjects of the "National Survey of Family Income and Expenditure," 80% re-extracted (re-sampling) households with 8 or more members were removed (removal of unusual records); in the event a person was aged 85 years or above, the notation was written as

deduction on married women's labor supply, we consider that the head of household's income also has an effect. Therefore, data on households in which the head of household was not working were excluded from the sample.

The data on income includes "annual income," which is the income obtained in a year, and "average income," which is the average of monthly income during the survey period. "Annual income" is not income per the unit of member but per the unit of household and the income is not broken down; therefore, only the data on "work income" within the category of "total income" weren't used. As the average data was on monthly units, they do not include bonuses. To calculate the spouse deductible amount, we need an annual income for each individual. So I first calculate the annual income by matching monthly wage data and bonus data. In particular, the data were matched with the "2004 Basic Survey on Wage Structure" by the Ministry of Health, Labour and Welfare, and annual bonuses were calculated. Specifically, the following tasks were performed.

First, using the attributes of industry, age, and gender as indexes, anonymous data from the National Survey of Family Income and Expenditure were matched with data in the "Basic Survey on Wage Structure." Participants confirmed as employed from the anonymous data were matched the "previously determined cash salary amount" and "annual bonus and other special salary amount" in the "Basic Survey on Wage Structure."

Second, as shown by Formula (1), the ratio of "annual bonus and other special salary amount" to the "previously determined cash salary amount" was calculated, and this ratio was multiplied by "work income" to derive the annual bonus.

$$\text{Annual bonus} = \text{''work income''} \times \frac{\text{''annual bonus and other special salary amount''}}{\text{''previously determined cash salary amount''}} \quad (1)$$

Third, in "employed or unemployed" in "work income," the calculated annual bonus was given to household members who were not part-time workers. Further, we multiplied the value for "work income" by 12 and added it as the annual bonus for individual income before income tax.

With regard to the tax burden, salary income deduction was calculated from the individual's income before tax, and this deduction was subtracted from income before tax in order to obtain salary income. Each type of income deduction was subtracted from the salary income to give the taxable income. To calculate the income tax amount and the resident tax amount, the calculated taxable income was multiplied by the income tax rate and resident tax rate. Table 1 shows the taxes used for analysis in this chapter. For insurance contributions, the Ministry of

85 years and above (top coating) and ages were expressed in 5-year groups; and the geographical divisions were limited to whether or not the household is in the three metropolitan areas (recoating).

Table 1 Tax systems used for analysis

Income tax			Resident tax		
Benefits income deduction	Amount up to 1.8 million yen	40%	Benefits income deduction	Amount up to 1.8 million yen	40%
	Amount up to 3.6 million yen	30%		Amount up to 3.6 million yen	30%
	Amount up to 6.6 million yen	20%		Amount up to 6.6 million yen	20%
	Amount up to 10 million yen	10%		Amount up to 10 million yen	10%
	Amount exceeding 10 million yen	5%		Amount exceeding 10 million yen	5%
	Lowest deduction amount	650,000 yen		Lowest deduction amount	650,000 yen
Basic deduction	380,000 yen		Basic deduction	330,000 yen	
Spousal deduction	380,000 yen		Spousal deduction	330,000 yen	
	Elderly spouse aged 70 years and above eligible for deduction, 480,000 yen			Elderly spouse aged 70 years and above eligible for deduction, 380,000 yen	
Spousal special deduction	Highest, 380,000 yen		Spousal special deduction	Highest, 330,000 yen	
	Eligible with a total income amount of less than 10 million yen			Total income amount 1,0 million yen or less is eligible (in the event of a spouse other than the spouse eligible for tax deduction)	
	Spousal income	Deduction amount			
	380,000 to less than 400,000 yen	380,000 yen		Income amount of less than 100,000 yen is eligible, 330,000 yen	
	400,000 to less than 450,000 yen	360,000 yen		Deduction from an income amount of 100,000 yen to 280,000 yen	
	450,000 to less than 500,000 yen	310,000 yen		Reduced by spousal income amount over 100,000 yen (in the event of a spouse other than the spouse eligible for tax deduction)	
		260,000 yen			

(continued)

Table 1 (continued)

Income tax			Resident tax		
	500,000 to less than 550,000 yen				
	550,000 to less than 600,000 yen			210,000 yen	Income amount of less than 450,000 yen, 330,000 yen
	600,000 to less than 650,000 yen	160,000 yen		Income amount of 450,000 yen to less than 500,000 yen, 310,000 yen	
	650,000 to less than 700,000 yen	110,000 yen		Income amount of 500,000 yen to less than 750,000 yen, from 60,000 yen	
	700,000 to less than 750,000 yen	60,000 yen		Reduced by spousal income amount exceeding 500,000	
	750,000 to less than 760,000 yen	30,000 yen		Income amount of 750,000 yen to less than 760,000 yen, 30,000yen	
	760,000 yen and above	0 yen		Income amount of 760,000 yen and above, 0 yen	
Dependent deduction	Dependent deduction, 380,000 yen		Dependent deduction	Dependent deduction, 330,000 yen	
	Specified dependent relatives (aged 16 years to less than 23 years), 630,000 yen			Specified dependent relatives (aged 16 years to less than 23 years), 450,000 yen	
	Elderly dependent relatives (aged 70 years and above), 480,000 yen			Elderly dependent relatives (aged 70 years and above), 380,000 yen	
Tax rate	Amount less than 3300,000 yen	10%	Income ratio	Prefectures (standard tax rate)	
	Amount exceeding 3300,000 yen	20%		7 million yen, amount less than	2%

(continued)

Table 1 (continued)

Income tax			Resident tax		
	Amount exceeding 9 million yen	20%		7 million yen, amount exceeding	3%
	Amount exceeding 18 million yen			20%	
	Municipalities (standard tax rate)				
	(Note) 1 A fixed rate tax reduction implemented from 1999 (20%, 250,000 yen limit)			Amount less than 2 million yen	3%
				Amount exceeding 2 million yen	8%
				7 million yen	10%
			(Note) fixed rate tax reduction implemented from fiscal 1999 (15%,40,000 yen limit)		
			Per capita ratio	Prefectures (standard Tax rate) 1000 yen	
Municipalities (standard Tax rate) 3000 yen					

Source Prepared by the author from the "Monthly Report on Government Finances and Financial Statistics: Special Feature on Taxation, Policy Research Institute of the Ministry of Finance, Japan"

Finance's simple calculation method was applied to calculate minimum taxation.[10] Household disposable income was calculated by subtracting income tax, resident tax, and insurance contributions from the head of household's and spousal income before tax.

4.2 Estimation Model

In this chapter, we will consider the effects of spousal deduction on the employment rate of married women. Here, spousal deduction is considered to have two effects.

First, the following hypothesis shall be tested: as spousal deduction exists and once a person's income exceeds a certain amount they cannot receive the deduction, in order to avoid a higher tax burden, married women adjust their employment.

The second hypothesis to be tested is that even if a married woman is eligible to receive spousal deduction, in low-income households, when the economic burden of childcare and long-term care of parents exceeds the tax burden, married women have to continue working

$$\begin{aligned} \text{Labor\_SupplyDummy} = {} & \beta_0 + \beta_1 \text{spousal\_deduction} + \beta_2 \text{spousal\_age} \\ & + \beta_3 X_{\text{dependent\_control}} + \beta_4 X_{\text{assets\_control}} \\ & + \beta_5 X_{\text{consumption\_control}} + \mu \end{aligned} \quad (2)$$

For the explained variable, Labor_SupplyDummy is a dummy variable as to whether a married woman is working or not working. For the explanatory variable, spousal_deduction, which is the amount of spousal deduction (the focus of this chapter), was used. The factors affecting the labor supply of married women used in the analysis included, married women's age, (spousal_age), a dependents factor*of*$X_{\text{dependent\_control}}$, an assets factor of $X_{\text{assets\_control}}$, a consumption factor of $X_{\text{consumption\_control}}$, and other factors were used.

For the dependents factor, dependents factor $X_{\text{dependent\_control}}$, we used the number of cohabiting dependents aged less than 23 years and not earning an income, and cohabiting dependents aged 70 years and older and not earning an income. For the assets factor $X_{\text{assets\_control}}$, we used the loan amount, savings amount, and whether or not the person had their own home and own car. For consumption factor$X_{\text{consumption_control}}$, we used consumption amounts of the 10 large consumption items—namely food, housing, fuel, light and water charges, furniture and household utensils, clothing and footwear, medical care, transport and communications, education, culture and entertainment—and other items.

[10]For persons with an income of less than 9 million yen, income is multiplied by 0.1, and for persons with an income of 9 million yen to less than 15 million yen, income is multiplied by 0.04 for an added amount of 540,000 yen, and an amount of more than 15 million yen becomes 1,140,000 yen.

5 Results of Estimations

Table 2 shows this chapter's descriptive statistics. Table 3 shows the results of the estimations by all income groups, by low- and high-income groups (Model 1 to Model 3), results of the estimations by age group (Model 4 and Model 5), and results of the estimation by income and age groups (Model 6 to Model 9).

First, from the results of the estimations from Model 1(all income groups), it was understood that spousal deduction has a statistically negative effect on married women's labor supply. On this point, the results were the same as for married women belonging to the high-income group, in which spousal deduction had a significantly negative effect on labor supply. Among the coefficient values, spousal deduction in the high-income group was greater than that of all the income groups. The opposite result was obtained for married women's labor supply in the low-income group. Therefore, the spousal deduction effect of suppressing married women's labor supply may not necessarily affect all households to the same extent, as this effect is not observed in the low-income group, suggesting that it differs according to the income group.

Second, according to Model 4 and Model 5, which are the results of estimations by age group, as with Model 1 and Model 3, a statistically significant negative result was obtained for spousal deduction for young women. Similarly, while a significantly negative result was obtained for spousal deduction for women other than young women, in the spousal deduction coefficients, spousal deduction was a smaller coefficient for the older women. In both Models 4 and 5, it was found that spousal deduction has a negative effect on married women's labor supply. Therefore, owing to the existence of spousal deduction, married women adjust their employment because the spouse is subject to income tax. The existence of spousal deduction is considered a barrier to married women working and has a negative effect on the supply of women labor.

Third, Models 6 to 9 show the results of the estimations across income groups and age groups. The results for the high-income group from Model 8 and Model 9 are the same as in Model 1 and Model 3, where spousal deduction had a statistically negative effect, both for young women and for women other than young women. In these coefficients, compared to young women, spousal deduction had a higher value for the older women. In the low-income group from Model 6 and Model 7, no statistically significant relation was observed between spousal deduction and employment. Therefore, in the low-income group, regardless of the age of married women, it can be seen that the mere existence of spousal deduction does not necessarily obstruct the supply of married women as labor.

Table 2 Descriptive statistics

	Unit	No. of samples	Average value	Standard deviation	Minimum value	Maximum value
Employed or unemployed (spouse)	Y/N	43,860	0.439	0.496	0	1
Spousal deduction	Yen	34,186	615,674	213,587	330,000	860,000
Spouse age	Years	39,702	54	13	20	90
No. of dependents (children)	People	43,860	1	1	0	5
No. of dependents (adults)	People	43,860	0	1	0	3
Savings amount	Yen	43,860	12,700,000	14,700,000	0	84,300,000
Loan amount	Yen	43,860	4,874,556	9,109,686	0	45,000,000
Own/do not own house	Y/N	43,860	0.778	0.415	0	1
Own/do not own car	Y/N	43,860	0.881	0.324	0	1
10 large consumption items						
Food	Yen	43,694	70,472	28,543	5707	185,401
Housing	Yen	43,357	13,364	24,540	0	161,511
Fuel, light, and water charges	Yen	43,626	19,486	7836	0	51,042
Furniture and household utensils	Yen	42,880	8192	7824	0	49,166
Clothing and footwear	Yen	43,060	11,611	11,501	0	65,583
Healthcare	Yen	42,834	10,497	10,339	0	63,112
Transport and communication	Yen	43,117	35,827	25,608	0	156,566
Education	Yen	43,459	12,355	29,653	0	230,481
Culture and recreation	Yen	43,029	28,003	23,422	0	132,690
Other	Yen	42,926	69,758	61,947	0	363,721

Table 3 Results of estimations

	Model 1	Model 2	Model 3	Model 4	Model 5	Model 6	Model 7	Model 8	Model 9
	All income groups	Low-income group	High-income group	Young females	Females other than young females	Low-income group young females	Low-income group of females other than young females	High-income group young females	High-income group of females other than young females
Spousal deduction amount	−5.11e−06***	3.01e−07**	−7.21e−06***	−5.54e−06***	−5.05e−06***	4.05e−07	2.21e−07	−6.77e−06***	−7.39e−06***
	(5.72e−08)	(1.40e−07)	(8.20e−08)	(1.43e−07)	(6.37e−08)	(4.39e−07)	(1.51e−07)	(1.80e−07)	(9.43e−08)
Spouse age	0.00458***	−0.0104***	0.0105***	−0.0190**	−0.0153***	0.0277	−0.0379***	−0.0274**	−0.00823***
	(0.00137)	(0.00230)	(0.00193)	(0.00920)	(0.00198)	(0.0190)	(0.00321)	(0.0111)	(0.00293)
No. of dependents (children)	0.0411***	−0.125***	0.164***	0.0510	−0.0245	−0.188**	−0.196***	0.103**	0.120***
	(0.0135)	(0.0262)	(0.0179)	(0.0343)	(0.0163)	(0.0753)	(0.0301)	(0.0413)	(0.0225)
No. of dependents (adults)	0.414***	0.234***	0.408***	0.426**	0.394***	0.305	0.221***	0.387	0.396***
	(0.0280)	(0.0444)	(0.0400)	(0.190)	(0.0286)	(0.318)	(0.0455)	(0.250)	(0.0415)
Savings amount	−4.10e−09***	−1.43e−09	−6.17e−09***	1.56e−09	−4.10e−09***	1.11e−08	−1.01e−09	−5.69e−09	−6.19e−09***
	(9.25e−10)	(1.44e−09)	(1.34e−09)	(4.57e−09)	(9.51e−10)	(9.74e−09)	(1.47e−09)	(5.59e−09)	(1.41e−09)
Loan amount	5.34e−09***	8.88e−09***	2.50e−09	3.67e−09	4.90e−09***	5.77e−09	6.52e−09***	4.09e−09	2.33e−09
	(1.18e−09)	(2.09e−09)	(1.63e−09)	(2.98e−09)	(1.32e−09)	(6.97e−09)	(2.23e−09)	(3.62e−09)	(1.88e−09)
Own/do not own house	0.165***	0.230***	0.117***	0.0101	0.185***	0.0259	0.186***	−0.0732	0.169***
	(0.0316)	(0.0550)	(0.0431)	(0.0777)	(0.0354)	(0.170)	(0.0599)	(0.0942)	(0.0496)
Own/do not own car	0.0147	−0.00640	0.0907	0.00299	0.00884	−0.0970	0.00832	0.0550	0.0851
	(0.0413)	(0.0656)	(0.0581)	(0.0945)	(0.0463)	(0.192)	(0.0713)	(0.114)	(0.0683)
10 large consumption items									
Food	3.81e−06***	3.65e−06***	4.88e−06***	5.48e−06***	2.62e−06***	3.14e−06	2.35e−06***	5.55e−06***	4.19e−06***
	(4.71e−07)	(8.22e−07)	(6.48e−07)	(1.38e−06)	(5.09e−07)	(3.15e−06)	(8.70e−07)	(1.65e−06)	(7.21e−07)
Housing	−1.02e−06**	−1.46e−06**	−9.94e−07*	−6.14e−07	−1.00e−06**	−2.93e−06	−1.21e−06	−2.58e−07	−1.22e−06*

(continued)

Table 3 (continued)

	Model 1	Model 2	Model 3	Model 4	Model 5	Model 6	Model 7	Model 8	Model 9
	All income groups	Low-income group	High-income group	Young females	Females other than young females	Low-income group young females	Low-income group of females other than young females	High-income group young females	High-income group of females other than young females
	(4.24e−07)	(7.25e−07)	(5.75e−07)	(1.03e−06)	(4.71e−07)	(2.67e−06)	(7.67e−07)	(1.21e−06)	(6.57e−07)
Fuel, light, and water Charges	5.79e−06***	5.06e−06**	1.11e−06	1.72e−06	5.00e−06***	1.15e−05	1.66e−06	−4.92e−06	1.10e−06
	(1.52e−06)	(2.44e−06)	(2.16e−06)	(4.60e−06)	(1.63e−06)	(9.44e−06)	(2.57e−06)	(5.63e−06)	(2.39e−06)
Furniture and household utensils	−4.67e−06***	−6.18e −06***	−3.59e−06**	−5.90e−06*	−3.77e−06***	4.11e−08	−5.53e −06**	−7.14e−06*	−2.17e−06
	(1.15e−06)	(2.11e−06)	(1.56e−06)	(3.28e−06)	(1.24e−06)	(9.14e−06)	(2.19e−06)	(3.76e−06)	(1.73e−06)
Clothing and footwear	2.06e−06**	6.84e−07	1.12e−06	7.25e−06***	1.45e−06	7.65e−06	2.51e−07	8.50e−06***	−4.06e−07
	(8.84e−07)	(1.58e−06)	(1.20e−06)	(2.21e−06)	(9.75e−07)	(5.60e−06)	(1.67e−06)	(2.65e−06)	(1.37e−06)
Healthcare	−5.95e−06***	−5.88e −06***	−5.21e−06***	−1.26e−05***	−4.23e−06***	−1.97e−05***	−3.56e −06**	−1.28e−05***	−3.25e−06**
	(9.54e−07)	(1.63e−06)	(1.32e−06)	(3.16e−06)	(1.01e−06)	(7.51e−06)	(1.69e−06)	(3.73e−06)	(1.45e−06)
Transport and communication	2.41e−06***	7.29e−07	3.73e−06***	2.54e−06**	2.21e−06***	7.20e−09	8.40e−07	3.90e−06***	3.55e−06***
	(3.87e−07)	(7.07e−07)	(5.25e−07)	(1.02e−06)	(4.23e−07)	(2.09e−06)	(7.71e−07)	(1.28e−06)	(5.84e−07)
Education	2.89e−06***	2.06e−06***	4.17e−06***	1.04e−05***	2.05e−06***	1.59e−05***	6.33e−07	1.01e−05***	3.68e−06***
	(2.97e−07)	(5.91e−07)	(3.90e−07)	(1.96e−06)	(3.04e−07)	(4.67e−06)	(6.03e−07)	(2.33e−06)	(4.08e−07)
Culture and recreation	−2.08e−06***	−2.75e −06***	−1.05e−06*	5.97e−08	−2.64e−06***	2.13e−06	−3.12e −06***	−1.88e−07	−1.54e−06**
	(4.73e−07)	(8.90e−07)	(6.31e−07)	(1.23e−06)	(5.18e−07)	(3.04e−06)	(9.44e−07)	(1.45e−06)	(7.14e−07)
Constant	1.983***	−0.356**	2.451***	2.647***	3.193***	−2.068***	1.494***	3.466***	3.609***
	(0.0838)	(0.163)	(0.112)	(0.320)	(0.126)	(0.692)	(0.226)	(0.391)	(0.180)
Pseudo R2	0.3616	0.0388	0.5562	0.3932	0.3566	0.077	0.0523	0.4983	0.5718
Observations	21,480	4958	16,522	4177	17,303	703	4255	3474	13,048

Remarks: 1. The upper row shows the coefficient and the lower row in parenthesis shows the standard error
Remarks: 2. ***, **, and * show significance at the levels of 1, 5, and 10%, respectively

6 Conclusion

In this chapter, an empirical analysis was conducted on the reduction in the supply of married women as labor resulting from spousal deduction. Individual questionnaire data from the "National Survey of Family Income and Expenditure" conducted by the Ministry of Internal Affairs and Communications, was used and the effects of spousal deduction were estimated. From the results of the estimations, it was clear that spousal deduction reduces the supply of married women as labor. As a result of spousal deduction, married women adjust their employment as the spouse is subject to income tax. Therefore, it is considered that the existence of spousal deduction obstructs the employment of married women and suppresses the supply of women as labor.

Alternatively, while the result obtained for married women in the high-income group was that spousal deduction obstructs the employment of married women, the opposite result was obtained for the supply of married women as labor in the low-income group. Therefore, it is not possible to infer that the effect of spousal deduction suppressing the supply of married women as labor necessarily affects all households to the same extent. Further, it was clarified that this differs according to the income group

From the above results, it can be seen that the spousal deduction system is not a desirable one owing to its impact on the supply of married women as labor. The government is strengthening social infrastructure to support the activities of women, with measures including promoting gender equality and holding the Council on Economic and Fiscal Policy. However, based on these results, it appears that the government should also investigate abolishing spousal deduction. Then again, the spousal deduction effect of suppressing the supply of married women as labor is limited to the high-income group and it is not seen in the low-income group, so it is clear that it does not affect all income groups in the same manner. Therefore, it is necessary to understand that spousal deduction is one factor, but not the key issue underlying married women's employment adjustment.

Part II
Economic Analysis of Social Security Policy

Chapter 5
Insurance Contribution Burden Structure: National Health Insurance System and Latter-Stage Elderly Medical Care System

1 Introduction

As indicated by the name of The Comprehensive Reform of Social Security and Tax, there has been an active and comprehensive discussion of the approach that should be adopted in order to secure financial resources for social security. In particular, it has been discussed in terms of whether insurance contributions or tax, and the social security system or the tax system should fund social security, given that insurance contributions and taxes have different advantages as financial resources.[1]

Within this situation, pensions, medical care, and long-term care form the basis for Japan's overall social security system. Insurance contributions are the most important financial resource for these social security systems. Therefore, when considering the question of whether insurance contributions or taxes, and the social security system or the tax system, are important in terms of presenting the problem, we must not forget that inherently, insurance contributions are an important component of the financial resources for Japan's social security system.

Insurance contributions are the main financial resource for pension, medical care, and long-term care because the social security system emphasizes the relationship between benefits and burdens. Benefit means the right to receive social security services. In principle, a person cannot receive the benefits available in the social security system if he/she does not pay insurance contributions. This corresponding relationship between benefits and burdens is very significant in a social security system.

[1]Please refer to the description in the Prologue p. 1 on the fact that insurance contributions and taxes have different qualities as financial resources.

The original version of the chapter was revised: Author corrections have been incorporated. The erratum to the chapter is available at https://doi.org/10.1007/978-981-10-7176-8_11

Y. Adachi, *The Economics of Tax and Social Security in Japan*,
https://doi.org/10.1007/978-981-10-7176-8_5

In Japan's social security system, not only insurance contributions, but also a large amount of national revenue is introduced as financial resources.[2] In herently, it is preferable to pay social security benefits out of the insurance contributions of households and companies. To strengthen the coverage and sustainability of the social security system, it is necessary to consider increasing insurance contributions.

However, in The Comprehensive Reform, the aim is to supplement these financial resources from taxes by hiking the consumption tax rate. The prevailing view is that it is not possible to increase insurance contributions as it has already reached its limits. Typically, taxation is a financial resource for general public services and not a financial resource specifically for the social security system. However, in The Comprehensive Reform, the share to be obtained from the hike in the consumption tax rate was determined to be a financial resource for social security. In other words, consumption tax has emerged as a financial resource for social security, specifically to cover the shortfall between the social security and tax systems.

The present state of the social security system indicates that the introduction of taxes as a financial resource seems inevitable, but that does not change the fact that insurance contributions are the most important financial resource. Therefore, in this chapter, from within the social security system, we shall consider the National Health Insurance system and the latter-stage elderly medical care system, and investigate the relationship between the benefits of medical care and the burden of insurance contributions.

Local governments, as the insurers, manage the National Health Insurance system and the latter-stage elderly medical care system. National revenue is introduced if financial resources are insufficient even when other insurers support the National Health Insurance system and the latter-stage elderly medical care system. This financial resource of national revenue is a burden that falls on the general taxpayer, while a feature of insurance contributions is the occurrence of regional disparities. Further, there are tax reductions and exemptions for low-income earners and other groups for insurance contributions toward the National Health Insurance system and latter-stage elderly medical care system. Naturally, it would seem that such measures affect the relationship between benefits and burdens.

In this chapter, in Sect. 1 we will consider the National Health Insurance contributions and in Sect. 2 the latter-stage elderly medical insurance contributions, and analyze the burden structure of insurance contributions. Each respective section includes an overview of the system and a description of the analytical methods. Finally, the results of the analysis will be summarized.

---

[2]Please refer to the description in the Prologue p. 3 and Fig. 2 on national revenue.

2 Burden Structure of National Health Insurance Contributions

The Japanese healthcare system is characterized by universal coverage, free choice of healthcare providers by patients, and fee-for-service practice. The health insurance systems that workers subscribe to include Health Insurance managed by the Health Insurance Society, which consists of the employees of enterprises, and the Japan Health Insurance Association-managed Health Insurance, which diversifies the risk using subscriptions from all the workers of small-and medium-sized enterprises in the Fig. 1 and Table 1. National Health Insurance is a health insurance system that is operated by municipalities, etc. and to which people who do not have any other insurance plan subscribe to. Furthermore, people aged 75 or older subscribe to the late-stage medical care system for the elderly.

As described above, everyone is covered by some form of public insurance system and thus can receive necessary medical services at low cost by paying certain insurance premiums and co-payments at reception desks. Patient charges vary depending on the age and other personal factors; 30% in general patients, 20% in children younger than 6 years and people older than 70 years, and 10% in people older than 75 years. In addition, "free access," which means that everyone can receive medical services at any medical institution nationwide, is also a characteristic of the Japanese health insurance system.

Figure 2 shows the framework of health insurance system. (1) Insured persons apply to insurers for a maximum payable amount certificate to be issued. (2) Insurers issue individually insured persons with maximum payable amount certificates according to the income of their household. (3) Insured persons send the maximum payable amount certificates at the counters of medical institutions. Medical and Clinic institutions calculate the amount of the co-payment of insured persons on an individual basis and do not collect the amount exceeding the maximum co-payment maximum. (4) Medical institutions will require from insurers the amount of high-cost medical benefits in addition to receipts. (5) Insurers will pay medical benefits and (6) send approved daim to the patient.

These health insurance system protects people's health and lives. Due to an increase in national medical expenditure, however, its financial management has been growing quite severe. The increase in medical expenditure has been mainly caused by an increase in medical expenditure on the elderly. Examining medical expenditure by age group revealed that medical expenditures increased as the age increased, with medical expenditure per elderly being 5 times that of young people. As aging further advances in the future in Japan, this situation can be expected to be even more severe.

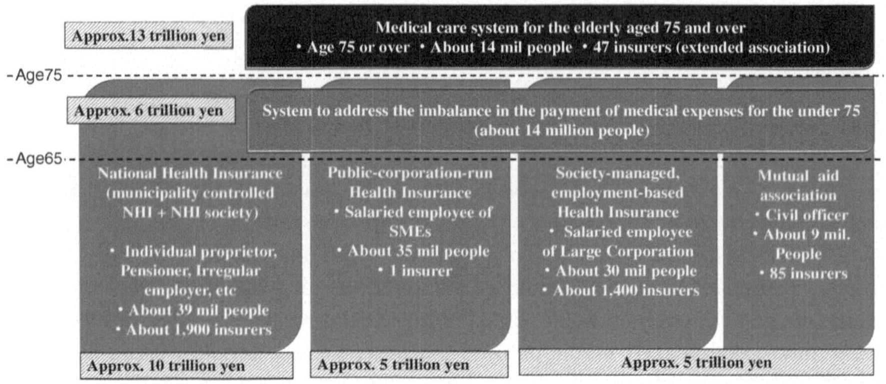

Fig. 1 System diagram of the insurer of the medical insurance system *Source* Based on "Overview of Medical Service Regime in Japan," by the Department of the Ministry of Health, Labour and Welfare, Japan

2.1 The National Health Insurance System as Seen from the Relationship Between Benefits and Burdens

In the benefits and burdens of the National Health Insurance system, the first problem is the balance between medical care benefits and insurance contributions.[3] Balance exists between insurers, within a region (intraregional), between regions (interregional), and between generations (intergenerational), but in this chapter, we will focus on the interregional and intraregional balance.[4] For reference, previous research is introduced below.

Suzuki et al. (2012), to clarify the extent of the burden of insurance contributions for social security benefits, used macro data on pensions, medical care, and long-term care, made long-term estimations by age, and showed there is an intergenerational imbalance. The "Current State of Municipal Health Insurance" study carried out by the Ministry of Health, Labour and Welfare (2012), showed that not all medical benefits can be covered by insurance premiums, and the regional disparity in insurance contributions is nearly three times, while the regional disparity in medical care benefits is more than four times, exceeding the disparity in insurance contributions.

The problem faced by the National Health Insurance system in terms of the burden relative to benefits is that compared to other medical care insurance systems, the payment rate for National Health Insurance contributions is low. The age of

[3]As the National Health Insurance system is a mixture of insurance contributions and insurance tax, National Health Insurance contributions (tax) is the correct notation, but for the sake of simplicity, below the term is unified to insurance contributions.

[4]Disparity has been discussed from various perspectives. For example, Urakawa (2012) focused on health disparity and indicated the problems in the public medical care insurance system.

Table 1 Comparison of Each Insurer *Source* Based on "on medical insurance in Japan," by the Department of the Ministry of Health, Labour and Welfare, Japan

	Municipality controlled National Health Insurance	Public-corporation-run health insurance	Society-managed, employment-based health insurance	Mutual Aid Association	Medical system for the elderly aged 75 and over
Number of insurers (End of March 2015)	1,716	1	1,409	85	47
Number of members (End of March 2014)	3,301mil. (1,981mil.households)	3,639mil. (The insured 2,090mil The dependents 1,549mil.)	2,913mil. (The insured 1,504mil The dependents 1,349mil.)	884mil. (The insured 449mil The dependents 434mil.)	1,577mil.
Average age of members (FY2014)	51.5	36.7	34.4	33.2	82.3
Amount used to work out the premiums per member (FY2014)	33.3mil.	16.7mil.	14.9mil.	15.2mil.	93.2mi.
Amount used to work out the premiums per member (FY2014)	86mil. (144mil. per household)	142mil. (246mil. per household)	207mil. (384mil. per household)	230mil. (451mil. per household)	83mil.
Average premium per member <amount including employers' contribution> (FY2014)	85,000yen (143,000yen per household)	107,000 yen <215,000 yen> 187,000 yen <373,000 yen> per insured person	118,000 yen <260,000 yen> 220,000 yen <483,000 yen> per insured person	139,000 yen <277,000 yen> 272,000 yen <544,000 yen> per insured person	6.9mil.
Government subsidies (Fixed rate portion only)	50% of benefits, etc.	16.4% of benefits, etc.	Fixed amount contribution to those associations that are in financial hardship	Nil	50% of benefits, etc.
Amount of government subsidies (Average based on FY2017 budget)	4,287.9 billion yen	1,122.7 billion yen	789 billion yen	Nil	7,849.0 billion yen

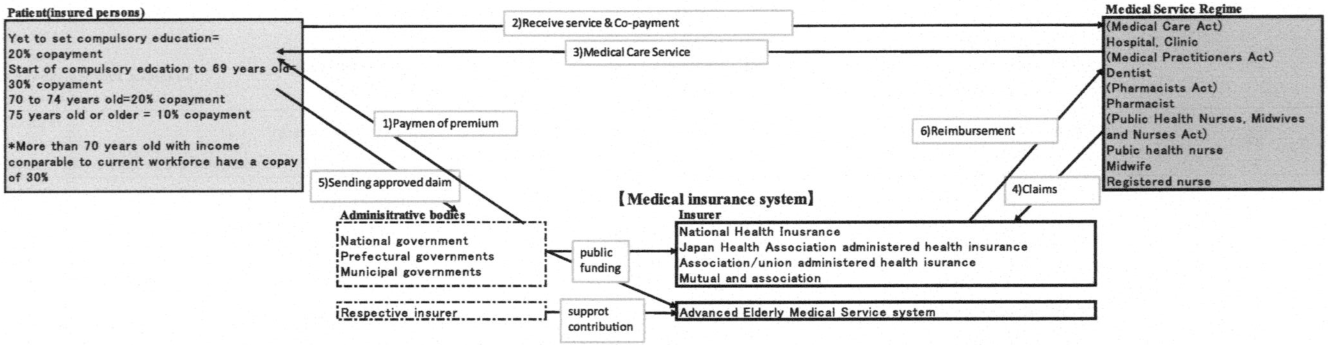

Fig. 2 A framework of Japanese Health Insurance System *Source* Based on "Overview of Medical Service Regime in Japan," by the Department of the Ministry of Health, Labour and Welfare, Japan

insured persons in the National Health Insurance system is high, as are the costs of medical care benefits per capita, while the income levels of the insured persons are low, leading to structural problems. With regard to the low income levels of the insured persons, as described by Kawaguchi and Ii (2010), Tanaka et al. (2011), this induces a rise in the relative insurance contribution burden rate and leads to a decline in the payment rate.[5]

Therefore, from the viewpoint of income redistribution, tax reductions and exemptions have been initiated for the low-income group, and national revenue has been introduced. However, with the introduction of national revenue to the financial resources available, the settings of insurance contribution amounts calculated in conjunction with the original costs of medical care benefits have been adjusted. Although the rise in the average insurance contribution is kept low, it is highly likely it will cause the balance between benefits and burdens in the National Health Insurance system to collapse.

In addition, the extent to which national revenue is introduced varies according to the municipalities, which are the insurers, and this causes interregional disparity in the burden. Not only this; it also causes a disparity in the burden between insurers, because the financial resource of national revenue is a burden that is placed on the general taxpayer.

The current state of the National Health Insurance system indicates that the introduction of national revenue into its financial resources is inevitable; but even so, there has been no change to the fact that insurance contributions are the most important financial resource for that system. Thus, in this section, on the unit of the insurers, the relationship between insurance contributions and the costs of medical care benefits is clarified, with focus placed on the interregional and the intraregional balance.

The specific analytical method is as follows. First, the interregional and intraregional disparity in insurance contributions will be verified based on the relationship between the costs of medical care benefits and insurance contributions. Second, the effects on tax reductions and exemptions and insurance contributions will be clarified, and the balance between the benefits from the costs of medical care and the burden of insurance contributions will be investigated from a coefficient of correlation.

In The Comprehensive Reform, to stabilize the National Health Insurance system, the unit areas for insurers will be expanded from municipalities to prefectures.

[5]According to Tanaka (2005) and the "Current State of Municipal Health Insurance" study by the Ministry of Health, Labour and Welfare (2012) while the burden rate of insurance contributions in municipalities' national health insurance is 9.1%, in contrast it is 6.2% for the Japan Health Insurance Association, 4.6% for union insurance, and 4.7% for mutual aid unions. The burden rate of insurance contributions is a value that is obtained by dividing the average income per capita for insured persons by the average insurance contributions per capita for insured persons. From this, we can see that the burden rate for National Health Insurance contributions is relatively high.

In this section, based on this trend, the effects of area expansion, shifting insurers from a municipality unit to a prefectural unit, will be investigated.

2.2 *The Financial Mechanism of National Health Insurance*

The various costs of medical care benefits in the National Health Insurance system include those for inpatient and outpatient care, in addition to medical benefit costs such as drug dispensing, medical treatment, and a combination of expensive medical treatment costs. The costs of medical care benefits also include the costs of other benefits such as transportation, childbirth, and childcare, and funeral costs.

As described above, insurance contributions, national revenue, and support funds cover the costs of medical care benefits. The contributions to National Health Insurance are of three types: insurance contributions for medical care (basic levied amount), insurance contributions for support funds (amount levied for funds for latter-stage elderly support, etc.), and insurance contributions for long-term care (amount levied to pay for long-term care).[6] To calculate insurance contributions for medical care, income-based contributions, asset-based contributions, per-capita contributions, and equal contributions from a pay-as-you go option are adopted; insurance contributions calculated using the pay-as-you-go system are known as the insurance contributions calculated amount.[7] The breakdown of the pay-as-you-go system differs depending on the insurer.

Figure 3 shows the relationship between National Health Insurance contributions and income. Fifty percent of contributions to National Health Insurance are taken from the ability-to-pay portion and the other 50% the benefit portion, with tax reductions and exemptions implemented. Specifically, for the ability-to-pay portion, targeting the middle-income group from the insurers' support systems, support is provided for insurance contributions compared to income. With regard to the benefits portion, in accordance with the system of reduced insurance contributions, reduction measures of 20, 50, and 70% are implemented for the low-income group. The system of reduced insurance contributions is applied to households with

[6]Insurance contributions differ according to age. For 0 to 39 years, they form the medical care portion and the support funds portion of insurance contributions; from 40 to 64 years, they are medical insurance contributions, and the support funds and long-term care portions of insurance contributions; for 65 years and above, they form the medical care portion and the support funds portion.

[7]As methods of calculating the income-based contributions of insurance contributions, the resident tax method and main text method were abolished from fiscal 2013, and were integrated into the former provisional method. The former provisional method is a method of applying insurance contributions to the sum of the previous year's total income amount, the forestry income amount, the long-term (short-term) transfer of shares income amount, etc., and subtracting the basic deduction amount of 330,000 yen. However, the carry-over deduction for miscellaneous losses is not deducted.

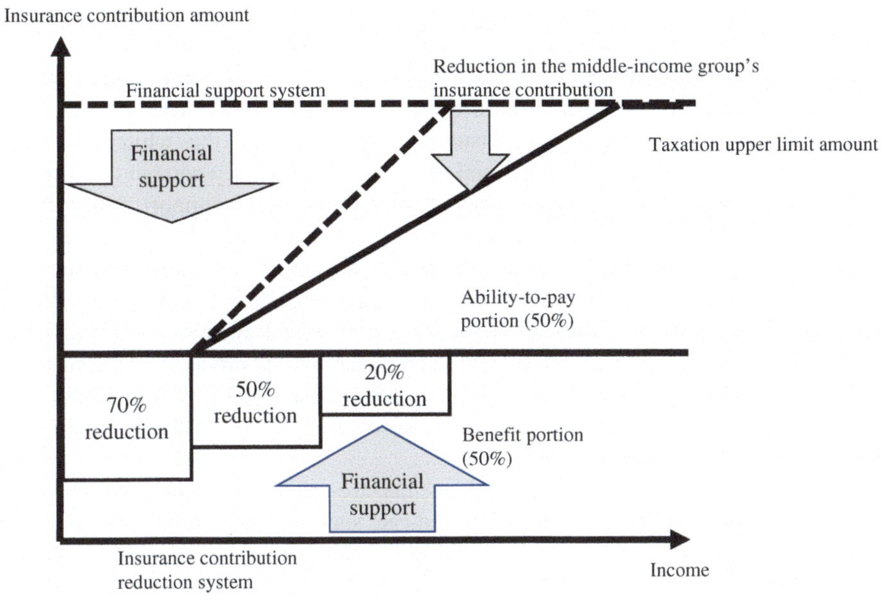

Fig. 3 Tax reductions and exemptions on National Health Insurance contributions. *Note* Based on the "The Upper Limit Amounts for the Imposition (Taxation) of National Health Insurance Contributions," Ministry of Health, Labour and Welfare (2015), Japan

total income below a defined amount in the previous year.[8] Further, with regard to the upper limit, the burden on the high-income group is also low as there is a limit on the payment amount. Thus, insurance contributions derived from these tax reductions and exemptions are the insurance contributions settled amount.

There are two types of insurance contribution collections; special collections as a deduction from the salary or pension, and ordinary collections using a payment form or bank transfer. Most insured persons pay their insurance contributions using the ordinary collection type. As most of the subscribers to the National Health Insurance system are in the low-income group, the burden rate of insurance contributions is high, but the insurance contributions payment rate is low.[9] Reflecting the payment rate, the insurance contributions amount that is actually collected is called the amount collected from insurance contributions.

[8]If a household's total income is less than 330,000 yen, a 70% reduction is applied; if total income is less than 330,000 yen on adding 260,000 per insured person (excluding head of the household), the reduction is 50%; and if the household's total income is less than 330,000 yen on adding 470,000 per insured person, the reduction is 20%.

[9]The municipalities' health insurance contributions payment rate exceeded 95% in the 1970s, the lowest recorded payment rate was 88.01% in fiscal 2009, and it has risen since then to 90.42% in fiscal 2013. Analysis of the National Health Insurance contributions payment rate is carried out in Chap. 7.

In order to pay for the costs of medical care benefits, not only insurance contributions, but large sums of national revenue and support funds are also introduced into the national health finances. Figure 4 shows the financial resources that support the payment of costs of medical care benefits in the National Health Insurance system. As shown in the figure, insurance contributions (the white part) are insufficient to cover the costs, so national revenue (the dark grey part) in the form of adjustment subsidies and state treasury contributions, and support funds from early-stage elderly subsidies (the dotted part) are also introduced.

Insurance contributions are set based on the status of the amount of insurance contributions collected in the past three years, and the deficit is paid from adjustment subsidies (financial stabilization support projects and insurance finances joint stabilization projects), and from a certain level of national revenue (the shaded part) each year, including expensive medical service costs, joint projects, and the insurers' support system. The types of national revenue described above are diverse and consist of the following items.

First, public expenses from the national tax are made up of the national government's adjustment subsidies and the fixed-rate state treasury burden. Adjustment subsidies are the regular adjustment subsidies that adjust for the imbalance in financial strength between municipalities, that is, the insurers (for example, at the

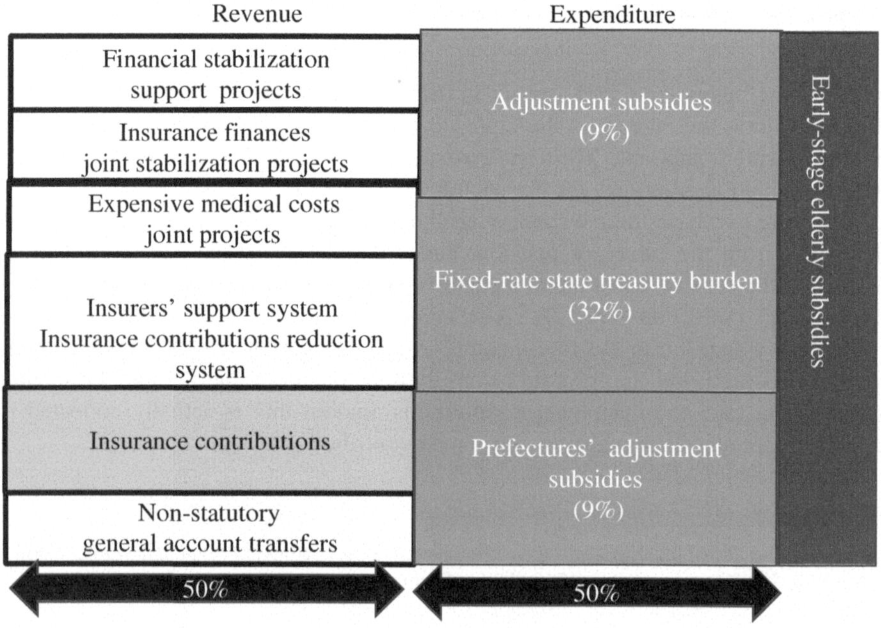

Fig. 4 Analysis of the financial resources used for the costs of medical care benefits in the National Health Insurance system. *Source* Based on "The Upper Limit Amounts for the Imposition (Taxation) of National Health Insurance Premiums," Ministry of Health, Labour and Welfare (2015), Japan

level of medical services costs and income), and special adjustment subsidies that are allocated for special situations, including disasters. The prefectures allocate prefectural adjustment subsidies in accordance with the actual situation in a region, in order to adjust imbalances at the level of medical services costs and income between the municipalities in their prefecture, and to respond to special situations within a particular region.

Second, early-stage elderly subsidies consist of support from employee insurance. There is an imbalance in the burden between insurers because among the subscribers to the National Health Insurance, the ratio of early-stage elderly aged between 65 and 74 years is high, compared to that of other insurers. Support subsidies are intended to adjust this imbalance.

Third, national revenue is introduced for expensive medical services costs that differ between the insurers. In expensive medical services costs joint projects, medical-services costs that exceed 800,000 yen per case are covered by the contribution from each municipality's National Health Insurance system. This financial resource adjusts the burden of costs placed on the prefectures and the national government, and each prefecture is responsible for a quarter of the municipality's contributions. Further, insurance finances joint stabilization projects support medical services costs exceeding 300,000 yen per case.

Fourth, financial support for low-income earners is provided by the insurers' support system and the insurance contributions reduction system. The insurers' support system provides support from the national revenue for a certain percentage of the insurance contributions amount, depending on the number of low-income earners. The insurance contributions reduction system uses national revenue to cover the reduction in insurance contributions that occurs owing to tax reductions and exemptions for low-income earners.

In the event that the financial resources to cover the costs of medical care benefits cannot be secured even from the diverse range of national revenue and support funds available, non-statutory transfers supplement them. A non-statutory transfer differs from a statutory transfer, such as the fixed-rate burden.[10] If we examining the allocation of non-statutory transfers by prefecture, we find that Metropolitan Tokyo accounts for around 30% of the total (353.4 billion yen), followed by Kanagawa Prefecture, Osaka Prefecture, Saitama Prefecture, and Aichi Prefecture, and the amount transferred in the top six prefectures was about 240 billion yen, which accounts for around 70% of the total amount.

The National Health Insurance system is supported by a large amount of public expenses and support funds, but in principle, the burden that corresponds to the benefits for the costs of medical care is insurance contributions. Therefore, a factor analysis of insurance contributions is conducted in the next section, and the medical care benefits that determine the cost of insurance contributions are shown.

---

[10]According to the "National Health Insurance Operations Annual Report" conducted by the Ministry of Health, Labour and Welfare (2009), those prefectures (which are the insurers) with non-statutory transferred funds per insured person exceeding 10,000 yen are Saitama Prefecture, Tokyo, Kanagawa Prefecture, Aichi Prefecture, Osaka Prefecture, and Okinawa Prefecture.

2.3 *Estimation Method for Factor Analysis of National Health Insurance Contributions*

In this section, we describe our method for factor analysis of the National Health Insurance contributions made by insurers. The unit for insurers in the analysis is the municipality. Table 2 explains the benefits. Figure 5 shows an image of the estimation procedure.

The costs per insured person Q can be broken down into the medical examination rate A, the number of days per case B, and costs per day C. The subscript i shows insurers ($i = 1, \ldots, I$). The subscript j shows the type of medical benefit costs; specifically, it expresses costs for hospitalization, non-hospitalization, dental, drug dispensing, food- and living-related medical-treatment, and home-visit care costs ($j = 1, \ldots, 6$).

$$\text{Costs per insured person } Q_{ij} = \text{medical examination rate } A_{ij} \times \text{the number of days per case } B_{ij} \times \text{costs per day } C_{ij} \tag{1}$$

Here, the variables on the right side can be broken down as follows.

$$\text{Medical examination rate } A_{ij} = \text{number of cases } a_{ij}/\text{number of insured persons } P_{ij} \tag{2}$$

$$\text{Number of days per case } B_{ij} = \text{number of days } b_{ij}/\text{number of cases } a_{ij} \tag{3}$$

$$\text{Costs per day } C_{ij} = \text{costs } c_{ij}/\text{number of days } b_{ij} \tag{4}$$

The data used in this section come from the "total number of general insured persons" (at the end of the relevant fiscal year) in "the general conditions" section of the "Report on the Status of National Health Insurance Operations (Annual Operations Report) Table A (fiscal 2010)," by the Ministry of Health, Labour and Welfare (2010). Data on the number of insured persons P by medical benefit costs and by insurer, number of cases by medical benefit costs, number of days b, and costs c were obtained, and medical examination rate A, number of days per case B, and costs per day C were calculated.

Next, medical treatment costs for which data on the number of days were unknown, expensive medical treatment costs and the costs of other benefits were broken down into costs per insured person Q, as described below. Medical treatment costs cover the following: general medical consultation, prosthetics, orthopedics-related treatment, massage therapy, acupuncture and moxibustion, other therapies, transportation costs, expensive medical treatment costs, expensive long-term care totaled medical treatment costs, childbirth and childcare benefits,

Table 2 Contents of benefits of public medical insurance *Source* Based on "on medical insurance in Japan," by the Department of the Ministry of Health, Labour and Welfare, Japan

Payment		National healthcare insurance	Healthcare insurance
Healthcare payments	Healthcare Benefits Visiting nursing healthcare	Until the entry into primary school: 80% After junior high school to 69 years: 70% 70–74 years: 80% Over 75 years: 90%	
	Meals during hospitalization expenses	Standard amount borne for meals: ¥260 per meal	Low-income persons: ¥210 per meal Low income persons after the 90th day of hospitalization: ¥160 per meal Persons of particularly low income (70 years old and over): ¥100 per meal
	Living care during hospitalization (65 years old and above)	Living care standard fee: ¥460 per meal (meal cost) + ¥320 (residential cost) ¥420 at the insurance medical institutions that calculate living care during hospitalization (II)	Low-income persons: ¥210 per meal (meal cost) + ¥320 (residential cost) Particularly low-income persons: ¥130 per meal (meal cost) + ¥320 (residential cost) Persons receiving senior citizens welfare benefits: ¥100 per meal (meal cost) + ¥0 (residential cost)
	High-cost medical care expenses (with individual limit)	Aged under 70 years (Figures in parenthesis are for the fourth month onwards) (High income) ¥252,600+(medical expenses – 842,000) × 1% (¥140,100) (General) ¥80,100+(medical expenses – 267,000) × 1% (¥44,400) (Low income) ¥35,400 (¥24,600)	Aged 70–74 years Hospitalization Outpatients (per person) (Working income level) ¥80,100+ ¥44,400 (medical expenses – 267,000) × 1% (General) ¥44,400 ¥12,000 (Low income) ¥24,600 ¥8,000 (Particularly low income) ¥15,000 ¥8,000
Cash payments	Lump-sum allowance for child birth	Contents of benefits are decided by separate regulations (Most insurers pay ¥420,000 (¥390,000 if the additional payment set out in the maternity medical care compensation scheme does not apply.)	420,000 paid in the instance of the insured person or their dependent giving birth (¥390,000 if the additional payment set out in the maternity medical care compensation scheme does not apply)
	Lump-sum funeral allowance, burial costs	Contents of benefits are decided by separate regulations. (Most local authorities pay at a rate between ¥10,000–50,000) Practiced by most local authorities	Burial costs: Fixed amount of ¥50,000 paid in the instance of the insured person dying Family burial costs: Fixed amount of ¥50,000 paid in the instance of the insured person's dependent dying
	Invalidity benefit	Voluntary benefit (Not practiced by any local authorities)	In the case that the insured person becomes unable to work because of medical treatment being received for a cause not related to work, an amount approximate to two thirds of that persons standards daily wage will be paid daily for a maximum period of I year and 6 months
	Maternity allowance		During the maternity leave taken by the insured person, an amount approximate to two thirds of that persons standards daily wage will be paid daily for a maximum period of from 42 days prior to the birth to 56 days after the birth

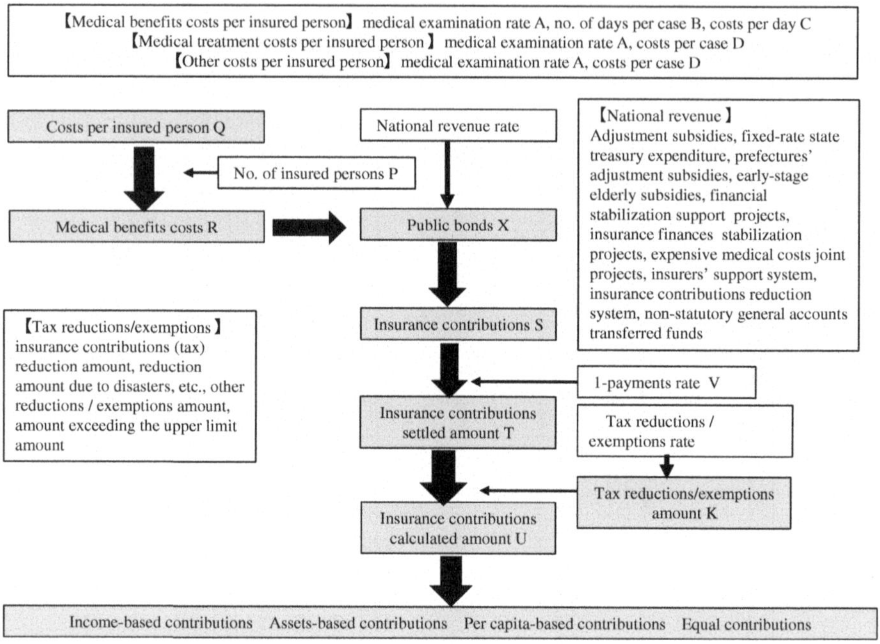

Fig. 5 Procedure for factor analysis of National Health Insurance contributions

funeral benefits, injury and sickness allowance, childbirth allowance, and other optional benefits (j = 7, …, 20).[11]

$$\text{Costs per insured person } Q_{ij} = \text{medical examination rate } A_{ij} \times \text{costs per case } D_{ij} \tag{5}$$

As above, costs per case D can be broken down as follows.

$$\text{Costs per case } D_{ij} = \text{costs } c_{ij}/\text{number of cases } a_{ij} \tag{6}$$

From the same report, the "Report on the Status of National Health Insurance Operations (Annual Operations Report) Table C (1) (fiscal 2010)," we obtained data on the number of cases a and costs c by insurer, including: benefit costs for general medical consultation, prosthetics, orthopedics-related treatment, massage therapy, acupuncture and moxibustion, other costs, transportation and medical treatment

[11]In order to calculate the costs of medical care benefits, we used the insurance benefits conditions shown in the "Form 15 Report on the Status of National Health Insurance Operations (Operations Annual Report) Table C (1) (fiscal 2010)". Medical care benefits costs and medical treatment costs were calculated from data on medical care benefits costs taken from the following section: "1. medical care benefits situation (1) Overall, expensive medical treatment costs," "2. The expensive medical treatment costs situation," and "3. Expensive long-term care totaled medical treatment costs situation," and the costs of other benefits from "4.The costs of other benefits situation."

costs, expensive medical treatment costs and expensive long-term care totaled medical treatment costs, childbirth and childcare benefits, funeral benefits, injury and sickness allowance, childbirth allowance, and other optional benefits. The data were used to calculate the medical examination rate A and costs per case D.

From the above relations, we obtained the medical benefit costs by insurer, medical treatment costs, expensive medical treatment costs, and the costs of other benefits were totaled and the costs of medical care benefits R, as follows:

$$\text{Costs of medical care benefits } R_i = \sum_j \text{number of insured persons } P_{ij} \times \text{ costs per insured person } Q_{ij} \tag{7}$$

National revenue X was subtracted from the costs of medical care benefits R to derive the amount collected from insurance contributions. Here, the following items were used for national revenue: administrative work costs, medical benefit costs and related expensive medical services costs, joint project contributions, specific health checkups and related costs, regular adjustment subsidies, special adjustment subsidies, childbirth and childcare lump sum subsidies, subsidies for special measures and other National Treasury expenditure, expensive medical services costs, contributions to support joint projects, specific health checkups and related costs, first prefectural adjustment subsidies, second prefectural adjustment subsidies, area expansion and related support funds, other prefectural expenditure, expensive medical services costs, subsidies for joint projects, insurance finances joint stabilization projects subsidies, and other subsidies to support joint projects.[12] Further, for the general account (municipal assistance) transferred funds, insurance-base stability (insurance tax reduction portion), insurance-base stability (insurers' support portion), costs exceeding the standard, employee salary costs, etc., childbirth and childcare lump sum payments etc., financial stabilization support projects, and other items were used. It is expressed by subscript $_m$ in national revenue X (m = 1, …, 23).

$$\text{Amount collected from insurance contributions } S_i = \text{the costs of medical care benefits } R_i - \sum_m \text{national revenue} X_i \tag{8}$$

On multiplying this by the amount collected from insurance contributions S (1-payment rate V), the insurance contributions settled amount T is obtained. Further,

[12]For national revenue, data from "Accounting conditions 1. Conditions of income and expenditure, and the status of assets, liabilities, etc., (1) Income station and expenditure situation," from "Form 14 Report on the Status of National Health Insurance Operations (Operations Annual Report) Table (1) (fiscal 2010)" were used.

by adding the tax reductions and exemptions amount K, the insurance contributions calculated amount U can be calculated.[13]

$$\text{Insurance contributions settled amount } T_i = \text{amount collected from insurance contributions } S_i \times (1 - \text{payment rate } V_i) \quad (9)$$

$$\text{Insurance contributions calculated amount } U_i = \text{insurance contributions settled amount } T_i + \text{tax reductions and exemptions amount } K_i \quad (10)$$

Here, with the subscript $_n$ showing the type of tax reduction and exemption, respectively, it represents the income-based contributions reduction ($n = 1$), per capita based contributions reduction ($n = 2$), reduction due to a disaster, etc. ($n = 3$), other reductions and exemptions ($n = 4$), and the amount exceeding the limit ($n = 5$) ($n = 1, \ldots, 5$).

2.4 *Factor Analysis and Regional Disparity in National Health Insurance Contributions*

First, the previous section model will be used to conduct a factor analysis of the medical care benefits from National Health Insurance contributions. We will investigate those medical care benefits within that system that are factors in determining the amount collected from insurance contributions, and the extent to which regional disparity occurs. Please refer to Fig. 6.

The costs of medical care benefits include medical benefit costs and medical treatment costs, expensive medical treatment costs, and the costs of other benefits. Studying the percentage share of the amount collected from insurance

[13]Insurance contributions were calculated using the insurance contributions calculated amount, insurance contributions reduction amount, reductions and exemptions amount from disasters etc., other reductions and exemptions amount, amount exceeding the tax upper-limit amount, increase/decrease amount, and insurance contributions settled amount from the payment rates from "2. Collection of insurance contributions conditions (general insured persons portion)" of "Form 14 Report on the Status of National Health Insurance Operations (Operations Annual Report) Table B (1) (fiscal 2010)"; ".Insurance contributions (medical care benefits portion) tax collection conditions (general insured persons portion)" in "Form 14-2 Report on the Status of National Health Insurance Operations (Operations Annual Report) Table B (2) (fiscal 2010)," "5.Insurance contributions (latter-stage elderly support funds portion) tax collection conditions (general insured persons portion)," from "Form 14-2 Report on the Status of National Health Insurance Operations (Operations Annual Report)Table B (3) (fiscal 2010)," "6.Insurance contributions (long-term care payment portion) tax collection conditions (long-term care insurance second insured persons portion)" from "Form 14-2 Report on the Status of National Health Insurance Operations (Operations Annual Report)Table B (4) (fiscal 2010)."

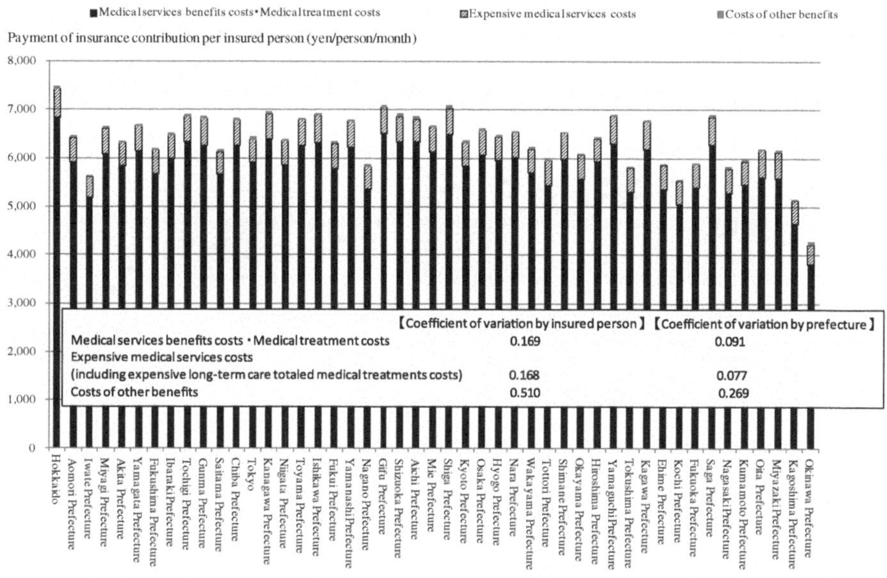

Fig. 6 Breakdown of amount collected from insurance contributions per insured person

contributions, medical benefit costs and medical treatment costs constitute more than 90%, while expensive medical treatment costs and the costs of other benefits are less than 10%. The coefficients of variation of the respective costs are 0.169 and 0.091 for medical benefit costs and medical treatment costs on the municipality unit and the prefectural unit, and 0.168 and 0.077 for expensive medical treatment costs. In contrast, the costs of other benefits are high values of 0.510 and 0.269.

Although most of the costs of medical care benefits are from medical benefit costs and medical treatment costs, their coefficients of variation are relatively low, which reduces the regional disparity levels. Regional disparity is also low for expensive medical treatment costs. Examining the coefficients of variation for the municipality and prefectural units, it can be seen that a common point for all the medical benefit costs and medical treatment costs, expensive medical treatment costs, and the costs of other benefits is that the values are lower for the prefectural unit than the municipality unit.

From this, it is clear that medical benefit costs and medical treatment costs constitute a large share of National Health Insurance contributions, regional disparity is small, and there is a tendency for regional disparity to reduce alongside the expansion from the municipality unit to the prefectural unit.

Second, we will verify the correlation between the coefficients of variation of the costs of medical care benefits and total taxable income (refer to Fig. 7). The average costs of medical care benefits per insured person and total taxable income per

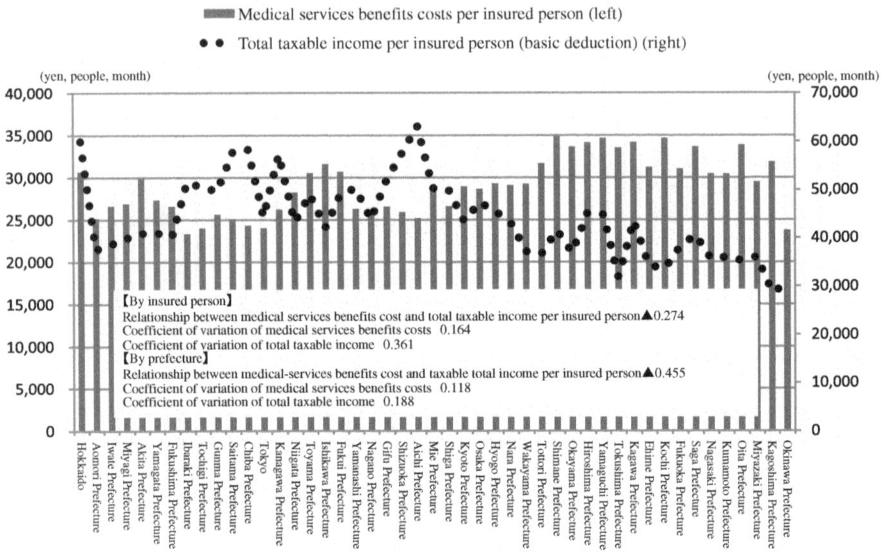

Fig. 7 Relationship between the costs of medical care benefits and total taxable income

insured person on the municipality unit are 28,380 yen and 45,742 yen, respectively.

On evaluating the coefficients of variation on whether there is regional disparity in the respective values, we find that the coefficient of variation for the costs of medical care benefits on the municipality unit is 0.164, but it is a smaller value on the prefectural unit, at 0.118. The coefficient of variation for total taxable income is 0.361 on the municipality unit, showing a value more than twice that of the coefficient of variation for costs of medical care benefits. With regard to total taxable income, as with the costs of medical care benefits, the coefficients of variation on the prefectural unit are smaller than on the municipality unit. Examining the differences in the coefficients of variation of the costs of medical care benefits and total taxable income, we see that they tend to be smaller on the prefectural unit than on the municipality unit.

The relationship between the costs of medical care benefits and total taxable income was evaluated using a correlation index from the municipality unit and the prefectural unit. From this, it was found that on the municipality unit, the correlation between the costs of medical care benefits and total taxable income was ▲0.274, while on the prefectural unit, the coefficient of correlation was ▲0.455, and there is a strong negative relation.

Therefore, compared to the costs of medical care benefits, total taxable income has greater regional disparity, and this disparity tends to reduce with the expansion from the municipality unit to the prefectural unit. For the correlation between the costs of medical care benefits and total taxable income, the results obtained show

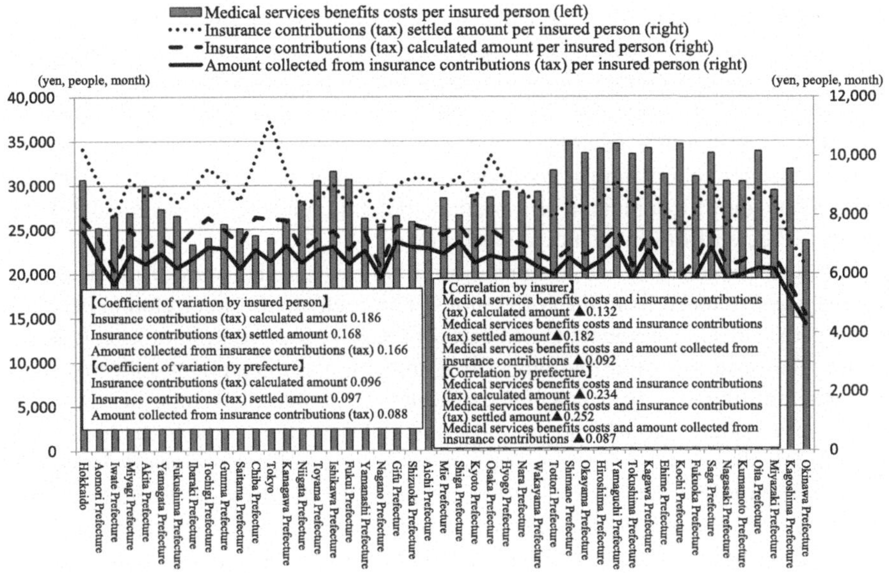

Fig. 8 Relationship between the costs of medical care benefits and insurance contributions

that it is a negative relation and that the value of the coefficient of correlation is higher for the prefectural unit than the municipality unit.

Third, we will look at the relationship between the costs of medical care benefits and insurance contributions (refer to Fig. 8). In this section, the effects are divided into the pay-as-you-go system, tax reductions and exemptions, and the payment rate. Three variables will be used for insurance contributions, namely insurance contributions calculated amount, insurance contribution settled amount, and amount collected from insurance contributions.

The average level of insurance contributions per insured person is 8730 yen for insurance contributions calculated amount, 6998 yen for insurance contributions settled amount, and 6399 yen for amount collected from insurance contributions. On comparing the insurance premiums based on insurance premium calculation and insurance premiums for insurance premiums due to tax reductions and exemptions, we find that insurance contributions were reduced by an average of nearly 20%. From the insurance contributions settled amount and the amount collected from insurance contributions, we understand that the collection conditions attract a 0.07% reduction in insurance contributions.

On calculating the disparity between municipalities in insurance contributions per insured person, the coefficient of variation for insurance contributions calculated amount is 0.186; in contrast, the coefficient for insurance contributions settled amount is 0.168, and that for the amount collected from insurance contributions is 0.166. In other words, at the calculation stage, tax reductions and exemptions decrease the disparity in insurance contributions, and a slight reduction trend is observed in the collection of insurance contributions. This coefficient of variation is a commonality shared by insurance contributions calculated amount, insurance contributions settled amount, the amount collected from insurance contributions, and the coefficient of variation for the prefectural unit trends below that of the municipality unit.

In comparing the municipality and the prefectural units, we see that for the insurance contributions calculated amount and insurance contributions settled amount, the prefectural unit's coefficient of variation is a higher value than the municipality unit's coefficient of variation, but this tendency is reversed for the amount collected from insurance contributions.

Next, the relation between insurance contributions and the costs of medical care benefits was evaluated from the correlations. The coefficients of correlation between the costs of medical care benefits and each of the insurance contributions calculated amount, the insurance contributions settled amount, and the amount collected from insurance contributions, were calculated to be negative values. This indicates that there is a negative correlation, whether on the municipality unit or on the prefectural unit.

From the above, it can be seen that tax reductions and exemptions decrease the regional disparity in insurance contributions, and that the disparity is reduced even further with the expansion of area from the municipality unit to the prefectural unit. Further, it is clarified that in the relationship between benefits and burdens, there is a negative correlation between the costs of medical care benefits and total taxable income, and the costs of medical care benefits and insurance contributions.

2.5 *Effects of Tax Reductions and Exemptions and the Relationship Between Benefits and Burdens*

Next, we will verify tax reductions and exemptions. Figure 9 shows a breakdown of tax reductions and exemptions, and in Fig. 10, the effects of tax reductions and exemptions on insurance contributions are investigated.

From Fig. 9, on calculating the tax reductions and exemptions amount per insured person, in the municipality unit, we find that the highest amount is in Sarufutsu Village in Hokkaido at 9131 yen, while the lowest is in Mikurashima Village at 331 yen. About 90% of that accounts for the reduction in insurance contributions amount and the tax upper limit.[14]

On calculating the regional disparity in tax reductions and exemptions, we find that the coefficient of variation of all tax reductions and exemptions for the municipality unit was 0.411, which is about the same value as for the insurance contributions reduction amount, while the reductions and exemptions amount from

[14]The maximum insurance contributions reduction amount of 2968 yen was in Aogashima Village in Metropolitan Tokyo, while the minimum was in Nogunikawa Village, Nara Prefecture, at 149 yen. With regard to the tax upper-limit amount, the maximum was in Sarufutsu Village, Hokkaido, at 8511 yen. Similarly, for the minimum, there were multiple insurers regardless of the limit. Specifically, Ueno Village in Gunma Prefecture and Aogashima Village in Tokyo did not have any insured persons corresponding to the reductions and exemptions from the tax upper-limit amount.

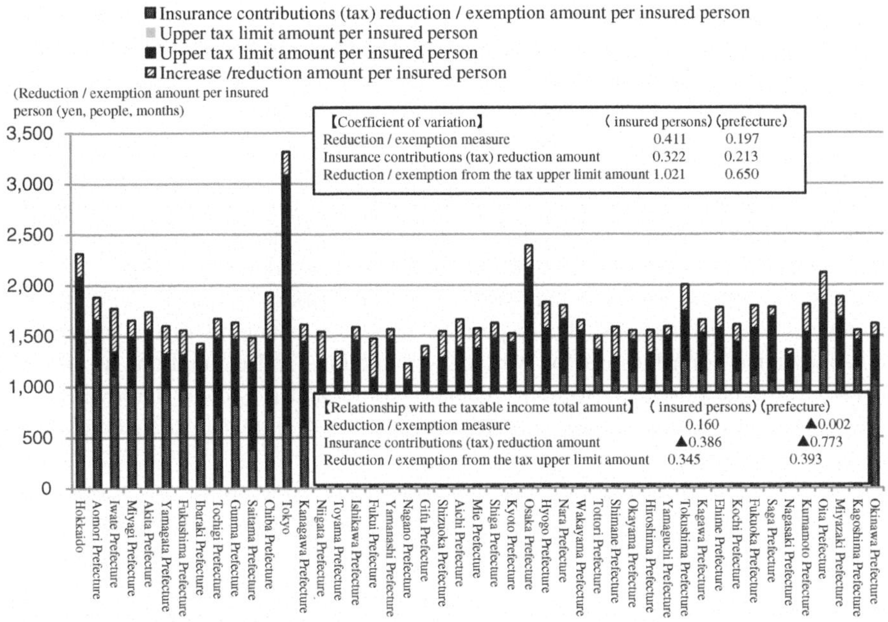

Fig. 9 Breakdown of tax reductions and exemptions

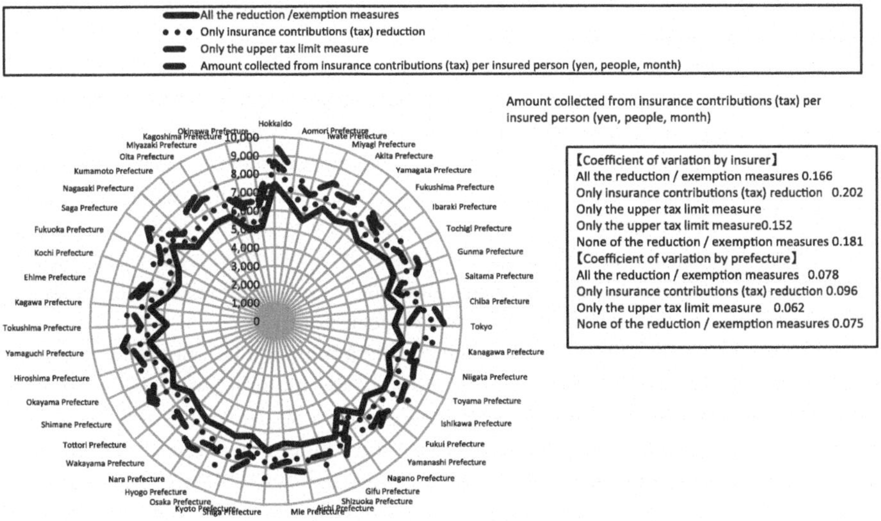

Fig. 10 Effects of tax reductions and exemptions on insurance contributions

the tax upper-limit amount was 1.021, indicating a strong regional disparity. However, when we expand the area to the prefectural unit, we see that the regional disparity is lower for all the values.

On verifying the relation between tax reductions and exemptions and total taxable income, we observe that a positive correlation exists between insurance contributions and total taxable income when implemented for all tax reductions and exemptions. However, when it is implemented only for insurance contributions reduction, the correlation is negative, and when implemented for reductions and exemptions from the tax upper-limit amount, it is a positive correlation.

From the above, we see that while regional disparity occurs owing to tax reductions and exemptions, the disparity reduces on changing to the prefectural unit. Insurance contributions for which tax reductions and exemptions are implemented correlate positively to total taxable income, and it is clear that even if tax reductions and exemptions are implemented, the result is that insurance contributions are large when income is high.

Further, while implementing tax reductions and exemptions, we verified the effects on the amount collected from insurance contributions per insured person. Figure 10 shows the estimates of how the amount collected from insurance contributions per insured person changes when all tax reductions and exemptions are implemented, when only the reduction in insurance contributions is implemented, when the tax upper-limit reductions and exemptions measure is implemented, and when none of the tax reductions and exemptions are implemented.

From the results on the amount collected from insurance contributions per insured person, considering only the municipalities unit, we find that when no tax reductions and exemptions were implemented, the largest value was in Sarufutsu Village in Hokkaido at 20,988 yen, while the smallest was in Aguni Village in Okinawa at 3407 yen.

On implementing the tax reductions and exemptions, the largest and the smallest amounts collected from insurance contributions per insured person were calculated as Hokkaido's Sarufutsu Village at 11,973 yen and Okinawa's Aguni Village at 2691 yen. In the results of estimations on the prefectural unit, when not implementing the tax reductions and exemptions, the largest value was Hokkaido at 9655 yen and the smallest was Okinawa Prefecture at 6593 yen, and when the tax reductions and exemptions were implemented, the values were reduced to 7456 yen in Hokkaido and to 5136 yen in Okinawa Prefecture.

Therefore, on examining the differences in the amounts when tax reductions and exemptions are not implemented, it is seen that in the municipality unit, when only insurance contribution reductions were implemented, the average reduction was 862 yen. Similarly, when only the tax upper-limit reductions and exemptions were implemented, the average reduction was 522 yen, and when all tax reductions and exemptions were implemented, the average reduction was 1579 yen.

Further, when considering the averages on the prefectural unit, if only the reduction in insurance contributions was implemented, the average reduction was 898 yen; when only the tax upper-limit reductions and exemptions were implemented, the average reduction was 475 yen; and when all tax reductions and exemptions were implemented, the average reduction was 1562 yen.

On the other hand, when considering the coefficients of variation, when no tax reductions and exemptions are implemented, we see that the amount collected from insurance contributions on the municipality unit is 0.181 and on the prefectural unit 0.075. In contrast, on implementing all tax reductions and exemptions, we find that the coefficient of variation for the municipality unit is 0.166 and the coefficient of variation for the prefectural unit is 0.078, indicating an expanding trend in the amount collected from insurance contributions.

On verifying the respective effects of tax reductions and exemptions, when implementing only the insurance contributions reduction amount, it can be seen that the coefficient of variation for the amount collected from insurance contributions is 0.202 on the municipality unit and 0.096 on the prefectural unit. Further, when we implement only the tax upper-limit reductions and exemptions measure, the coefficient of variation of the amount collected from insurance contributions is 0.152 on the municipality unit and 0.062 on the prefectural unit, indicating that the coefficient of variation differs depending on the type of tax reduction and exemption.

Therefore, from the results obtained, when implementing tax reductions and exemptions, although the amount collected from insurance contributions per insured person is low, the regional disparity in the amount collected from insurance contributions increases, and the coefficient of variation on the municipality unit exceeds that on the prefectural unit for this disparity.

In this section, we focused on the medical care benefits and insurance premiums of the the National Health Insurance system, and examined from regional disparity and benefits and burden. On conducting a factor analysis of insurance contributions from the content of benefits, the same tendency is seen in all the regions; namely, that medical benefit costs constitute the largest share of total costs and the coefficient of variation is small. Regional disparity was observed in insurance contributions for each calculated amount, the settled amount, and the collection amount. Moreover, for the relation between the costs of medical care benefits and insurance contributions, it was clarified that the balance between benefits and burdens collapses when tax reductions and exemptions are implemented.

3 Burden Structure of Latter-Stage Elderly Medical Insurance Contributions

3.1 Latter-Stage Elderly Medical Care System as Seen from the Relationship Between Benefits and Burdens

Based on the law concerning the security of healthcare treatment for senior citizens, the latter-stage elderly medical care system was enforced from April 2008; only the latter-stage elderly aged 75 years and above are eligible. The latter-stage elderly medical care system, designed to address issues in the National Health Insurance system, was established with the aim of achieving a suitable balance between medical care benefits and the burden of paying insurance contributions.

The background for the establishment of this system is the range of difficulties that originated when medical services were made free for the elderly in 1973. This move invited problems such as the so-called "salonization" of medical care and "social hospitalization," and produced a structure in which the excessive burden of the costs of medical care benefits is placed on the working generation. The factors behind this include the separation of financial burden and the management of insurers, an unclear burden of costs between the working generation and the elderly generation, and the regional disparity between insurers. After reflecting on these issues, the government introduced the latter-stage elderly medical care system with the aim of constructing a system in which insurance contributions are set appropriately in accordance with the level of medical services costs, and in which the elderly themselves bear the burden. The insurers are latter-stage elderly medical care wide-area unions within the prefectural units.

However, the problem of intragenerational income inequality occurs even among the latter-stage elderly and this causes health disparity among them. Otake (1994, 2005), Iwamoto (2000), Shirohase (2002), Oshio (2004), and Oshio et al. (2006) found that income inequality within age groups is expanding, particularly within the elderly age group. Wilkinson (1992), Subramanian and Kawachi (2004), and Wilkinson and Pickett (2006) found that income inequality affects the subjective evaluation of health, while within Japan, Kondo (2005), Kawakami et al. (2006), Oshio and Kobayashi (2009), Oshio (2010) reached the same conclusion. Also, Ichida et al. (2009), Oshio and Kobayashi (2009) examined the relation between socioeconomic disparity and elderly health using the Gini coefficient as an indicator in regions of different sizes.

The latter-stage elderly, considered to have poor income-earning potential, are highly likely to face health problems. While setting appropriate insurance contributions in accordance with medical care benefits costs and requiring that the latter-stage elderly bear this burden, it would seem important to reflect the income of insured persons in the calculation of insurance contributions.

Thus, a shortfall for medical care benefits, specifically for the part that cannot be covered by insurance contributions, will occur. As a result, there will be no choice but to consider the introduction of national revenue as a financial resource. However, this would mean there would be a disparity between benefits and burdens. Komatsu (2008) focused on the regular adjustment subsidies introduced to address income inequality between insurers in the latter-stage elderly medical care system, theoretically showing that although the method of calculating regular adjustment subsidies excludes income inequality, it causes a distortion in the burden of insurance contributions.

From the above, the important aim is to achieve a balance between the burdens and benefits for the working generation, who bear a relatively large share of the tax and insurance contributions, and the elderly generation, who receive a large amount of the benefits, and a balance within the elderly generation. However, it is highly likely that the expansion of intragenerational income inequality among the elderly will lead to an expansion in health disparity; therefore, from this perspective, it is considered necessary to introduce national revenue to a certain extent.

In this section, we examine the balance between benefits and burden of medical benefits and insurance premiums in the latter-stage elderly medical care system. Insurance contributions include the calculated amount, which is estimated from the pay-as-you-go system according to income and number of insured persons, and the settled amount, which takes into consideration tax reductions and exemptions in the insurance contributions calculated amount. In this section, these two types of insurance contributions shall be used and the relationship between the benefits and burden of the costs of medical care benefits and insurance contributions, and the redistribution effects of tax reductions and exemptions, will be verified.

3.2 *Financial Mechanism of the Latter-Stage Elderly Medical Care System*

There are four financial resources for the latter-stage elderly medical care system: national revenue, support funds, insurance contributions, and self-payments. Self-payments are the responsibility of insured persons who are working or who receive an income, and other insured persons. The total area of Fig. 11 shows the costs of medical care benefits excluding self-payments for the latter-stage elderly medical services costs. Analyzing this, 50% of financial resources come from national revenue, 40% from support funds, and the remaining 10% is the burden borne by the latter-stage elderly.[15]

Breaking down the composition of national revenue, 8.3% is adjustment subsidies, 25% is the fixed-rate state treasury contribution, 8.3% is the fixed-rate prefectural contribution, and 8.3% is the fixed-rate contribution by municipalities. Adjustment subsidies include regular adjustment subsidies, which are intended to equalize the disparity in the financial strengths of wide-area unions, and special adjustment subsidies that are allocated in the event of a disaster or other special circumstances.

Public expenses that clarify the use for the latter-stage elderly medical insurance system have also been introduced. National revenue is introduced after it is clarified for intended use. Financial stabilization funds are set to cover the risk of non-payment of insurance contributions and benefits-related risks, and to reduce the increase in insurance contributions. With regard to support for expensive medical services costs and special expensive medical services costs, joint projects have been established to alleviate the impact of the rapid increase in medical services costs as a result of the provision of expensive healthcare services.

As shown in Fig. 12, the latter-stage elderly medical care system's insurance contributions are made by means of a pay-as-you-go system per individual, and are composed of per capita-based contributions for all insured persons, and a

[15]Support funds are contributions from insured persons who subscribe to the municipalities' national health insurance and to the health insurance plan. Unlike support funds from the elderly healthcare system, they are linked to the results of specific health checkups and specific health guidance, and the monetary amounts are determined from these results.

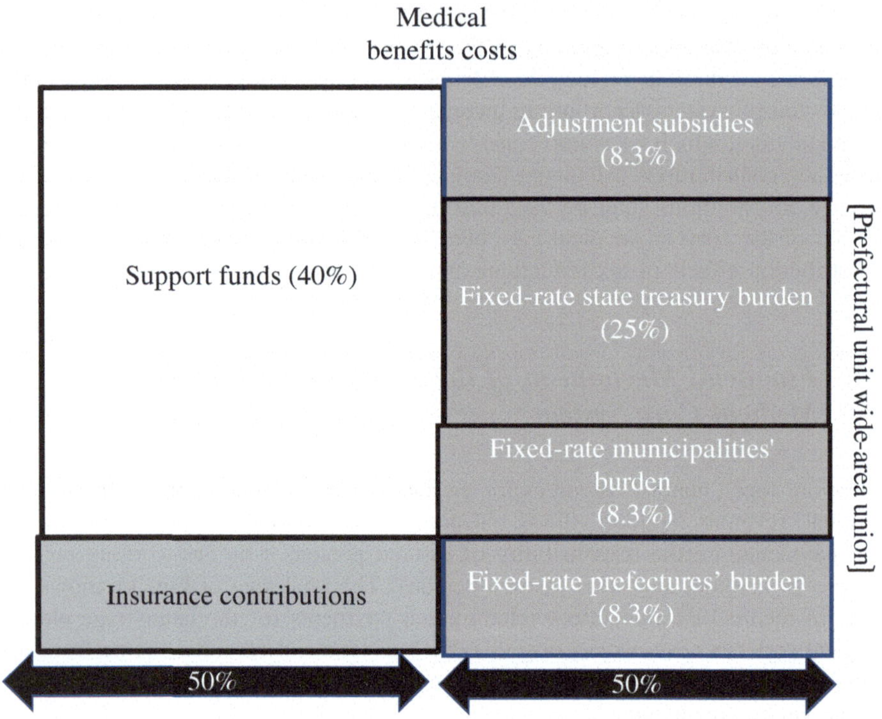

Fig. 11 Breakdown of financial resources for the costs of medical care benefits in the latter-stage elderly medical care system. *Note* Based on the Ministry of Health, Labour and Welfare (2008), "Overview of the Latter-stage Elderly Medical Care System."

percentage of income levied on people with a certain level of income. In the elderly healthcare system in the past, elderly persons who subscribed to insurance because they were eligible as dependents were not obligated to pay, but they are now required to pay insurance contributions to the latter-stage elderly medical care system. The system also incorporates various measures intended for low-income earners at the insurance contributions calculation stage.

First, tax reductions and exemptions are implemented. There are reduction and exemption measures for income-based contribution reductions, per capita-based contributions reductions, and the tax upper-limit amount; reduction and exemption measures for disasters; and other reduction and exemption measures. Here, the income-based contributions reduction indicates that the amount of income underlying the imposition (for example, the former provisional income) is below a certain level, and the reduction amount is determined in accordance with this amount.[16] For

[16]For the income-based contributions reduction, an income-based contributions reduction of 50% is applied to income of less than 580,000 yen after the basic deduction for the insured person who bears the income-based contributions.

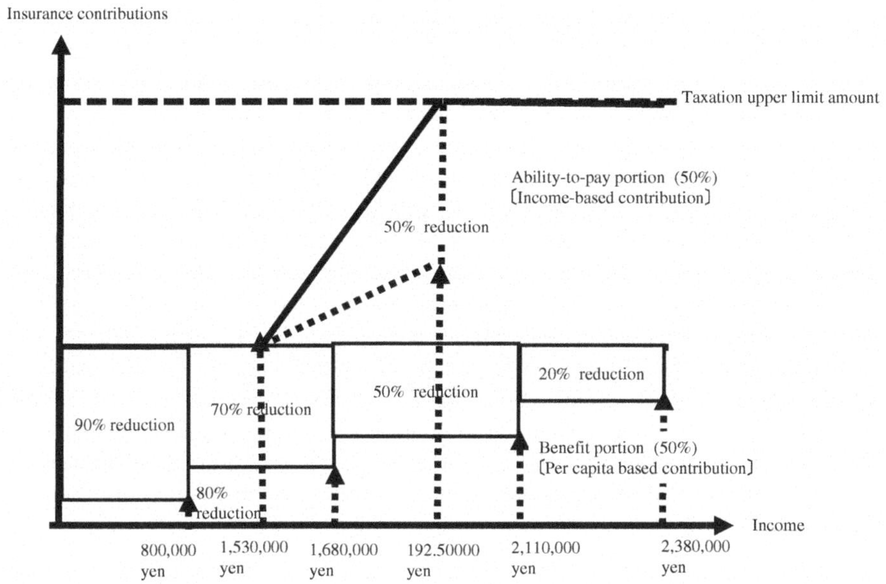

Fig. 12 Tax reductions and exemptions on insurance contributions. *Note* Based on the Ministry of Health, Labour and Welfare (2008), "Overview of the Latter-Stage Elderly Medical Care System."

the households in which all the insured persons of the same household and the head of household "total amount of gross income sum" are equal to or less than a certain amount, the equal amount of insurance premium portion is reduced.[17]

Insurance contributions for latter-stage elderly medical care were established with an upper limit of 500,000 yen per year when the system was established in fiscal 2008. This was to ensure that the burden did not fall excessively on insured people with a high income. However, alongside the rise in the per capita costs of medical care benefits, the average insurance contribution has also risen and the burden on the low-income group has expanded.[18] Further, in order to maintain a

[17]The per capita-based contributions are reduced by 70, 50, and 20% according to income from the locally imposed burden. It is reduced when the total income of insured persons is within the same household and the head of household's income is below a certain level. Moreover, with regard to the 70% reduction, the state treasury bears a reduction of 90% for all insured persons in the latter-stage elderly medical care system and for households with income of less than 800,000 yen and a reduction of 85% for all others.

[18]In the latter-stage elderly medical care system, it is limited to 35% for households that bear income-based contributions. Compared to the National Health Insurance in which approximately 60% of households bear income-based contributions, it signifies that the slope of the income-based contribution rate becomes higher. A hike in the tax upper-limit amount aims to achieve a structure in which payments are made according to the ability to pay by reducing the slope of the rate of income-based contributions.

balance with the National Health Insurance contributions, the upper-limit amount was reduced by 10% in 2012.[19]

The reduction and exemption measures for disasters and related problems are implemented in the event that an insured person's house, household belongings, or other assets suffer considerable damage because of a disaster. Following an application, the monthly insurance contributions are reduced by half or the insured person is completely exempt for not more than one year from the month the damage occurs.

Second, the latter-stage elderly medical care system incorporates generous insurance contribution reduction measures into a supplementary budget, mainly for the low-income group. A measure has been implemented to reduce the burden of insurance contributions on the dependents of employee insurance by 90%.[20]

Financial resources for the latter-stage elderly medical care system are insurance contributions, national revenue, support funds, and self-payments. In consideration of the above-described medical care system, in the next section, a factor analysis of latter-stage elderly medical insurance contributions by prefecture shall be carried out, and the effects of the tax reductions and exemptions on insurance contributions shall be estimated.

3.3 Estimation Method for Factor Analysis of the Latter-Stage Elderly Medical Insurance Contributions

In this section, the estimation method for the factor analysis of the latter-stage elderly medical insurance contributions by insurers is described. The unit used for insurers in the analysis is the prefecture. Figure 13 shows an image of the estimation procedure.

Costs per insured person O can be broken down into medical examination rate A, number of days per case B, and costs per day C. Subscript i shows the prefecture ($i = 1, \ldots, 47$). Moreover, subscript j ($j = 1, \ldots, 7$) indicates the type of medical benefit cost; specifically, it represents costs covering hospitalization, non-hospitalization, dental, drug dispensing, food- and living-related medical treatment, and home visits.

$$\begin{aligned}\text{Costs per insured person } O_{ij} &= \text{medical examination rate } A_{ij} \\ &\times \text{ the number of days per case } B_{ij} \times \text{costs per day } C_{ij}\end{aligned} \tag{11}$$

Here, the variables on the right side can be broken down as follows.

---

[19]The upper-limit amount for National Health Insurance contributions was 590,000 yen in 2008, which was the year when the latter-stage elderly medical care system was established, but rose by 10% over three years and was 650,000 in 2011.

[20]From April 2012, 50% of the insurance contributions burden of dependents was the local burden as a legal measure and up to 90% was borne by the state treasury as a budgetary measure.

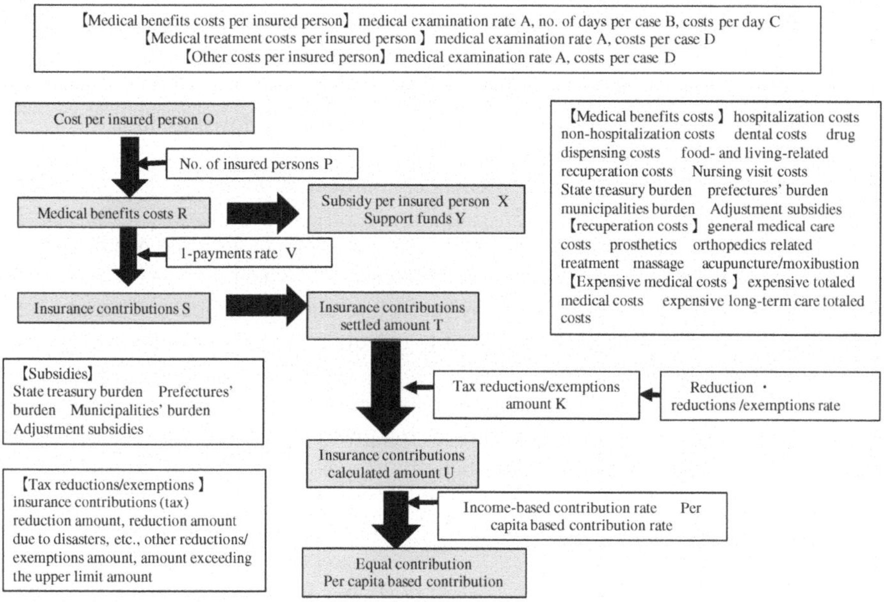

Fig. 13 Estimation procedure

$$\text{Medical examination rate } A_{ij} = \text{number of cases } a_{ij}/\text{number of insured persons } P_{ij} \tag{12}$$

$$\text{Number of days per case } B_{ij} = \text{number of days } b_{ij}/\text{number of cases } a_{ij} \tag{13}$$

$$\text{Costs per day } C_{ij} = \text{costs } c_{ij}/\text{number of days } b_{ij} \tag{14}$$

Data used in this section are from the Ministry of Health, Labour and Welfare's (2010) "Report on the Status of Latter-Stage Elderly Medical Care Operations, 2nd Table, Status of Prefectural Medical-services Costs." Data were obtained on the number of insured persons P by prefecture and by medical benefit costs, number of cases by medical benefit costs, number of days b, and costs c; and medical examination rate A, number of days per case B, and costs per day C were calculated.

Next, medical treatment costs for which data on the number of days were not known were broken down into costs per insured person O, as described below. Here, medical treatment costs (j = 8, …, 14) were general medical consultation, prosthetics, orthopedics-related treatment, massage therapy, acupuncture and moxibustion, transportation, and other costs. There are also expensive medical treatment costs (j = 15), expensive long-term care totaled medical treatment costs (j = 16), and funeral costs (j = 17).

$$\text{Costs per insured person } O_{ij} = \text{medical examination rate } A_{ij} \times \text{costs per case } D_{ij} \tag{15}$$

The same as previous, costs per case D can be broken down as follows.

$$\text{Costs per case } D_{ij} = \text{costs } c_{ij}/\text{number of cases } a_{ij} \tag{16}$$

From the same "Report on the Status of Latter-stage Elderly Medical Care Operations, the 2nd Table, Status of Prefectural Medical-services Costs," we obtained data on the number of cases by prefecture and by medical treatment costs, and on costs c. These data were then used to calculate the medical examination rate A and costs per case D.

From the above-described relations, medical benefit costs by prefecture, medical-treatment costs, expensive medical treatment costs, and funeral costs were totaled, and the costs of medical care benefits R was obtained, as follows.

$$\begin{aligned}\text{Costs of medical care benefits } R_i = & \sum_j \text{number of insured persons } P_{ij} \\ & \times \text{ costs per insured person } O_{ij}\end{aligned} \tag{17}$$

Subsidies X and support funds Y were subtracted from the costs of medical care benefits R to derive the amount collected from insurance contributions. With subsidies X expressed by subscript m, it was used to represent (m = 1, ..., 4), which are the adjustment subsidies (m = 1), the fixed-rate state treasury contribution (m = 2), the fixed-rate prefectural contribution (m = 3), and the fixed-rate municipality contribution (m = 4), respectively.

$$\begin{aligned}\text{The amount collected from insurance contributions } S_i = & \text{ the costs of medical care benefits } R_i \\ & - \sum_m \text{subsidies } X_i - \text{ support funds } Y_i\end{aligned} \tag{18}$$

On multiplying the amount collected from insurance contributions S by (1-payment rate V), insurance contributions settled amount T is obtained. Further, on adding the tax reductions and exemptions amount K, insurance contributions calculated amount U can be calculated.

$$\begin{aligned}\text{Insurance contributions settled amount } T_i = & \text{ amount collected from insurance contributions } S_i \\ & \times (1 - \text{payment rate} V_i)\end{aligned} \tag{19}$$

$$\begin{aligned}\text{Insurance contributions calculated amount } U_i = & \text{ insurance contributions settled amount } T_i \\ & + \sum\nolimits_n \text{tax reductions and exemptionsamount } K_i\end{aligned} \tag{20}$$

Here, with subscript n showing the type of tax reduction and exemption, n represents ($n = 1, \ldots, 5$), which includes the income-based contributions reduction amount ($n = 1$), the per capita-based contributions reduction amount ($n = 2$), the reduction amount owing to a disaster, etc. ($n = 3$), other reduction and exemption amounts ($n = 4$), and amount exceeding the upper limit ($n = 5$), respectively.

3.4 Factor Analysis and Regional Disparity in the Latter-Stage Elderly Medical Insurance Contributions

Using the estimation model constructed in the previous section, a factor analysis of insurance contributions by prefecture will be conducted in this section. The estimation model used here makes it possible to break down the insurance contributions settled amount according to medical care benefits services. In Fig. 14, the effects of each type of medical care benefits service on the insurance contributions settled amount per capita is verified.

In terms of the percentage of costs of medical care benefits in insurance contributions, the largest item is hospitalization costs, which at 46.1% constitutes nearly half of the benefit costs. Next are non-hospitalization and drug dispensing costs at 28.4 and 14.4%, respectively. Besides these items, other costs such as for dental, food- and living-related medical treatment, home-care visits, medical

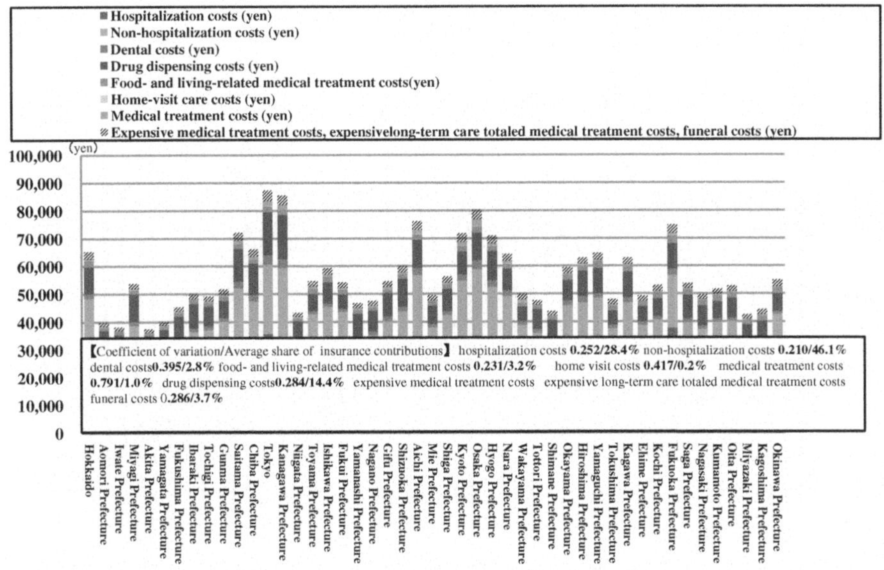

Fig. 14 Breakdown of costs of medical care benefits in insurance contributions per insured person

treatment, expensive medical treatment and expensive totaled medical treatment, and funerals constitute less than 5.0%.

On examining the disparity by prefecture between the respective medical care benefits services from their coefficients of variation, the coefficient of variation for medical treatment costs was the highest at 0.791, followed by costs for home-care visits at 0.417. On the other hand, the values for hospitalization costs, non-hospitalization costs, and drug dispensing costs, with each constituting a large share of the total costs of medical care benefits, were 0.210, 0.252, and 0.284, respectively, and from this, we understand that their regional disparity is small compared to other benefits services.

Therefore, medical care benefit services can be explained as almost 90% form inpatient costs, outpatient care costs, and drug dispensing costs; further, while regional disparity exists between prefectures for these cost items, it is small compared to the disparity for other benefit services.

As the second analysis, we compare the medical benefit cost per insured person and the premium adjustment amount per insured, the relationship between the medical benefit cost per insured person and the insurance premium calculation amount per insured by prefecture. Figure 15 shows the results of the estimations.

Looking at the coefficients of variation by prefecture for each cost, we see it was 0.115 for the costs of medical care benefits per insured person, while it was comparatively high for the calculated amount per insured person, at 0.196. When

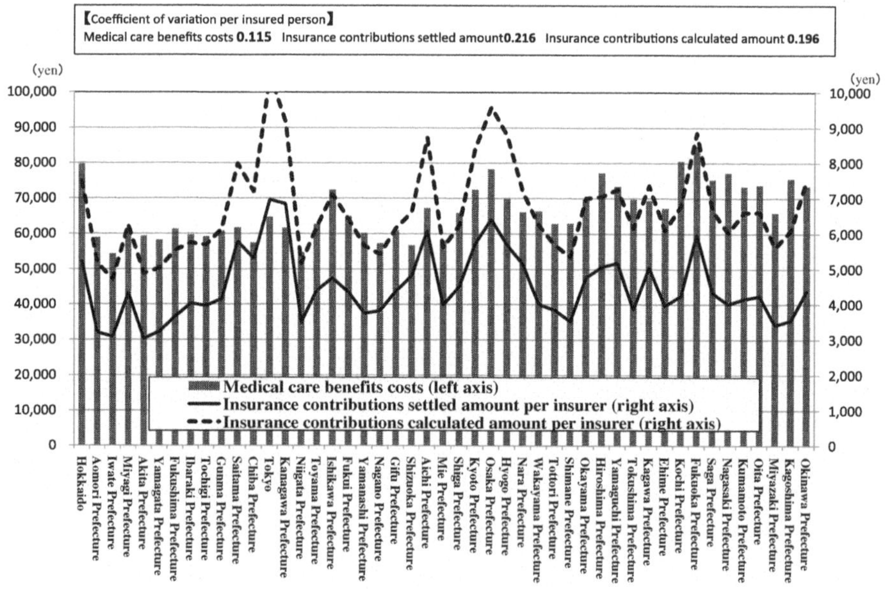

Fig. 15 Relationship between costs of medical care benefits per insured person and insurance contributions

we applied tax reductions and exemptions, the insurance contributions settled amount per insured person was even higher, at 0.219.

Finally, we will look at the relation between costs of medical care benefits and insurance contributions. In order to verify the effects of the pay-as-you-go system and tax reductions and exemptions, two values were calculated, namely the costs of medical care benefits and the insurance contributions calculated amount, and the costs of medical care benefits and the insurance contributions settled amount. The results show that the coefficient of correlation for costs of medical care benefits and insurance contributions settled amount was 0.366, while the coefficient of correlation for costs of medical care benefits and insurance contributions calculated amount was 0.493.

In other words, we understand that if we compare the coefficients of variation by prefecture for the burden of insurance contributions with the benefits of receiving medical care services, the burden is larger. Further, with regard to insurance contributions, the coefficient of variation is higher for the insurance contributions settled amount after the implementation of reduction measures than the insurance contributions calculated amount before the implementation of reduction measures. The aim of tax reductions and exemptions, intended for low-income earners, is to reduce income inequality within a prefecture, but it was shown that they widen the regional disparity between prefectures. In addition, while a positive correlation was observed for the relation between the costs of medical care benefits and insurance contributions, the results indicated that the positive correlation for redistribution is weak owing to the tax reductions and exemptions.

3.5 *Effects of Tax Reductions and Exemptions on Latter-Stage Elderly Insurance Contributions*

Based on the results of the previous section, the effects of tax reductions and exemptions were verified. Figure 16 shows the results of this verification.

In Fig. 16, with the per-insured person settled amount as the indicator, four patterns were estimated for the 2010 per-insured person insurance contributions: tax reductions and exemptions were not implemented; only the income-based contribution reduction measure was implemented; per capita-based contribution reduction measures were implemented; and only reduction measures for amounts exceeding the upper limit were implemented.

From the results, it can be seen that when tax reductions and exemptions were not implemented, the average insurance contributions calculated amount was 80,336 yen, but when all were implemented, the average insurance contributions settled amount declined to 56,134 yen (down 31% on the insurance contributions calculated amount). Here, it is shown that the fluctuations in the values differ

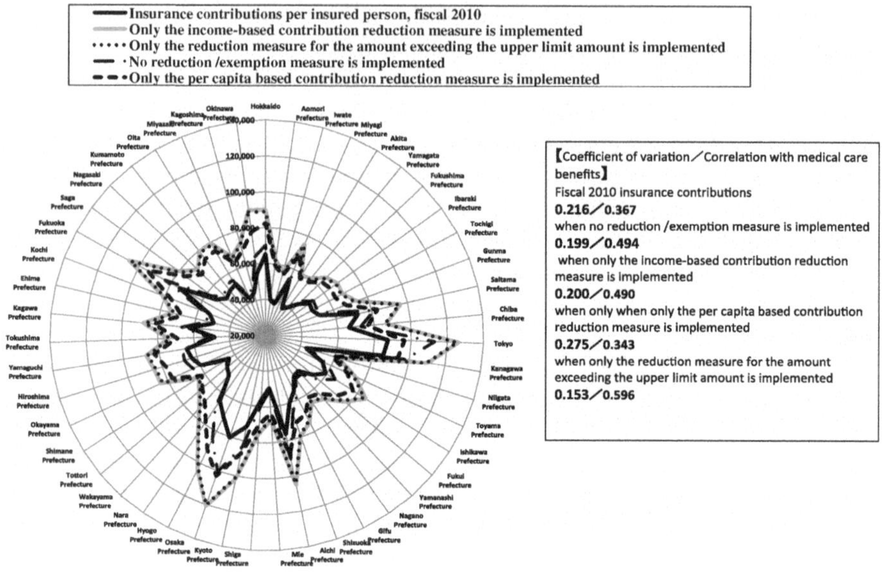

Fig. 16 Effects of reduction and exemption measures on insurance contributions per insured person

depending on the tax reductions and exemptions. Specifically, when only the income-based contributions reduction was implemented, the average of the insurance contributions settled amount remained at 79,468 yen (down 0.02% on the insurance contributions calculated amount). Likewise, when the per capita-based contributions reduction was implemented, it declined to 61,181 yen; the extent of the reduction is greater (down 24% on the insurance contributions calculated amount), and we understand that the insurance contributions settled amount is reduced. Moreover, the value calculated for the reduction measure for amounts exceeding the upper limit amount was 73,256 yen (down 9% on the insurance contributions calculated amount).

The costs of medical care benefits per insured person were the highest in Fukuoka Prefecture at 1,019,205 yen, which is 1.56 times the lowest costs, those of Iwate Prefecture, at 651,489 yen. The calculated amount per insured person was 125,957 yen in Metropolitan Tokyo, while the lowest was in Iwate Prefecture at 56,644 yen. Insurance contributions per insured person settled amount was the highest in Tokyo at 83,596 yen, which is more than twice that of Akita Prefecture at 30,306 yen. The difference in the amounts was the largest in Metropolitan Tokyo at 42,361 yen and the lowest in Nagano Prefecture at 19,234 yen.

Examining the prefectural disparity, the coefficient of variation for the 2010 insurance contributions settled amount, when all tax reductions and exemptions were implemented, was 0.219, but the coefficient of variation for insurance contributions calculated amount, when tax reductions and exemptions were not implemented, was small, at 0.199. Further, in terms of the types of tax reductions and exemptions, when reduction and exemption measures were implemented for only the upper-limit amount, the coefficient of variation for insurance contributions settled amount was 0.153. However, after the income-based contributions reduction measure it was 0.200, and after the per capita-based contributions reduction measure it was 0.275, so the coefficients of variation are higher.

We have seen that tax reductions and exemptions widen the disparity between prefectures and that the effects differ depending on their type. Among them, the per capita-based contributions measure constitutes a large share of the tax reductions and exemptions, and the disparity between the prefectures is greater only when this measure is implemented.

In this section, the per capita-based contributions reduction measure, which is the tax reduction and exemption measure that causes disparity to widen the most, was verified. Figure 17 shows the results of the verification. In the per capita-based contributions reduction, the percentage it is reduced to changes depending on the income of the respective household, and there are four reduction percentages: 90, 85, 50, and 20%. Each of these respective reduction percentages were verified, and it was found that when each reduction was implemented, the average settled amount per insured person was 72,941 yen when only the 90% reduction was implemented,

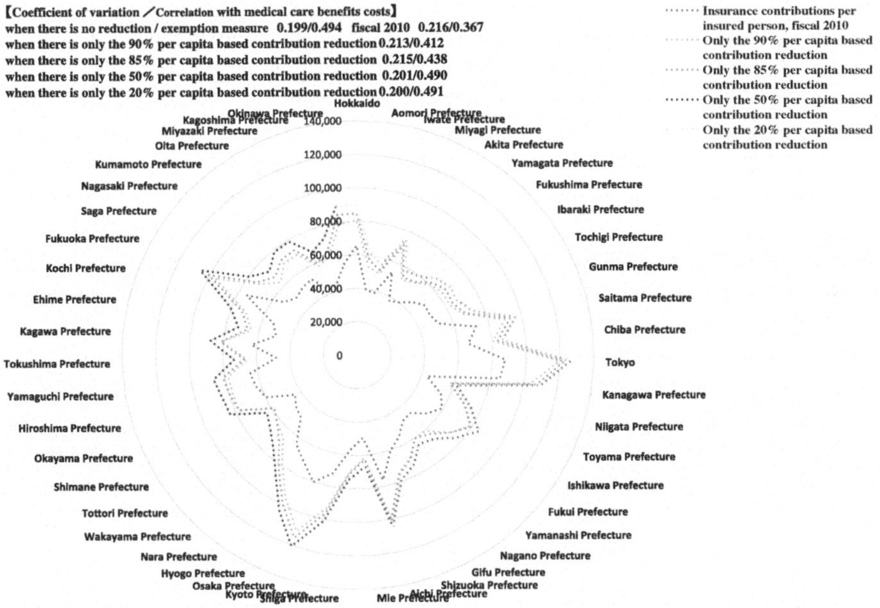

Fig. 17 Effects on insurance contributions per insured person from the per capita-based contributions reduction measure

but 75,153 yen for the 85% reduction, 79,802 yen for the 50% reduction, and 79,824 yen for the 20% reduction.

In other words, the results showed that if the reduction rate increases, the settled amount per insured person decreases. Here, when implementing only the 90% reduction, the 85% reduction, the 50% reduction, and 25% reduction, the results showed that the prefectures with the largest and the smallest settled amount per insured person were Metropolitan Tokyo and Iwate Prefecture, respectively.

On calculating the disparity between prefectures, the coefficients of variation for the 90% reduction, which is the highest reduction rate, and the 85% reduction, were 0.213 and 0.215 respectively. In contrast, the values for the 50% reduction and the 20% reduction were smaller, at 0.201 and 0.200, respectively. From the above, it was clarified that while there is the tendency for the settled amount per insured person to rise as the per capita-based contributions reduction percentage is reduced, it reduces the disparity between prefectures.

4 Conclusion

This chapter has focused on the costs of medical care benefits and insurance contributions in the National Health Insurance system. Further, regional disparity and the relationship between benefits and burdens were verified. A breakdown of the National Health Insurance system's medical care benefits shows that medical benefit costs and medical treatment costs, which include hospitalization and non-hospitalization, constitute a large percentage of the benefit costs, and their regional disparity is small. In the latter-stage elderly medical care system, the contents of the benefits were investigated in more detail, and on dividing the costs into hospitalization, non-hospitalization, and medical treatment costs and breaking down the elements, it was shown that hospitalization and non-hospitalization costs constitute the majority of the benefit costs, and that their regional disparity is small.

In terms of the relationship between medical care benefits and the burden of insurance contributions, there are differences depending on the insurance contributions calculated amount derived from the pay-as-you-go system, the insurance contributions settled amount from which tax reductions and exemptions are deducted, and the amount collected from insurance contributions that takes the payment rate into consideration. Here, due to the redistribution effect from tax reductions and exemptions, the correlation between the costs of medical care benefits and insurance contributions is weakened, which is a point that the National Health Insurance system and the latter-stage elderly medical care insurance system have in common. At the same time, it was shown that reduction and exemption measures have the effect of widening regional disparity.

In other words, it was shown that the coefficient of variation, which is an indicator of regional disparity, increases more for the insurance contributions settled amount after the implementation of reduction measures than for the insurance contributions calculated amount before the implementation of reduction measures. This result suggests that although the aim of tax reductions and exemptions is to reduce income inequality within prefectures, they are actually widening disparity between regions.

Chapter 6
Analysis of the Regional Disparity in Long-Term Care Insurance Contributions

1 Introduction

The National Health Insurance system and the latter-stage elderly medical care system, which were dealt with in the previous chapter, play important roles in the provision of medical care services as social security systems. However, in this chapter, we shall consider long-term care, and the social security system for this is long-term care services.

As with the National Health Insurance system and the latter-stage elderly medical care system, long-term care is also a regional insurance, and its main financial resource is insurance contributions, which places importance on the relationship between benefits and burdens. The main insurers for long-term care are municipalities, and this is another point in common with the National Health Insurance system.[1] However, the National Health Insurance system is not a regional insurance plan that covers all citizens, while a major feature of long-term care is that it is one.

Established in fiscal 2000, long-term care is comparatively new as a social security system. In the context of the rapidly aging population, there have been questions about the sustainability of long-term care since it was first established. Looking at the trend of the total costs of long-term care as shown in Fig. 1, we can see that they are growing steadily.

When the long-term care system was established, the total costs of long-term care contributions were approximately 3 trillion yen, but within just 10 years, the total costs had tripled to nearly 9 trillion yen. In the future also, the total costs of long-term care will likely continue to increase alongside an aging population.

Insurers formulate long-term care insurance operations plans on a time frame of three years equals one period and, in this situation, based on the anticipated costs of services prescribed in the operations plan, they review the long-term care insurance

[1]In some cases, wide-area unions and partial-affairs associations manage them.

Y. Adachi, *The Economics of Tax and Social Security in Japan*,
https://doi.org/10.1007/978-981-10-7176-8_6

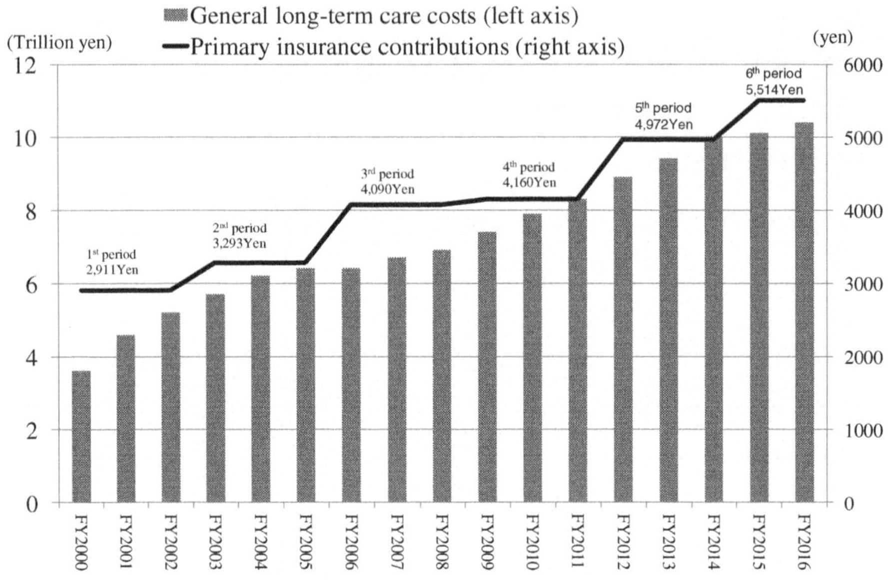

Fig. 1 Trends in the total costs of long-term care (annual amounts) and long-term care insurance contributions (nationwide average monthly amounts). *Note* Based on the Ministry of Health, Labour and Welfare (2012), "Process of Formulating Municipalities' Long-term Care Insurance Operations Plan, 5th Period."

contributions to try to maintain a financial balance over the years. Overall, long-term care insurance contributions are increasing, but the costs of long-term benefits are rising at a pace surpassing the extent of the increase in contributions.

As in other social security systems, self-payments account for the total costs of long-term care, insurance contributions, and national revenue. The amount remaining when self-payments are subtracted from the total costs of long-term care corresponds to the costs of long-term care benefits. Insurance contributions pay for about a half of the costs of long-term care benefits, with national revenue supporting the remaining half. Long-term care insurance contributions are set according to the income of the insured person and based on the insurance contributions standard amount defined by the insurer. As shown in Fig. 1, the costs of long-term care benefits are rising, as are the total costs of long-term care.

Long-term care insurance contributions include primary insurance contributions and secondary insurance contributions. Primary insurance contributions are a fixed-amount burden paid by insured persons aged 65 years and above. Persons aged between 40 and 64 years pay the secondary insurance contributions, which are also a fixed-rate burden.

In Fig. 1, long-term care insurance contributions standard amounts use the nationwide average. The municipalities, which are the insurers, determine the actual long-term care insurance contributions and, therefore, regional disparity occurs. The standard amount also fluctuates depending on the benefits level, which further widens the regional disparity.

If considered from the viewpoint of the national minimum, inherently it is preferable that the insured person's benefits and burdens are about the same, regardless of where they live. However, if insurance contributions in specific regions rise and the disparity between the burdens placed on the insured persons widens, this disparity can cast a shadow of doubt on the sustainability of the system.

With regard to the burden and benefits of long-term care, the Japan Business Federation's (2004) "Summary of the Reforms to Long-term Care" showed the disparity in the burden of long-term care insurance contributions as a problem in the system, in addition to the concerns about the increase in the total costs of long-term care. Moreover, the Federation concluded that the balance between benefits and burdens is a problem caused by an increase in the costs of long-term care benefits, mainly for those who need support and those at the mild level of necessary long-term care.[2]

To investigate the benefits and burdens of long-term care systems, it is necessary to estimate the individuals pay premiums and service costs of long-term care. Representative previous studies include Tajika and Yuri (2001, 2003), Tanaka and Kikuchi (2003, 2004), Kikuchi et al. (2005), and Kikuchi (2008), which simulated the total costs of long-term care and primary insurance contributions by gender, age, level of necessary long-term care, and by long-term care services.[3]

However, these previous studies did not sufficiently take into account the self-payment ratio specific to long-term care, and long-term care insurance contributions according to income stage, in their estimates of the total costs of long-term care and their simulations of primary insurance contributions. Further, as these previous studies used macro data, they did not ascertain the actual situation for long-term care insurance contributions for which regional disparity occurs. If the insurance contributions of specific regions rise and the disparity of the burden placed on insured persons widens, then the sustainability of the system will be called into question by this regional disparity. To clarify this point, it would seem important to conduct a verification using data on the unit of regions.

Further, the long-term care systems of other countries could serve as a reference for future long-term care insurance contributions. Japan's long-term care system is modeled on the German system. Moreover, in fiscal 2008, following Germany and Japan, South Korea started a full-fledged long-term care system. As will be described in detail later, on comparing the systems of both countries, it can be seen that Japan's benefits system is a relatively generous one. In addition, the insured

[2]According to the Ministry of Health, Labour and Welfare's (2009) "Policy Report (Preventative Long-term Care)," "Japan's population is aging and the number of elderly people who require long-term care is increasing … in particular, the number of people at the mild level of necessary long-term care (necessary support level 1 and 2) has increased. Mild (necessary support 1, 2) refers to the state in which the person requires some support for everyday life such as with housework and other daily tasks, but they are not at the level of requiring long-term care."

[3]Estimations of the macro total costs of long-term care in the future include/and Iwamoto (2007).

persons the systems target and their self-payment ratios are different. In Japan's long-term care system, the burden of long-term care insurance contributions is limited to insured persons, and the self-payment ratio that is paid when using long-term care insurance services is low. This means it is possible that long-term care insurance contributions will rise.

Bearing in mind the problem described above, in this chapter, based on prefectural data, including the number of insured persons and the costs of benefits per insured person, first a model is constructed to conduct a factor analysis of long-term care insurance contributions. Second, I evaluated the benefits and burden of the long-term care system in Japan, while referring to the long-term care systems of Germany and South Korea. Specifically, a quantitative analysis is conducted to determine the extent to which the "optimization of benefits" lowers the total costs of long-term care and the costs of benefits per insured person. This includes prioritization of home services and restrictions on the provision of facilities-related services, and "optimization of the burden" from raising the self-payment ratio and increasing the number of insured persons.

2 Overview of Long-Term Care

The Long-term Care Insurance System has been steadily established as a scheme to support needs for care since the start in April 2000. Table 1 shows the historical transition and the institutional problems of the elderly health system and the elderly medical care system before the long-term care insurance system. Figure 2 shows insured individuals pay premiums from the pension or pay in person using payment slips, apply for care need certification before using services, can use certified services based on mental and physical conditions, and pay user fees in using services, generally 10% or 20% of the service cost.

The users of the Long-term Care Insurance have increased rapidly. While the number of insured persons aged 65 or older has increased by approximately 1.5 times over 15 years since 2000, when the Long-term Care Insurance System was established, that of care service users has increased by approximately 3 times over the same period. The surge in the number of in-home care users accounts for the threefold increase of the care service users.

The municipal governments formulate Long-term Care Insurance Service Plan which designates 3 years as one term and is reviewed in every 3 years. As ageing proceeds, premiums estimated to rise to 6, 771 yen in 2020 and 8, 165 yen in 2025. As the system is steadily established, the total expense of the Long-term Care Insurance is drastically growing.

The population aging will progress further and all of the "first baby boomer generations" will be 75 years old and over in the early 2020s. The establishment of the sustainable social security system is urgently needed because the medical care and long-term care benefits per capita increase sharply with the increase in age. While meeting the needs of the elderly and their families, a sustainable system is

Table 1 Transition to the Long-Term Care Insurance System *Source* Based on "Long-Term Care Insurance System of Japan," by the Department of the Ministry of Health, Labour and Welfare, Japan

Period	Main outline	Aging rate (year)	Enforcement year	Major policies
1960s	Beginning of welfare policies for the elderly	5.7% (1960)	1963	Enactment of the Act on Social Welfare Services for the Elderly ●Intensive care homes for the elderly created ●Legislation on home helpers for the elderly
1970s	Expansion of healthcare expenditures for the elderly	7.1% (1970)	1973	Free healthcare for the elderly
1980s	Social hospitalization" and Bedridden elderly people" as social problem	9.1% (1980)	1982	Enactment of the Health and Medical Services Act for the Aged ●Adoption of the payment of co-payments for elderly healthcare, etc.
			1983	Establishment of the Gold Plan (10-year strategy for the promotion of health and welfare for the elderly) ●Promotion of the urgent preparation of facilities and in-home welfare services
1990s	Promotion of the Gold Plan	12.0% (1990)	1994	Establishment of the New Gold Plan (new 10-year strategy for the promotion of health and welfare for the elderly) ●Improvement of in-home long-term care
	Preparation for adoption of the Long-Term Care Insurance System	14.5% (1995)	1997	Enactment of the Long-Term Care Insurance Act
2000s	Introduction of the Long-Term Care Insurance System	17.3% (2000)	2000	Enforcement of the Long-Term Care Insurance Syste

Institutional Problems

Welfare System for the elderly

【Services provided】

- Intensive Care Home for the Elderly, etc.
- Home-help service, Day service, etc.

【Problems】

●Users could not choose services
Municipal governments decided services and service providers.
●Psychological resistance
Means test was required when applying services.
●Services tended to be unvarying without competition
Services were basically provided by municipalities or organizations entrusted.
● Service fee could be heavy burden for the middle/upper income group
The principle of ability to pay according to income of the person/Supporter under Duty.

Medical System for the elderly

【Services provided】

- Health center for the elderly, Sanatorium medical facility, general hospital, etc.
- Home-visit nursing, day care, etc.

【Problems】

● Long-term hospitalization to be cared in hospitals ("social hospitalization") increased
hospitalization fee is less expensive than welfare services for middle/upper income group, as well as basic maintenance of the welfare service was insufficient.
→Medical cost increased: Hospitalization fee was more expensive comparing with Intensive Care Home for the Elderly and Health center for the elderly.
→Facilitation of hospital was not sufficient enough for long-term care with staff and living environment: Hospitals are expected to provide "cure" (e.g. Limited room area for care, dining hall or bathrooms)

To solve institutional problems

the Long-Term Care Insurance System

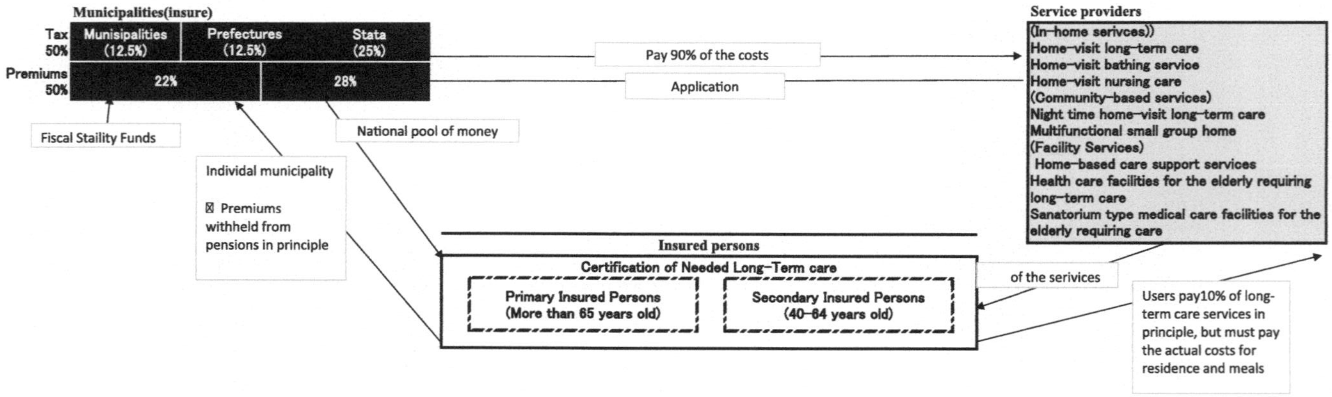

Fig. 2 Structure of the Long-Term Care Insurance System *Source* Based on "Long-Term Care Insurance System Diagram," by the Department of Ministry of Health, Labor and Welfare, Japan

essential so that it can be handed over to the future generation. Consumption Tax resources are used to establish a fund in each prefecture to promote a development of infrastructure and a securing human resources for long-term care.

Almost 10 years have passed since the introduction of long-term care in Japan, and long-term care services have become established in Japanese society. It is highly likely that the number of households using long-term care services will increase in future, and therefore, it seems inevitable that the total costs of long-term care will rise.

The main factor behind the increase in the total costs of long-term care is the aging population, which is a nationwide phenomenon, although there are differences between regions. Going forward, the population will likely age rapidly mainly in the urban areas of metropolitan cities, particularly Saitama Prefecture, Chiba Prefecture, and Kanagawa Prefecture.[4] In the long-term care system in which insured persons are aged 40 years and above, not only long-care insurance contributions expanding due to aging determine long-care insurance premiums. long-term care insurance contributions Long-term care insurance contributions are set proportionally for primary insured persons, aged from 40 to 64 years, and secondary insured persons, aged 65 years and above. Therefore, the declining birth rate also affects the rise in long-term care insurance contributions. The question is whether population factors will create regional disparity in long-term care insurance contributions in future.

The aging will affect not only the number of people who need long care but also the degree of need for long care. Among senior citizens aged 65 years and above, in the context of the increase in those with cognitive impairment at level II and above for their level of independence in daily life, in households with members aged 65 years and above, the number of single-person households and couple-only households are rapidly rising.[5] The weakening of family ties increases the burden of long-term care. The change in the composition of the aging population will not only

---

[4]According to the Ministry of Health, Labour and Welfare (2012), "The Process for Formulating the 5th Period Municipalities Long-term Care Insurance Operations Plan," in fiscal 2010, 11.1% of the population were latter-stage elderly aged 75 years and above, but by fiscal 2055, this is forecast to have more than doubled to 26.1%. Also, in fiscal 2005, the number of people in single-person households or in couple-only households was 8.53 million people, but by fiscal 2025 this will have likely increased to 12.67 million people, with households with members aged 65 years and over accounting for 60% of this number. Further, as of fiscal 2005, the elderly population of Saitama Prefecture was 1.16 million people, Chiba Prefecture was 1.06 million people, and Kanagawa Prefecture was 1.49 million people, but by 2015, the elderly populations of these three prefectures were 1.79 million people (+55%), 1.60 million people (+50%), and 2.18 million people (+47%), respectively. It is considered that in these prefectures, population aging is occurring more rapidly than in some other prefectures, where the percentage of the elderly is increasing at a rate of around 10%, as in Akita Prefecture, Yamagata Prefecture, and Kagoshima Prefecture.

[5]The evaluation criteria for level II degree of independence in the daily life of the elderly with cognitive impairment is that, "They are able to live independently if someone is watching over them, even if to a certain extent they exhibit symptoms and behavior that may interfere with their daily lives and they have problems in communicating."

lead to an increase in benefit costs for long-term care services, but will also require the provision of services according to the diverse needs.

While aiming to reduce the total costs of long-term care, Japan's long-term care insurance administration has set the goal of constructing an "integrated community care system" so that people can receive a certain level of long-term care services in their own community. In terms of content, the system aims to realize a society in which people can receive medical care and long-term care services regardless of where they live, and to strengthen at-home medical care.

Specifically, assuming a junior high school district with a population of around 10,000 people as the integrated community care unit, the system prioritizes community-based at-home long-term care services. This includes providing medical care services in the form of enhanced at-home medical care and home-visit care, and a 24-hour system of regular visits, group homes, and small-scale multifunction services.

The above describes the developments in Japan's long-term care, but next we will compare it with the systems for long-term care in Germany and South Korea. Table 2 shows the differences in the long-term care provided in Japan, Germany, and South Korea and the procedure for use of Long-term Care Service in Japan.

First, we consider the scope of insured persons. Japan's long-term care insurance system is a requirement of insured persons over 40 years old. Meanwhile, in the German nursing care insurance system, all members of public medical insurance are insured persons. In addition, in South Korea's long-term care system, the subscribers to National Health Insurance are insured persons. In other words, in both these countries, the scope of the insured persons who bear the burden of long-term care insurance contributions is wider than in the Japanese system.

There are also major differences between the three countries in terms of users who are eligible to use the services and their composition. In Japan, everyone who needs necessary long-term care, from the mild to the severe level, is eligible, and various long-term care services are provided, from preventive services through at-home, community-based, and facilities services. However, in Germany and South Korea, if we speak in terms of Japan's necessary long-term care levels, only at-home services and facilities services are provided and only to people at the serious level receive necessary long-term care.

Further, the self-payment ratios when using the services are different. In principle, in Japan, the burden is 10%, but in South Korea, it is 10% for home services and 20% for facilities services, so the self-payment ratios vary depending on the content of the service.[6]

In Germany and South Korea, the original designs of the long-term care systems are different to that of Japan. If keeping long-term care insurance contributions low is important in Japan, then with reference to the long-term care provided in

[6]As of August 2015, the self-payment rate of users with income above a certain level was raised to 20%.

Table 2 Comparison of the long-term care systems in Japan, Germany, and South Korea *Source* Based on "Long-Term Care Insurance System of Japan," by the Department of the Ministry of Health, Labour and Welfare, Japan

	Japan	Germany	South Korea
Name	Nursing Care Insurance Law	Act on the social protection of the risk from the necessary long-term care system	Act on Long-term Health Care for the Elderly
Insurers	Municipalities (approx. 1700 nationwide)	Public long-term nursing care insurers (nationwide, approx. 280)	National Health Insurance Public Corporation(nationwide, 1)
Insured persons	40 years and above	Subscribers to public health insurance	Subscribers to the National Health Insurance
Necessary long-term care system	stages (necessary support and necessary long-term care	3-stages (severity only)	3-stages (severity only)
Description of insurance benefit	Preventative services Home services Community-based services Facilities services	Home services Facilities services	Home services Facilities services
No. of necessary long-term care certified persons	Approx. 4.40 million people	Approx. 2 million people	Approx. 280,000 people
Self-payment rate	10% burden	None	Home services, 10% burden Facilities services, 20% burden
Financial resources structure	Other than the user's burden, half is from public expenses and insurance contributions	All insurance contributions burden	Other than the user's burden, borne by public expenses and insurance contributions. State treasury burden is equivalent to around 20% of the public expenses burden.

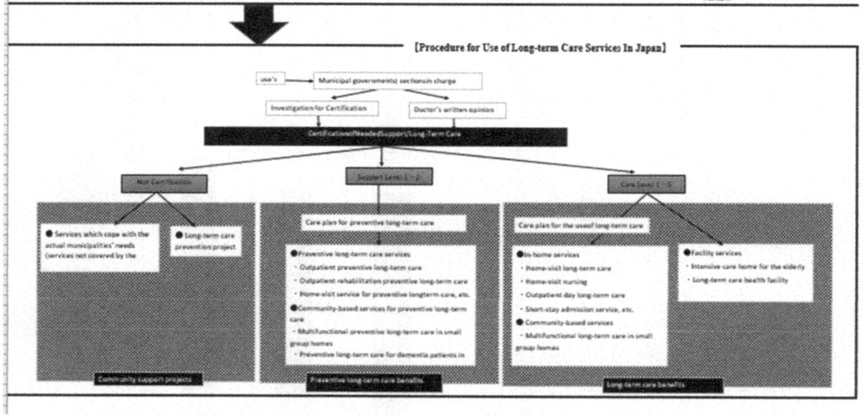

Germany and South Korea, it would seem necessary to investigate the possibility of a policy to keep long-term care insurance contributions lower.

Based on the above discussion, in the next section, Japan's long-term care insurance contributions will be estimated by prefecture from a factor analysis.

3 Estimation Method for Factor Analysis of Long-Term Care Insurance Contributions

This section describes the estimation method for a factor analysis of the long-term care insurance contributions by prefecture. Figure 3 shows the estimation procedure.

First, from the October 2010 edition of the Ministry of Health, Labour and Welfare's "Report on the Status of Long-term Care Insurance Operations Monthly Report (Preliminary Version)," we obtained data on the number of primary insured persons P_1 by prefecture for those aged 65 to 74 years, and by gender for those aged 75 years and above. In addition, data on the number of secondary insured persons P_2 by gender for those aged less than 65 years were obtained from the National Institute of Population and Social Security Research's report, "Future Population Estimations by Prefecture (May 2011 Estimates)."

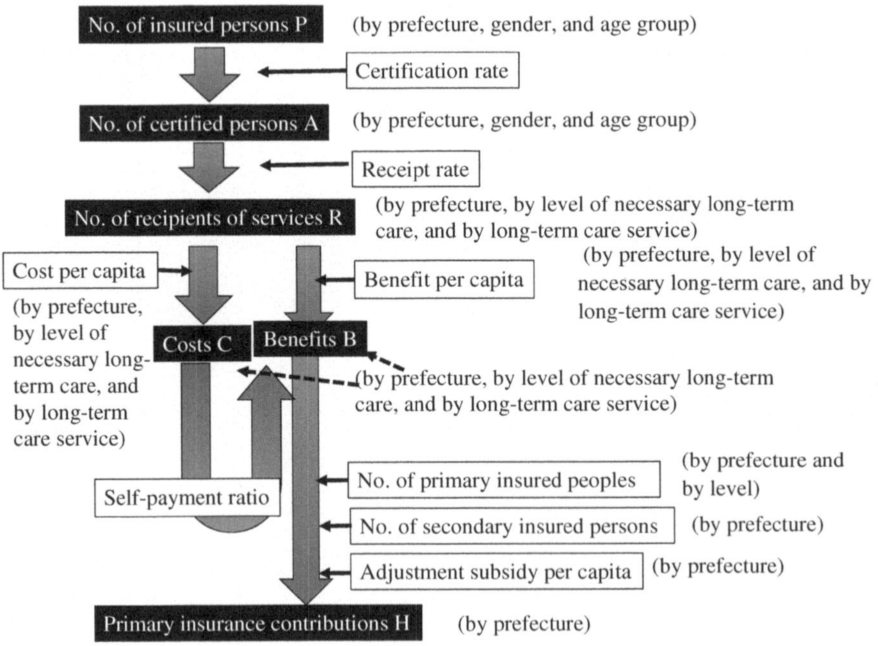

Fig. 3 Factor analysis estimation for first insurance contributions by prefecture

Second, from the October 2010 edition of the "Monthly Report on the Survey of Actual Conditions for the Costs of Long-Term Care Benefits (Each Month's Examined Part)," we obtained data on the number of certified persons A by gender, age, and level of necessary long-term care. From the October 2010 edition of the Ministry of Health, Labour and Welfare's "Report on the Status of Long-term Care Insurance Operations Monthly Report (Preliminary Version)," we obtained data on secondary insured certified persons A for those aged 65 to 74 and 75 years and above by prefecture and by level of necessary long-term care.

Based on the data for number of insured persons P and number of certified persons A, the certification rate was calculated from Formula (1) shown below. Subscript i indicates the prefecture ($i = 1, \ldots, 47$), j indicates gender, ($j = 1, 2$) k shows age (5-year groups) ($k = 1, \ldots, 13$), and l shows whether the insured person is primary or secondary type ($l = 1, 2$).[7]

$$\begin{aligned} \text{Number of certified persons } A_{ijkl} &= \text{certification rate } a_{ijkl} \\ &\times \text{number of insured persons } P_{ijkl} \end{aligned} \tag{1}$$

Third, data were obtained from the October 2010 edition of the "Monthly Report on the Survey of Actual Conditions for the Costs of Long-Term Care Benefits (Each Monthly Examined Part)," and the October 2010 edition of the Ministry of Health, Labour and Welfare. Data on the number of recipients R by the level of necessary long-term care and long-term care services were collected from the "Report on the Status of Long-term Care Insurance Operations Monthly Report (Preliminary Version)."

Based on the data for number of certified persons A and number of recipients R, receipt rate r was calculated from Formula (2) shown below. Subscript m shows the level of necessary long-term care (necessary support) ($m = 1, \ldots, 7$) and n indicates the type of long-term care service ($n = 1, \ldots, 40$).[8]

---

[7]There are 13 age groups: 30 to 34, 35 to 39, 40 to 44, 45 to 49, 50 to 54, 55 to 59, 60 to 64, 65 to 69, 70 to 74, 75 to 79, 80 to 84, 85 to 89, and 90 years and above.

[8]The types of long-term care services considered in the model in this chapter are as follow; (1) preventative long-term care, home-visit long-term care, (2) preventative long-term care, home-visit bathing long-term care, (3) preventative long-term care, home-visit care, 4) preventative long-term care, home-visit rehabilitation, (5) preventative long-term care, day-care, long-term care, (6) preventative long-term care, day-care rehabilitation, (7) preventative long-term care, loan of welfare equipment, (8) preventative long-term care, short-term admission living care, (9) preventative long-term care, short-term admission recuperative care (healthy old age), (10) preventative long-term care, short-term admission recuperative care (hospitals, etc.), (11) Guidance for Management of In-home Medical Long-term Care, (12) living and long-term care at specified residential facilities, (13) preventative long-term care support, (14) preventative long-term care for outpatient dementia patients, (15) preventative long-term care, small-scale multifunctional residential long-term care, (16) preventative long-term care, living care for dementia patients (short-term use), (17) preventative long-term care, living care for dementia patients (other than short-term use), (18) home-visit long-term care, (19) home-visit bathing long-term care, (20) home-visit care, (21) home-visit rehabilitation, (22) day-care long-term care, (23) day-care rehabilitation, (24) loan of welfare equipment, (25) short-term admission living care,

$$\text{Number of recipients } R_{imn} = \text{receipt rate } r_{imn} \times \sum_j \sum_k \sum_l \text{number of certified persons } A_{ijkl} \quad (2)$$

Fourth, from the fiscal 2010 "Report on the Status of Long-term Care Insurance Operations (annual report)," data on the costs amount C by level of necessary long-term care and by long-term care services were obtained. Based on data for number of recipients R and costs amount, the costs amount per capita c was calculated from Formula (3), as shown below.

$$\begin{aligned}\text{Long-term care costs}_i &= \sum_m \sum_n \text{costs amount } C_{imn} \\ &= \sum_m \sum_n \text{per capita costs amount per capita } c_{imn} \\ &\quad \times \text{the number of recipients } R_{imn}\end{aligned} \quad (3)$$

Fifth, from the March 2010 to April 2011 editions of the Ministry of Health, Labour and Welfare's "Report on the Status of Long-term Care Insurance Operations Monthly Report (preliminary version)," we obtained data on benefit costs B by level of necessary long-term care and by long-term care services. Based on data for number of recipients R and benefit costs B, benefit costs per capita b was calculated from Formula (4), as shown below.

$$\begin{aligned}\text{Costs of long-term care benefits}_i &= \sum_m \sum_n \text{benefit costs } B_{imn} \\ &= \sum_m \sum_n \text{per capita benefit costs } b_{imn} \\ &\quad \times \text{the number of recipients } R_{imn}\end{aligned} \quad (4)$$

Based on long-term care costs and costs of long-term care benefits by prefecture estimated from these data sets, the primary insurance contributions by prefecture were estimated. For this, the composition of financial resources for long-term care costs and the costs of long-term care benefits were considered. Figure 4 shows the revenue and expenditure for long-term care insurance operations.

(26) short-term admission recuperative care (healthy old age), (27) short-term admission recuperative care (hospitals, etc.), (28) Guidance for Management of In-home Medical Long-term Care, (29) living and long-term care at specified residential facilities, (30) at-home long-term care support, (31) evening visit-compliant type home-visit long-term care, (32) cognitive impairment-compliant type day-care, long-term care, (33) small-scale multifunctional residential long-term care, (34) cognitive impairment-compliant type shared living care (short-term use), (35) living care for dementia patients (other than short-term use), (36) community-based living and long-term care at specified residential facilities, (37) community-based long-term care elderly welfare services, (38) long-term care welfare facilities services, (39) long-term care insurance facilities services, and (40) long-term care recuperation facilities services.

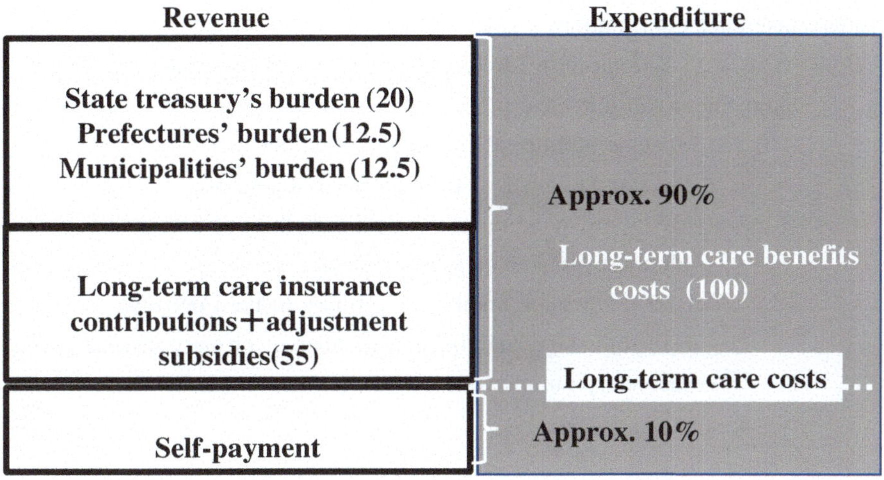

Fig. 4 Composition of the financial resources for total costs of long-term care and costs of long-term care benefits

In the breakdown of the expenditure for total costs of long-term care, the self-payment ratio corresponds to approximately 10%, the remaining 90% being the costs of benefits. The self-payment ratio is approximately 10%, but in this chapter, as the total costs of long-term care and costs of long-term care benefits by prefecture are estimated, the self-payment ratios by prefecture, by level of necessary long-term care, and by long-term care services are obtained as follows.

$$\text{Self-payment ratio } d_{imn} = (\text{costs amount } C_{imn} - \text{benefit costs } B_{imn})/\text{costs amount } C_{imn} \quad (5)$$

Further, revenue other than from self-payments is a financial resource used to pay for the costs of long-term care benefits. As shown in Fig. 4, when the costs of long-term care benefits are set as 100%, national revenue that corresponds to the burden of the national government, prefectures, and municipalities is 45%, while insurance contributions and adjustment subsidies pay for the remaining 55%. Based on the above, the primary insurance contributions (monthly amount) by prefecture can be obtained as follows.

Primary insurance contributions

$$\begin{aligned} H_i = {} & \{0.55 \times \Sigma_m \Sigma_n \text{ long-term care costs}_{imn} \times (1 - \text{self-payment ratio } d_{imn}) \\ & -\text{adjustment subsidies, etc . , } f_i\} \\ & \div (0.5 \times \text{1st stage number of primary insured persons}_i \\ & \quad \times \text{2nd stage number of primary insured persons}_i \\ & \quad + 0.75 \times \text{3rd stage number of primary insured persons}_i \\ & \quad + \text{4th stage number of primary insured persons}_i \\ & \quad + 1.25 \times \text{5th stage number of primary insured persons}_i \\ & \quad + 1.5 \times \text{6th stage and beyond number of primary insured persons}_i \\ & \quad + \text{Secondary number of insured persons}_i) \div 12 \end{aligned} \tag{6}$$

A major factor in this section's model is that it not only estimates the primary insurance contributions by prefecture, but it also takes into consideration the calculation method for the self-payment ratio, adjustment subsidies, and so on, and insurance contributions by income stage.[9] The weight multiplied by the number of primary insured persons at each stage gives the rate of change of the standard amount of insurance contributions. The rates of change by income stage were calculated with reference to the calculation formulas by income stage of the Ministry of Health, Labour and Welfare. The adjustment subsidies, etc., were set by adjusting the results of the estimations from Formula (6) so they matched the 5th period insurance contributions standard amount by prefecture.[10]

4 Factor Analysis and Regional Disparity of Long-Term Care Insurance Contributions

Factor analysis was conducted for primary insurance contributions. This chapter's estimation model can be broken down into primary insurance contributions by long-term care services. Figure 5 shows the effects of the benefit costs of each type of long-term care services, on the burden level from primary insurance contributions.

The effects of benefit costs for long-term care preventive services on primary insurance contributions are an average of only 6.70%, and the benefit costs for

[9] In the model in the previous research, primary insurance contributions = 0.5 × benefit costs ÷ (the number of primary insured persons + number of No. 2 insured persons) ÷ 12 was used. That is to say, it did not take into consideration a method of calculating insurance contributions by the self-payment rate, and the income stage, such as adjustment subsidies.

[10] However, as long-term care preventative services are not eligible for adjustment subsidies, they were excluded from the calculations.

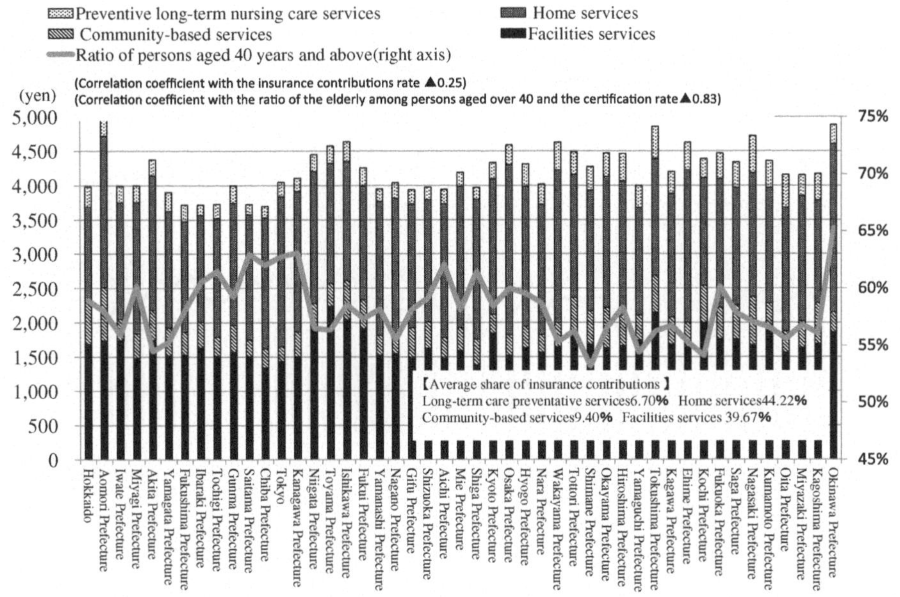

Fig. 5 Primary insurance contributions by long-term care services (monthly amount). *Note* Ratio of aging population aged 40 years and above = population aged 65 years and above/population aged 40 years and above

home services and facilities services constitute more than 80% of the primary insurance contributions. In other words, approximately 80% of long-term care insurance contributions are for the benefit costs of home services and facilities services.

Figure 5 shows the ratio of the aging population aged 40 years and above by prefecture, but the coefficient of correlation with primary insurance contributions is low, at ▲0.25. In other words, it is understood that primary insurance contributions are not necessarily high in prefectures where the population is aging. From this, we understand that primary insurance contributions are a factor that also affects the number of secondary insured persons. On considering the future of the system, we understand that not only the aging population but also the declining birth rate will affect primary insurance contributions.

Next, similar to Figs. 4 and 5 shows primary insurance contributions broken down by the level of necessary long-term care. On looking at the level of necessary long-term care, we see that the "mild" level of level 2 and below accounts for around 30%, but the "medium" level from levels 3 to 5 and the "serious" level, above level 5, constitute most of the primary insurance contributions.

Further, Fig. 6 shows the certification rate and the receipt rate. The coefficients of correlation with the primary insurance contributions are 0.63 for the certification rate and 0.62 for the receipt rate, and both were positive correlations. On considering that the correlation between the previously mentioned ratio of the aging

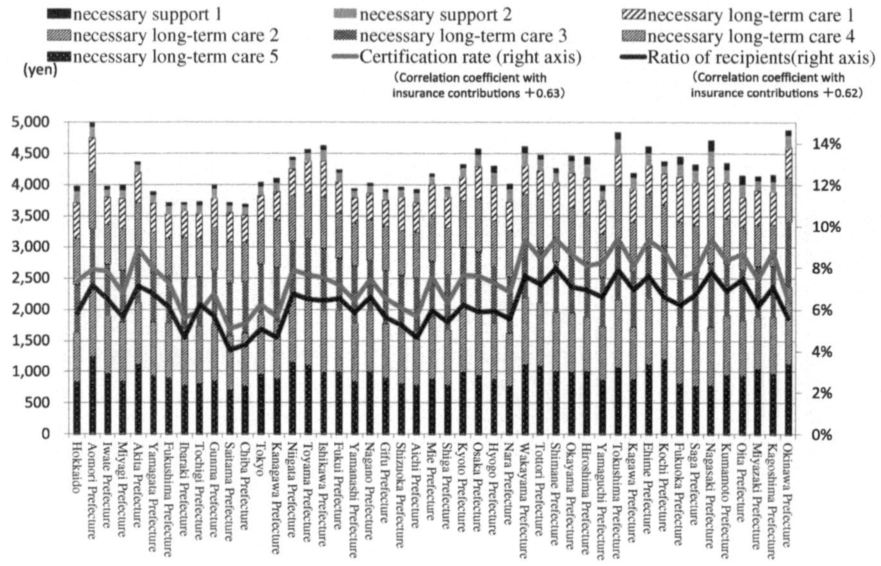

Fig. 6 Primary insurance contributions by necessary long-term care (monthly amount). *Note* Certification rate = number of certified persons/number of insured persons, receipt rate = number of recipients ÷ number of insured persons

population and the primary insurance contributions is low, we understand that the increase in certified persons has more of an effect on the cost of primary insurance contributions than the aging population.

In other words, the situation is that if insurers set a high certification rate, this contributes to an increase in primary insurance contributions. At the same time, the receipt rate is correlated with the primary insurance contributions and moves in the same way as the certification rate, which indicates that if the certification rate is raised, the number of recipients using the services will also increase.

The above can be summarized as follows. On breaking down the primary insurance contributions factor into long-term care services, we see that home services and facilities services constitute most of it. In the same way, on breaking it down by the level of necessary long-term care, we find that people who need necessary long-term care on the medium and serious levels of level 3 and above constitute most of it. Further, it was clarified that the correlation between primary insurance contributions and the ratio of the aging population aged 40 years and above is low, but that it is highly correlated with the certification rate and the receipt rate.

Based on the above-described features of primary insurance contributions, in the next section, we will verify whether primary insurance contributions can be reduced by aiming to "optimize the benefits and burdens."

5 The Benefits and Burdens of Long-Term Care Insurance Contributions

In this section, the policies intended to primary insurance contributions low will be quantitatively investigated from the perspectives of "optimizing the benefits" and "optimizing the burdens."

"Optimizing the benefits," which is first investigated in this chapter, entails prioritizing home services and placing restrictions on the content of long-term care services. In the simulation, by moving the number of recipients R by the level of necessary long-term care or by long-term care services from Formula (4), the primary insurance contributions from Formula (6) are increased or decreased. For "optimizing the benefits," cases 1–4 in Table 3 are assumed.

"Optimizing the burden," which is investigated second in this chapter, entails increasing the self-payment ratio or implementing measures to increase the number of insured persons. Specifically, in the simulation, by moving the self-payment ratio d from Formula (6), or the number of insured persons P from Formulas (1) and (6), the primary insurance contributions from Formula (6) are increased or decreased. For "optimizing the burden," cases 5–8 in Table 3 are assumed.

In the above simulations of policies which aim to keep insurance contributions down, primary insurance contributions in fiscal 2010 were used as the standard for comparisons. The extent to which primary insurance contributions can be reduced compared to the primary insurance contributions in fiscal 2010 are shown by prefecture. These results are presented as laser charts in Figs. 7 and 8.

From the results for case 1 and case 2 for the effects of keeping primary insurance contributions down, the effects from case 2, of shifting from facilities services to home services, are greater than the effects from case 1, of shifting from facilities services to home-based facilities services. From the results of case 3 and case 4, it was found that the effects of keeping primary insurance contributions down by implementing case 3, that of abolishing long-term care preventive services, are small, but the effects are large from case 4 of abolishing services for people at the necessary long-term care level 2 and below.

From the results, it can be seen that the effects of keeping insurance contributions lower in case 5, whereby the self-payment ratio for facilities services was set at 20% and at 10% for all other services, were the same as in case 6, whereby the self-payment ratio for necessary long-term care at level 2 and below was set at 20%, and at 10% for all other levels. However, cases 7 and 8, in which the self-payment ratio remains constant, but the scope of insured persons is expanded, were observed to have much greater effects in terms of keeping the primary insurance contributions lower when compared to changing the self-payment ratio.

Table 3 "Optimizing the benefits and burdens" by case

Optimizing the benefits	Case 1	Recipients of necessary long-term care at level 3 and below facilities services are transferred to home-based facilities services. Necessary long-term care level 4 and above-facilities-services recipients remain unchanged
	Case 2	Necessary long-term care level 3 and below-facilities-services recipients are transferred to home services. Necessary long-term care level 4 and above-facilities-services recipients remain unchanged
	Case 3	As in South Korea and Germany's long-term care systems, long-term care preventative services are abolished
	Case 4	As in South Korea and Germany's long-term care systems, services for persons at necessary long-term care level 2 and below are abolished
Optimizing the burdens	Case 5	As in South Korea's long-term care system, the self-payment ratio of facilities services is raised from 10% to 20%
	Case 6	Bearing in mind the fact that Germany and South Korea's long-term care does not cover those at necessary long-term care level 2 and below (Japanese standards), the necessary long-term care level 2 and below self-payment ratio is raised to 20%
	Case 7	Bearing in mind the fact that Germany and South Korea's age groups for insured persons for long-term care are wider, the scope of insured persons is widened to 35 years and above
	Case 8	Bearing in mind the fact that Germany and South Korea's age groups for insured persons for long-term care are wider, the scope of insured persons is widened to 30 years and above

Specifically, there are cases of sorting the recipients of facilities services of 38) long-term care welfare facilities services, 39) long-term care insurance facilities services, and 40) long-term care recuperation facilities services) (however, at level 3 and below of necessary long-term care) by half into 29) living and long-term care at specified residential facilities, which corresponds to home-based facilities services, and 34) cognitive impairment-compliant type shared living care (short-term use)

Specifically, there are cases of sorting recipients of facilities services (however, at level 3 and below of necessary long-term care) into 18) home-visit long-term care to 30) at-home long-term care support, which correspond to home services, while fixing the fiscal 2010 use ratio of recipient

How much does the premium control policy affect regional disparity of premiums? The standard amount for the fiscal 2010 primary insurance contributions average was 4229 yen and the coefficient of variation was 0.078. The results of the analysis are summarized in Table 4.

In "optimizing the benefits," abolishing services for necessary long-term care at level 2 and below (case 4) has the effect of keeping insurance contributions down, but widens regional disparity. Abolishing long-term care preventative services (case 3) was observed to have the effect of keeping insurance contributions down and to reduce regional disparity.

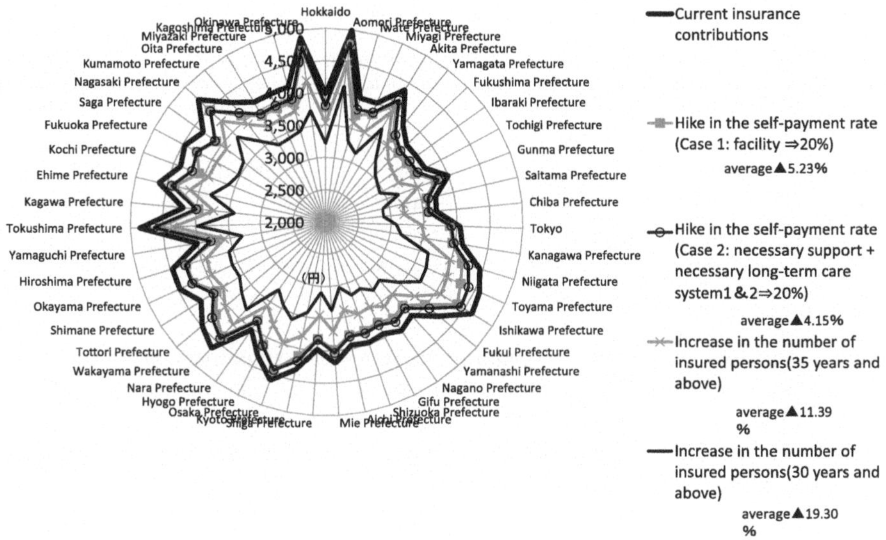

Fig. 7 "Optimizing the benefits" from primary insurance contributions (monthly amount: cases 1 to 4)

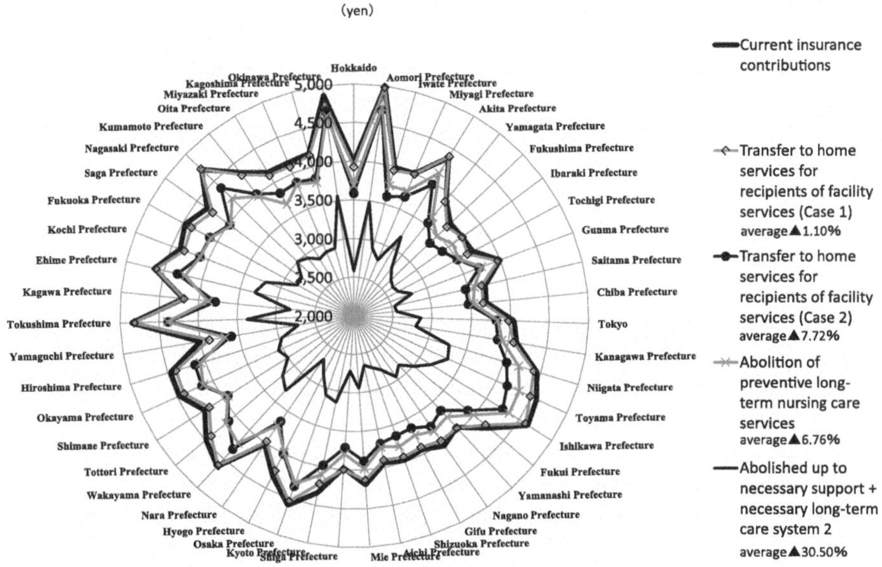

Fig. 8 "Optimizing the burden" for primary insurance contributions (monthly amount: cases 5 to 8)

Table 4 Average insurance contributions and coefficient of variation

"Optimizing the benefits"	Average insurance contributions (yen)	Coefficient of variation	"Optimizing the burden"	Average insurance contributions (yen)	Coefficient of variation
Case 1	4182	0.078	Case 5	4008	0.077
Case 2	3903	0.082	Case 6	4053	0.076
Case 3	3943	0.072	Case 7	3747	0.082
Case 4	2939	0.086	Case 8	3413	0.087

In "optimizing the burden," expanding the scope of insured persons (cases 7 and 8) contributes to keeping insurance contributions down, but widens regional disparity. Further, it was confirmed that raising the self-payment ratio (cases 5 and 6) not only has a certain amount of effect in terms of keeping insurance contributions down, it can also reduce regional disparity.

6 Conclusion

This chapter has presented an analysis of the burden structure of long-term care insurance contributions in long-term care. It can be seen that regional disparity occurs in such contributions in long-term care also. With reference to the systems in Germany and South Korea, whilst considering the benefits and burdens for insured persons and the regional disparity in insurance contributions, specific policies to keep insurance contributions lower were investigated.

From the results of the analysis, it can be seen that those policies that contribute the most to keeping down long-term care insurance contributions were the cases in which necessary long-term care at level 2 and below was abolished, and which expanded the scope of insured persons to 30 years and above. Moreover, when referring to the long-term care systems of South Korea and Germany, we should keep in mind not only the policy of expanding the scope of insured persons, but that of abolishing long-term care preventive services and services for necessary long-term care at level 2 and below.

By merely accumulating the effects from these policies, it actually becomes possible to keep long-term care insurance contributions down by 50% or more. However, it is understood that they could widen regional disparity in long-term care insurance contributions, particularly the policy of expanding the scope of insured persons. On the other hand, raising the self-payment ratio has a smaller effect on keeping insurance contributions lower than cases 4 and 8, but it also reduces regional disparity.

From the results of the analysis in this section, it can be observed that to a certain extent optimizing the benefits and burdens has the effect of keeping long-term care insurance contributions low, but it was also found that the effects on regional disparity in long-term care insurance contributions differ subject to the case. The burden structure for insurance contributions in long-term care was clarified by looking at the relationship between benefits and burdens, while the existence of regional disparity and related was also noted. As it is a form of regional insurance, to a certain extent the existence of regional disparity in insurance contributions is unavoidable; however, any widening of the disparity to the extent that it threatens the sustainability of the system must be avoided. If we clarify the burden structure of insurance contributions, results will indicate that it is preferable to review the approach taken for benefits in a region and to shift to a system that is more efficient and sustainable.

Chapter 7
Analysis of the Payment Rate of National Health Insurance Contributions

1 Introduction

Households and companies bear the burden of insurance contributions in return for government providing services. The burden is imposed collected in the form of insurance contributions based on the conditions of the households and companies. However, not all households and companies are able to pay taxes and social insurance premiums. Having a sufficiently high tax collection rate and insurance contribution payment rate is very important for the government to pay for administrative services.

If tax and insurance contributions are not steadily collected, there is no prospect of securing the necessary financial resources. If there are problems with the collection, the government will also not be able to provide administrative services. In addition, if the collection rate and the payment rate are low, it will be difficult to maintain horizontal fairness. For example, if there were two people who earned the same wage income, it would not be fair to collect insurance contributions from one and not from the other. Maintaining a high collection rate or payment rate is vital for the tax system and the social security system.

However, the situation is that the collection rate or the payment rate are at low levels for some taxes and insurance contribution, particularly the payment rate for insurance contributions in the National Health Insurance system, which is discussed in this chapter. It is widely known that the insurance contributions payment rate of the National Health Insurance system is extremely low.

There are two methods for collecting National Health Insurance contributions: special collections as a deduction from salary or pension, and ordinary collections paid through a payment form or bank transfer. Most insured persons pay their National Health insurance contributions using the ordinary collections method. As most subscribers to the National Health Insurance system are in the low-income group, the insurance contributions burden rate is high and the insurance contributions payment rate is low.

Y. Adachi, *The Economics of Tax and Social Security in Japan*,
https://doi.org/10.1007/978-981-10-7176-8_7

The National Health Insurance finances of insurers, which are mainly municipalities, are in a difficult condition. The insurance benefits costs for the fiscal 2010 National Health Insurance finances increased 1.1% compared to the previous year (the average for the previous three years was an increase of 0.3%).[1] Conversely, insurance contributions income in the fiscal 2010 National Health Insurance finances decreased 2.1% compared to the previous year (the average for the previous three years was a decrease of 0.6%).[2] The insurers, facing a shortage of financial resources, were obliged to use non-statutory transfers from the municipalities' general account and the previous fiscal year's carry-forward funds.[3]

The slump in insurance contributions payment rate has been cited as a factor causing the decline in National Health Insurance finances. Figure 1 shows the trend in the current year's payment rate.[4] The current year's payment rate trended around 95% in the 1960s and then gradually declined, and has been below 90% in recent years. In fiscal 2010, the insurance contributions current year settled amount was 41,097 billion yen, but because of the low insurance contributions payment rate, the current year's collection amount remained at 27,434 billion yen, of which a vast amount was uncollected. Further, the payment rate of carried-forward delinquent payments is at a low level and far below the insurance contributions payment rate of 20%.

However, we cannot acquire averages for these payment rates. From Table 1, according to the average of the current year's payment rate and the delinquent portion's payment rate, the standard deviation, the minimum value, and the maximum value, the payment rate varies depending on the insurer. Figure 2 shows the distribution of the current year's payment rate for 2010, and the payment rate conditions vary greatly depending on the insurer. In addition to the insured persons and the regional characteristics that the insurers have, it is considered that the performance in collection work of the insurance premium on the administrative side reflects the variations in the payment rates.

In this chapter, data is used to analyze the factors that determine the payment rate of National Health Insurance contributions. As we consider that the different methods for the adjustment of finances and the method of paying insurance contributions play an important role, the analysis is divided into two. First, an overview

---

[1]The payment rates were derived from the Ministry of Health, Labour and Welfare's "Report on the Status of National Health Insurance Operations." Here, the payment rates cited are for the insurers of municipalities, partial-affairs associations, and wide-area unions.

[2]There are two methods for collecting insurance contributions: the insurance contributions method of collecting them as national health "insurance contributions," and the insurance tax method of collecting them as national health "insurance tax." According to the Ministry of Health, Labour and Welfare's (2010) "National Health Insurance Operations Report (Operations Annual Report)," slightly under 90% of insurers use the national health "insurance tax" method. Insurers can select the insurance contributions or the insurance tax method, but below they are collectively called "insurance contributions," unless otherwise specified.

[3]Please refer to Chap. 4 pp. x for non-statutory transfers and previous fiscal year carry-forward funds.

[4]Please refer to Sect. 3 of this chapter for a definition of the current year's payment rate.

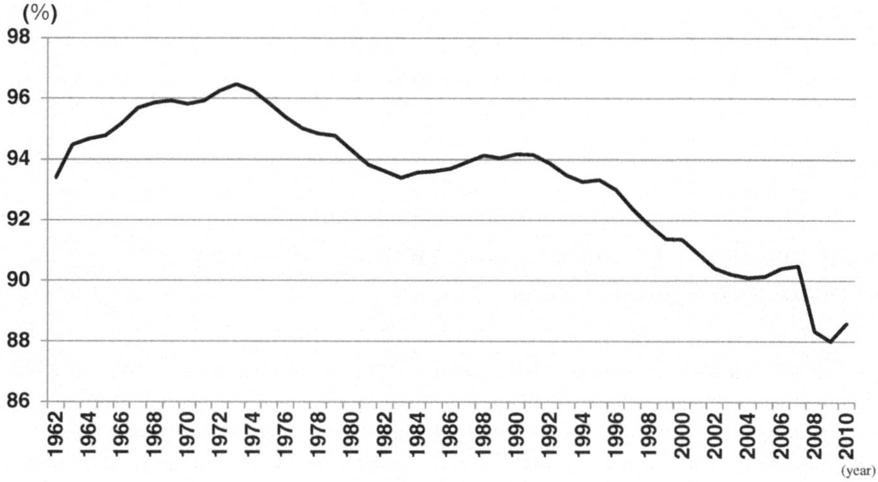

Fig. 1 Trends in the current year's payment rate. *Note* Based on materials from the Ministry of Health, Labour and Welfare

Table 1 Current year's payment rate and payment rate of carried-forward delinquent payments

Fiscal year	Average (%)	Standard deviation	Lowest (%)		Highest (%)
Current year's payment rate					
2008	92.12	0.04	75.29	Yachimata City, Chiba Prefecture	100.00
2009	91.91	0.04	76.33	Yachimata City, Chiba Prefecture	100.00
2010	92.37	0.04	76.64	Yachimata City, Chiba Prefecture	100.00
Payment rate of carried forward delinquent payments					
2008	17.22	0.10	0.69	Oshika Village, Nagano Prefecture	100.00
2009	16.77	0.08	0.00	Oshika Village, Nagano PrefectureMikurajima Village, Tokyo	100.00
2010		0.08	1.17	Oshika Village, Nagano Prefecture	100.00

Note Prepared based on the Ministry of Health, Labour and Welfare, "National Health Insurance Operations Report"

is provided of the current situation with regard to the adjustment of finances, the insurance contributions payment rate, and methods of paying insurance contributions and the insurance contributions payment rate. After that, we describe the analytical method and the results of the analysis; finally, the main points from those results are set out in the conclusion.

2 Adjustment of Finances and Methods of Paying Insurance Contributions

In order to improve payment rates, each issuer has invested in policies for the collection of National Health Insurance contributions. At the national, prefectural, and municipal government levels, attempts are being made to promote effective collection of insurance contributions by the adjustment of finances. The three systems for adjusting finances relating to the payment rate are described below.

First, we shall describe the National Treasury's regular expenditure adjustment subsidies. Various types of National Treasury expenditure have been introduced in the National Health Insurance system, and among them, regular adjustment subsidies relate to the payment rate. The national government provides regular adjustment subsidies to correct the imbalance between municipalities' levels of financial strength—specifically, to adjust medical services costs and income levels. The amount of regular adjustment subsidy is reduced as a penalty if the payment rate in the previous fiscal year was low. Therefore, regular adjustment subsidies require insurers to maintain the payment rate.

Second, let us examine prefectural adjustment subsidies for expenditure. Prefectural adjustment subsidies are divided into regular adjustment subsidies and special adjustment subsidies. Special adjustment subsidies relate to the payment rate and increase if the payment rate in the previous fiscal year was higher. Therefore, special adjustment subsidies are considered to function as an incentive for insurers, requiring them to improve the payment rate.

Third, insurance-base stability (insurance tax reduction portion) funds are transferred from the municipalities' general account. Insurance-base stability transferred funds from national revenue compensate for the reduction in insurance contributions for low-income insured persons.[5] The reduction in insurance contributions promotes payment by the insured persons and as a result, it is considered to affect the payment rate.

As described above, in the National Health Insurance system, the aim is to maintain or improve the payment rate from these three systems to adjust finances.

[5]With regard to the benefit portion of insurance contributions, insurance contributions are partially reduced, mainly for low-income insured persons, through supplementing funds from national revenue. This reduced portion is transferred from municipalities' general accounts; three quarters of financial resources are derived from the prefecture and one quarter from the municipality.

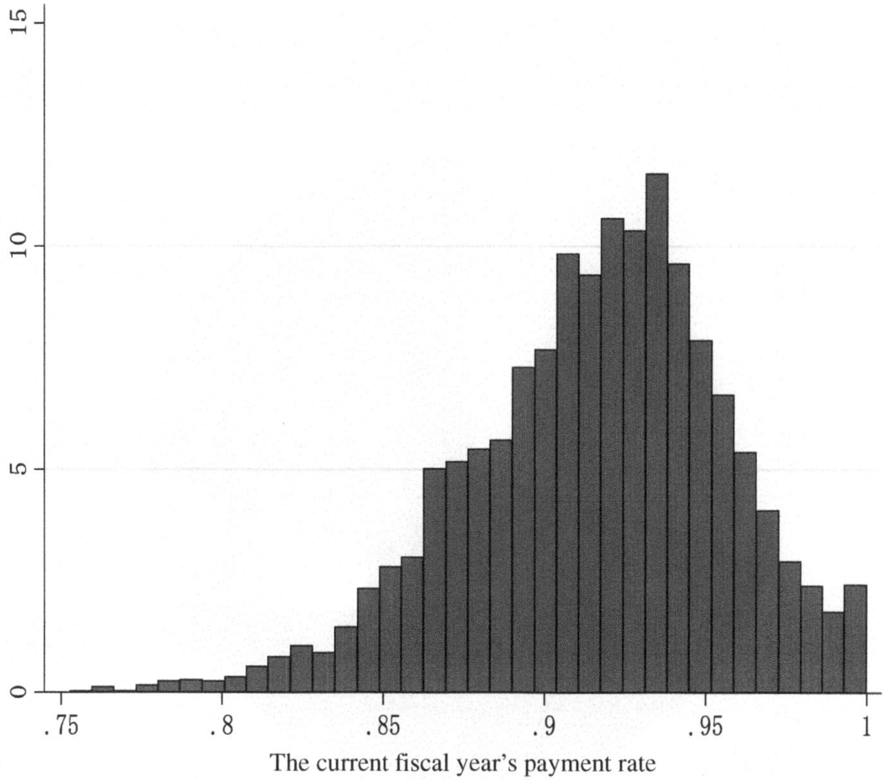

Fig. 2 Distribution of the current fiscal year's payment rate (fiscal 2010). *Source* Based on the Ministry of Health, Labour and Welfare (2010), "Report on the Status of National Health Insurance Operations (Operations Annual Report)"

The first objective of this chapter is to use the data on insurers to verify the effects these systems have in adjusting finances on the payment rate.

In addition, a fourth method is the pay-as-you-go system of National Health Insurance contributions. The payment rate for National Health Insurance contributions is influenced by these systems. Therefore, in this chapter, the effects of the pay-as-you-go systems on the payment rate for insurance contributions are investigated.

Insurers can choose a combination of these pay-as-you-go systems. Specifically, the burden portion and the benefit portion are divided equally into income-based contributions, that is, the insurance contributions portion corresponding to income

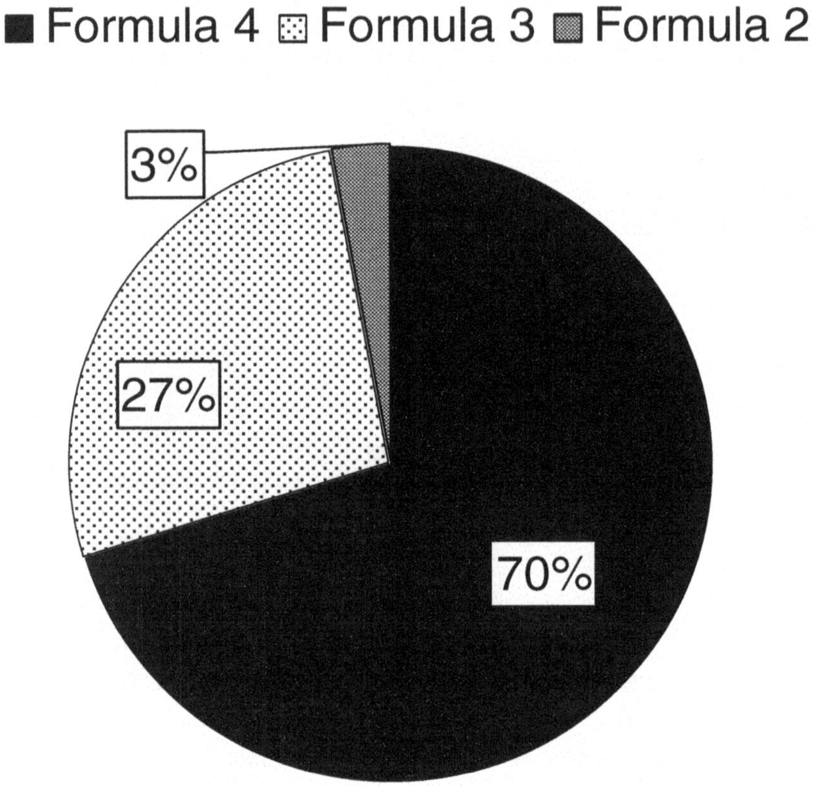

Fig. 3 Percentage of insurers by the method of paying insurance contributions (fiscal 2010). *Note* Based on the Ministry of Health, Labour and Welfare, "National Health Insurance Operations Report."

is income-based contributions and the portion corresponding to fixed assets is assets-based contributions.[6]

Figure 3 shows the percentage of insurers for each method of paying insurance contributions. About 70% of insurers adopt formula (4) which uses all the methods: income-based contributions, assets-based contributions, equal contributions, and per capita-based contributions. Fewer than 30% use formula (3) and only a small percentage uses formula (2).

[6]The insurance contributions portion corresponding to income is income-based contributions and the portion corresponding to fixed assets is assets-based contributions, and these are ability-to-pay contributions, according to the person's ability to bear the burden. On the other hand, there are also benefit contributions according to benefits, such as equal contributions that are levied on each household and the per capita-based contribution levied on each insured person as an individual. Insurers collect insurance contributions as a combination of these four types.

Table 2 National Health Insurance contributions rate

Fiscal year	Average	Standard deviation	Lowest		Highest	
Income ratio						
Fiscal year	Average (%)	Standard deviation	Lowest (%)		Highest (%)	
2008	5.85	1.46	0.98	Fujimi Town, Nagano Prefecture	12.20	Sendai City, Miyaki Prefecture
2009	5.90	1.46	2.04	Hinoemata Village, Fukushima Prefecture	12.20	Hayama Town, Kanagawa Prefecture
2010	6.04	1.44	2.10	Miyake Village, Tokyo	12.60	Nagoya City, Aichi Prefecture
Per capita ratio						
Fiscal year	Average (yen)	Standard deviation	Lowest (yen)		Highest (yen)	
2008	19248.28	4886.14	2000	Niiza City, Saitama Prefecture	42,000	Sarufutsu Village, Hokkaido
2009	19585.42	4971.63	2000	Niiza City, Saitama Prefecture	42,000	Sarufutsu Village, Hokkaido
2010	20109.26	4961.66	2000	Niiza City, Saitama Prefecture	42,000	Sarufutsu Village, Hokkaido
Asset ratio						
Fiscal year	Average (%)	Standard deviation	Lowest (%)		Highest (%)	
2008	27.98	11.87	2.00	Tendo City, Yamagata Prefecture	100.00	Nosegawa Village, Nara Prefecture
2009	27.72	11.69	2.00	Tendo City, Yamagata Prefecture	100.00	Nosegawa Village, Nara Prefecture
2010	27.44	11.59	3.40	Yuzawa City, Akita Prefecture	100.00	Nosegawa Village, Nara Prefecture
Equal ratio						
Fiscal year	Average (yen)	Standard deviation	Lowest (yen)		Highest (yen)	
2008	20808.56	5784.51	1200	Fukushi City, Tokyo	60,500	Ogata Village, Akita Prefecture
2009	20991.03	5722.61	1200	Fukushi City, Tokyo	60,500	Ogata Village, Akita Prefecture
2010	21271.90	5670.04	1200	Fukushi City, Tokyo	60,500	Ogata Village, Akita Prefecture

Note Based on the Ministry of Health, Labour and Welfare, "National Health Insurance Operations Report."

The levels of the rate of insurance contributions also vary greatly between insurers. Table 2 shows the average of insurance contributions, standard deviation, and the lowest and highest values. The fiscal 2010 rate of insurance contributions for income-based contributions was lowest in Miyake Village and Metropolitan Tokyo at 2.10%, and the highest rate was in Nagoya City and Aichi Prefecture at 12.60%. Thus, the highest contributions were six times the level of the lowest contributions. In the same way, there are large standard deviation between insurers for assets-based contributions, equal contributions, and per capita-based contributions. The national health insurance system falls into a difficult financial situation and the sustainability of the system becomes difficult. How to secure insurance premium income is an important issue; therefore, improving the payment rate is vital for income from insurance contributions.

Prefectures aim to stabilize their National Health Insurance finances by formulating support policies such as targeting area expansion. This means attempting to expand the area targeted for operations through implementing joint projects in the prefectural units. However, as the pay-as-you-go systems and insurance contributions are different for each insurer, this impedes the implementation of joint projects.

Integrating the two methods of income-based contributions and per capita-based contributions is cited as a future area of expansion support policy. What would be the impact on the payment rate of consolidating the pay-as-you-go insurance contribution systems into income-based contributions and per capita-based contribution? In order to investigate this, it is important to empirically investigate the effects that the differences in the pay-as-you-go systems have on the payment rate.

3 Previous Research on the Payment of Insurance Contributions

There is little previous research on the collected payments and delinquent payments of National Health Insurance contributions.[7] In this section, we will describe the previous research on the collected and delinquent payment of insurance contributions including National Health Insurance contributions, focusing on the differences in these studies' analytical approaches. First, with regard to payment behavior for national pension insurance contributions, Ogura and Chiba (1991) performed an analysis using data aggregated on a nationwide level, while Komamura (2001) used data aggregated by prefecture and Maruyama and Komamura (2005) used data aggregated by municipalities.

Ogura and Chiba (1991) conducted a factor analysis of non-payments using the non-payment rate and non-subscription rate for national pension insurance contributions from 1972 to 1988. Komamura (2001) used panel data by prefecture from

[7]Yamada (1998), Kishida (2002), Izumida (2003), and Yuda (2010) focused on the costs of administrative work and management work in the National Health Insurance, and clarified that economies of scale have an effect on improving the efficiency of finances. Also, as noted in Yuda (2010), many of the studies on the theme of National Health Insurance contributions have focused on the relationship between scale in terms of number of insured persons and financial problems.

1991 to 1998 to conduct a factor analysis of the non-payment of national pension insurance contributions and showed that it relates to the consumption amount, effective job vacancy rate, and the university entrance rate. Maruyama and Komamura (2005) used panel data by prefecture and by municipality from 1994 to 2002 and clarified that irregular labor and unemployment cause the payment rate for national pension insurance contributions to decline. A particular feature of Komamura (2001) and of Maruyama and Komamura (2005) was that these studies used data on local governments.

Previous research that also used the same approach as in this chapter to analyze the non-payment of National Health Insurance contributions includes Izumida (2003). Izumida (2003) clarified that the payment rate affects the costs of administrative work in the National Health Insurance system (general affairs costs) by using data "Municipalities National Health Insurance" from 1995 to 1998 by the Ministry of Health, Labour and Welfare document.[8] Shikata et al. (2012) conducted hearing direct interviews with local governments having the lowest payment rates for National Health Insurance contributions and clarified the factors determining payments.

Within the previous research, Tajika and Yuri (1999) and Suzuki (2001) examined the relationship between the collection of payments and adjustment of finances. These studies on the National Health Insurance system's financial resources verified that in addition to income from insurance contributions, financial resources include the introduction of various subsidies and transfers from the general account, and that there are soft budget constraints.

However, finances are adjusted in the National Health Insurance system by including the national government's regular adjustment subsidies, the special adjustment subsidies of prefectures, and the insurance-base stability transferred funds of municipalities. Different methods are adopted for these adjustment subsidies, alongside measures aiming to improve the payment rate by imposing penalties and offering incentives to encourage the collection of insurance contributions.

Therefore, the first problem we shall consider in this chapter is that of the relations between each of these adjustments of finances and payments, and the methods that lead to an improvement in the payment rate will be examined. Previous research has not focused on this problem, and this chapter represents the first attempt to do this. Another feature of this chapter is that the factors on the insurers' side determining the payment rate—the expenses associated with measures for the collection of payments, different collection methods, and collection conditions—will be analyzed.

A different approach from that of using local government data is the method of focusing on individual questionnaire data on households' payment of insurance

[8]Yuda (2006) analyzed that National Health Insurance contributions influence non-subscriptions by using the data of "Panel Survey on Consumption Life" of the Institute for Research on Household Economics.

contributions. For national pension insurance contributions, Suzuki and Makoto (2001) used data from the Institute for Posts and Telecommunications Policy's "Survey on Households' Selections of Financial Assets" to conduct a factor analysis of non-subscribers. Abe (2001) used data from the Ministry of Health, Labour and Welfare's "1996 Survey on Income Redistribution, Individual Questionnaires" to show that the behavior of non-subscribers and non-payers is structurally different.

Komamura and Yamada (2007) used the "Attitude Survey on Pensions" by the "Research Project on the Pension System Corresponding to the Diversification of Employment Type," while Shikata et al. (2010) used the "Attitude Survey on Public Pensions" by the Research Institute for Socionetwork Strategies (RISS) in Kansai University to conduct an attitude survey on national pension insurance contributions. These previous research analyzed the National Health Insurance contributions' behaviour focusing on the individual non-subscribers and non-payers toward insurance contributions.

Previous research studied behavior with regard to payment collection of insurance contributions, but no studies have focused on the amount of insurance contributions collected. National Health Insurance contributions differ according to the respective insurer. That is, to calculate insurance contributions, insurers have adopted various pay-as-you-go systems of income-based contributions, assets-based contributions, equal contributions, and per capita-based contributions.

Therefore, the second task of this chapter is to show by means of an empirical analysis the effects National Health Insurance contributions, which are determined by each respective insurer in accordance with their pay-as-you-go system, have on the payment rate. Previous research has not considered this connection, and this chapter is the first attempt to show this.[9]

Based on the above, in this chapter, an empirical analysis will be conducted focusing on the collection of National Health Insurance contributions. As insurers —mainly municipalities—manage the National Health Insurance system, data arranged by insurers is used. Specifically, after controlling for the insured person's situation with regard to the National Health Insurance system, we will consider the effects on the payment rate of the adjustment of finances and the insurance method.

This chapter's empirical analysis is divided into two parts. First, it analyzes the insurance contributions payment rate and the adjustment of finances, and the second part deals analyzes the method of paying insurance contributions and the insurance contributions payment rate. These analyses will be conducted in the following sections.

The Ministry of Health, Labour and Welfare's "Report on the Status of National Health Insurance Operations (Operations Annual Report)" is used as the main

[9]This chapter is based on Adachi and Uemura (2013c).

source of data in this chapter.[10] The analysis period is from fiscal 2008 to fiscal 2010.[11] However, owing to the progress in the merger of municipalities and the formation of associations for segments of administrative affairs (hereafter, partial-affairs associations) and wide-area unions, the total number of insurers in each fiscal year is different. Therefore, to reflect the actual state of the merger of municipalities and the formation of partial-affairs associations and wide-area unions, the total number of insurers in fiscal 2008 and fiscal 2009 were adjusted to match the number in fiscal 2010, the final fiscal year of the analysis period, and a balanced panel data set was created for the three years.[12]

The above data were used to create the variables described below. The items within parentheses are the insured data from the "Report on the Status of National Health Insurance Operations (Operations Annual Report)."

4 Analysis of the Adjustment of Finances, Method of Paying Insurance Contributions, and Insurance Contributions Payment Rate

The explained variable is the current year's payment rate. There are two types of collection amounts for National Health Insurance contributions: the "current year's collection amount" and the "carried-forward delinquent payments collection amount." The "carried-forward delinquent payments collection amount" includes the collection amount for overdue National Health Insurance contributions. The point in time at which that the carried-forward delinquent payment will be collected is unknown; therefore, in this chapter, the payment rate for carried-forward delinquent payments is not adopted as an explained variable. The current year's payment rate is obtained by dividing the "current year's collection amount" by a figure derived by deducting the

[10]From the "Report on the Status of National Health Insurance Operations (Operations Annual Report)," the following were used: "Table 13 Report on the Status of National Health Insurance Operations (Operations Annual Report) Table A," "Table 14 Report on the Status of National Health Insurance Operations (Operations Annual Report) Table B (1)," and "Table 14–2 Report on the Status of National Health Insurance Operations (Operations Annual Report) Table B (2)."

[11]From the implementation of the latter-stage elderly medical care system in April 2008, the categories of latter-stage elderly aged 75 years and above and early-stage elderly with a disability were withdrawn from health insurance and incorporated into the latter-stage elderly medical care system. Therefore, data on the persons in question collected before and after fiscal 2008 shows differences in the "Report on the Status of National Health Insurance Operations (Operations Annual Report) (https://www.e-stat.go.jp/stat-search/files?page=1&toukei=00450396&result_page=1: Browsing date February 5, 2018)." In this chapter, data from fiscal 2008 and onward were used in consideration of the implementation of the latter-stage elderly medical care system.

[12]The number of insurers in fiscal 2008 was 1646, and in fiscal 2009 and 2010, it was 1587. In preparing the panel data, the number of insurers in each fiscal year was unified as 1587.

"current year's whereabouts-unknown persons' settled amount" from the "current year's settled amount."[13]

- Explained variable

$$\text{Current year's payment rate} = \text{``current year's collection amount''}/(\text{``current year's settled amount''} - \text{``current years whereabouts-unknown persons' settled amount''}) \quad (1)$$

I mention four explanatory variable is the "finances factor." Insurers pay for the costs of measures for the collection of payments out of "general affairs costs." Therefore, general affairs costs per insured person, which is obtained by dividing "general affairs costs" by the "number of insured persons," will be used as an explanatory variable.[14] The costs of measures for the collection of payments are considered to have the effect of increasing the current year's payment rate, so the coefficient is expected to be positive.

In addition, the explanatory variables from "the National Treasury expenditure (regular adjustment subsidies)" are adopted. The national government grants the National Treasury a certain amount of expenditure (regular adjustment subsidies) to adjust imbalances in financial strength between the municipalities. A feature of regular adjustment subsidies is that the amount is reduced if the payment rate in the previous fiscal year is lower than it had been the year before.[15] Therefore, regular adjustment subsidies have the function of encouraging insurers to maintain the current year's payment rate.

Next, the explanatory variable from "prefecture expenditure (special adjustment subsidies)" is adopted. Prefecture expenditure (special adjustment subsidies) is granted in the current fiscal year if the previous fiscal year's payment rate for National Health Insurance contributions was high. As special adjustment subsidies are considered to provide an incentive for raising the current year's payment rate, the coefficient is expected to be positive.

Further, "insurance-base stability (insurance tax reduction portion)" is also considered. These transferred funds are paid from the general account.[16] As it is

[13]The definition of payment rates for the current year's portion and carried-forward delinquent payments use the calculation formulas actually used by the insurers.

[14]In the "Report on the Status of National Health Insurance Operations (Operations Annual Report)," as it is not possible to separate the costs of measures for the collection of payments from "general affairs costs," in this chapter, "general affairs costs" is used.

[15]The reduction rate is determined by the rate of collection of insurance contributions, according to the number of insured persons.

[16]The methods for calculating income-based contributions include the resident tax method, the main text method, and the former provisional method, with practically all the insurers adopting the former provisional method. In these methods, the basis for calculating income-based contributions is different. Therefore, in this chapter, data on the insurance contributions rate of income-based contributions of insurers adopting the former provisional method is used for analysis, and data on insurers using the other methods is not adopted. For the future, the policy is to unify the methods into the former provisional method.

considered that the current year's payment rate will be raised by the partial reduction of insurance contributions, mainly for low-income insured persons, the coefficient is expected to be positive.

- Explanatory variable (finance factor)

$$\text{General affairs costs per insured person} = \text{"general affairs costs"}/\text{"number of insured persons"} \quad (2)$$

$$\begin{aligned}&\text{National Treasury expenditure per insured person (regular adjustment subsidies)}\\&\quad = \text{"National Treasury expenditure (regular adjustment subsidies)"}/\text{"number of insured persons"}\end{aligned} \quad (3)$$

$$\begin{aligned}&\text{Prefecture expenditure per insured person (special adjustment subsidies)}\\&\quad = \text{"Prefecture expenditure (special adjustment subsidies)"}/\text{"number of insured persons"}\end{aligned} \quad (4)$$

$$\begin{aligned}&\text{Insurance-base stability per insured person (insurance tax reduction portion)}\\&\quad = \text{"Insurance-base stability (insurance tax reduction portion)"}/\text{"number of insured persons"}\end{aligned} \quad (5)$$

I adopt "insurance contributions factor" as the second explanatory variable.[17] Insurers can select either the insurance contributions method or the insurance tax method for National Health Insurance contributions. According to the National Health Insurance Law, the extinctive prescription period on insurance contributions is two years; with the Local Taxation Law, the extinctive prescription period on insurance tax is five years. If the extinctive prescription period has lapsed, insurers lose the right to collect insurance contributions. The extinctive prescription for insurance tax, which has a longer extinctive prescription period, is less likely to be applied.

Delinquency processing, such as seizure of property, is enforced for delinquent payments of insurance contributions. The order of priority for delinquency processing is different for insurance contributions and insurance tax. Insurance contributions come after resident tax, but insurance tax has the same place in the order as resident tax. The extinctive prescription period is longer for insurance tax than insurance contributions, and its order of priority for delinquency processing is higher. These differences in handling the methods legally may affect the current year's payment rate.

[17]Insurers adopting an unequal pay-as-you-go system as a result of mergers or other reasons are given a 0 in the insurance contributions data in the "Report on the Status of National Health Insurance Operations (Operations Annual Report)." Therefore, in this chapter, insurers with an unequal pay-as-you-go system were removed from the data set to be analyzed.

The Insurance tax dummy is a dummy variable in which insurers adopting insurance tax are 1 and insurers adopting insurance contributions are 0. The incentive to collect payments may differ from the different extinctive prescriptions for tax and insurance contributions. In other words, as the extinctive prescription period for tax is five years, which is longer than the two years for insurance contributions, the carried-forward delinquent payments balance increases by three years. Because of the different ways in which methods are handled legally, it is considered that the current year's payment rate will increase more for insurance tax than for insurance contributions, so its coefficient is expected to be positive.

• Explanatory variable (insurance contributions factor)

Insurance tax dummy: a dummy variable that is 1 in the case of insurance tax and 0 in the case of insurance contributions (6)

"Carried-forward delinquent payments factor" is the third explanatory variable. If the National Health Insurance contribution is not paid, it becomes a carried-forward delinquent payment. It is also necessary to collect the carried-forward delinquent payments, and insurers' efforts to collect them are considered to affect the current year's payment rate. In other words, it is possible that insurers whose payment rate for carried-forward delinquent payments in previous fiscal years is low are neglecting these efforts to collect insurance contributions, and that the payment rate of the current fiscal year may also decrease. Conversely, insurers whose payment rates for carried-forward delinquent payments in previous fiscal years is high would seem to be working to collect insurance contributions, so that the current fiscal year's payment rate increases.

In terms of the current year's payment rate and the payment rate of the carried-forward delinquent payments, as the payment rate for carried-forward delinquent payments is for past fiscal years relative to the current year's payment rate, there is no simultaneity bias as it is considered that there is a time lag. Therefore, the payment rate for carried-forward delinquent payments is set as an explanatory variable. A rise in the payment rate for carried-forward delinquent payments is considered to positively affect the insured persons' willingness to pay. Therefore, the payment rate for carried-forward delinquent payments is expected to have a positive coefficient.

Further, the rate of loss following non-collection of carried-forward delinquent payments was created as the explanatory variable for the "amount of loss from the non-collection of carried-forward delinquent payments." The unpaid amount, not collected from delinquency processing, may be treated as the amount of loss owing to non-collection, at the discretion of the insurers. "The amount of loss from the non-collection of carried-forward delinquent payments" relates to the collection efforts of insurers.

Insurers who actively conduct delinquency processing may also focus their efforts on improving the payment rate. In this case, the coefficient of the rate of loss from the non-collection of carried-forward delinquent payments will be positive. Conversely, an increase in the "amount of loss from the non-collection of carried-forward delinquent payments" may have a negative effective on the insured persons' willingness to pay. In this case, the coefficient of the rate of loss from the non-collection of carried-forward delinquent payments is expected to be negative. Therefore, it is not possible to know a priori what the coefficient of the rate of loss resulting from the non-collection of carried-forward delinquent payments will be.

- Explanatory variable (carried-forward delinquent payments factor)

Payment rate for carried-forward delinquent payments
= "carried-forward delinquent-payments collection amount"/
("carried-forward delinquent payments settled amount"
− "carried-forward delinquent payments of whereabouts unknown persons' settled amount") (7)

Rate of loss from the non-collection of carried-forward delinquent payments
= "amount of loss from the non-collection of carried-forward delinquent payments"/
("carried-forward delinquent payments settled amount"
− "carried-forward delinquent payments of whereabouts unknown persons' settled amount" (8)

"Environmental factor" is the fourth explanatory variable. First, bearing in mind that the current year's payment rate is affected by the insured persons' income, income per insured person was prepared as an explanatory variable.[18] Further, because the current year's payment rate depends on the insurers' population composition and area, the early-stage elderly rate and number of insured persons per habitable area were prepared as explanatory variables.

Specifically, the early-stage elderly rate was calculated based on the "Report on the Status of National Health Insurance Operations (Operations Annual Report)," and set as a variable expressing the financial situation and the aging population.[19]

---

[18]In this chapter, for taxable income, insurance contributions in the "National Health Insurance Operations Report (Operations Annual Report)" are used. The various forms of insurance contributions include income-based contributions, assets-based contributions, equal contributions, and per capita-based contributions, but income-based contributions are related to the income of the insured person. The basis for calculating income-based contributions are "① taxable income amount (basic deduction)," "② taxable income amount (various types of deductions)," "③ municipal resident tax income-based contributions tax amount," "④ municipal resident tax amount, etc.," and "⑤ other." But in this chapter, data on insurers adopting the method of income after the basic deduction from "① taxable income amount (basic deduction)" was used. The reasons for this were that these data were abundant compared to other data; that from fiscal 2013 onwards, it was decided to unify the methods into the method of income after the basic deduction, and it is also considered to be the most suitable as data on the income of insured persons.

[19]Following the introduction in fiscal 2008 of the latter-stage elderly medical care system, the National Health Insurance system is intended for the early-stage elderly aged less than 75 years. So, in this chapter, the effects of population aging on the early-stage elderly rate 】 are analyzed.

For area, habitable area by municipality was extracted from the Ministry of Internal Affairs and Communications, "Survey of Financial Conditions by Municipality." As previously mentioned, as the number of municipalities and the number of insurers did not match because of the progress made in municipal mergers, panel data was aggregated so that the total number of insurers matched.

- Explanatory variable (environmental factor)

$$\text{Income per insured person} = \text{“breakdown of the income-based contributions insurance contributions calculated amount” “income-based contributions”/“number of insured persons”} \tag{9}$$

$$\text{Early-stage elderly rate} = \text{“early-stage elderly, total number“/“number of insured persons“} \tag{10}$$

$$\text{Number of insured persons per habitable area} = \text{“number of insured persons“/“habitable area“} \tag{11}$$

Further, the "insurance method factor" explanatory variables of income-based contributions, assets-based contributions, equal contributions, and per capita-based contributions toward insurance were adopted as the explanatory variables. Income-based contributions are levied according to the previous fiscal year's income. Assets-based contributions are imposed based on the insured person's fixed assets. Equal contributions are charged uniformly on each household with insured persons. Per capita-based contributions are levied on individual insured persons.

Broadly, it is considered that the higher the insurance contributions, the lower the current year's payment rate and the expected coefficient is negative. However, since insured persons holding assets are considered relatively wealthy, it is deemed that the coefficient for assets-based contributions will be positive. Further, the collection of insurance contributions was set as an explanatory variable. It is assumed that the greater the number of collections, the higher the current year's payment rate will be; therefore, the coefficient is expected to be positive.

- Explanatory variables (insurance method factor)

$$\text{Income-based contributions} = \text{“income-based contributions“ of insurance contributions rate} \tag{12}$$

$$\text{Assets-based contributions} = \text{“assets-based contributions“ of insurance contributions rate} \tag{13}$$

$$\text{Equal contributions} = \text{“equal contributions“ of insurance contributions} \tag{14}$$

$$\text{Per capita-based contributions} = \text{"per capita-based contributions" of insurance contributions} \quad (15)$$

$$\text{Number of collections} = \text{"number of collections"} \quad (16)$$

From the above, the explanatory variables such as "finances factor," "insurance contributions factor," "carried-forward delinquent payments factor," and "environmental factor" were used. It was assumed that the estimation model (17) was determined by the following logarithmic linear function.[20] Here, μ is the error term.

$$\ln(y_{it}) = a_0 + a_1\ln(Z_{it}) + a_2\mathrm{DUM}_{it} + a_3\ln(H_{it}) + a_4\ln(M_{it}) + a_5\ln(E_{it}) + \mu_{it} \quad (17)$$

The left side explained variable y_{it} is the current year's payment rate. On the right side, the explanatory variable Z_{it} shows the "finances factor," while the general affairs costs per insured person, the National Treasury expenditure per insured person (regular adjustment subsidies), prefecture expenditure per insured person (special adjustment subsidies), and insurance-base stability per insured person (insurance tax reduction portion) were used. For the "insurance contributions factor," DUM_{it} is the insurance tax dummy and H_{it} is income-based contributions. For the "carried-forward delinquent-payments factor" M_{it} , the payment rate for the carried-forward delinquent payments and the rate of loss from the non-collection of carried-forward delinquent payments were used. For the "environmental factor" E_{it}, income per insured person, the early-stage elderly rate, and number of insured persons per habitable area were used. Subscript i shows insurers and t each fiscal year.

Further, in order to analyze the method of paying insurance contributions, an estimation model (18) was prepared.

$$\ln(y_{it}) = a_0 + a_1\ln(Z_{it}) + a_2\mathrm{DUM}_{it} + a_3\ln(H_{it}) + a_4\ln(M_{it}) + a_5\ln(E_{it}) + a_5\ln(W_{it}) + \mu_{it} \quad (18)$$

That is, on the right side of the explanatory variable described above were added "insurance method factors" of the number of collections, income-based contributions, assets-based contributions, equal contributions, and per capita-based contributions to give W_{it}. Table 3 shows the descriptive statistics of the variables.

[20]It was decided to use a logarithmic linear function in order to interpret the coefficients obtained from the estimations as elastic values.

Table 3 Descriptive statistics

	Average value	Standard deviation	Minimum value	Maximum value
Current year's payment rate (%)	91.574	4.018	75.290	100.000
General affairs costs per insured person (yen/person)	6932.674	6240.145	41.689	98470.930
State treasury expenditure per insured person(regu!ar adjustment subsidies) (yen/perso	15493.650	9319.048	0.000	68482.920
Prefecture expenditure per insured person (special adjustment subsidies) (yen/person)	3511.125	5523.787	27.339	96631.070
Insurance-base stability per insured person (insurance tax reduction portion) (yen/perso	8715.828	3035.611	710.870	21605.590
Insurance tax dummy	0.890	0.313	0.000	1.000
Carried-forward of delinquent payments rate (%)	16.504	8.331	0.000	100.000
Rate of loss from non-collection of carried-forward delinquent payments (%)	8.452	7.726	0.000	71.223
Income per insured person (yen/person)	560.137	191.742	137.913	3476.295
Early-stage elderly rate (%)	32.426	6.218	7.955	56.088
No. of insured persons per habitable area (person/Km^2)	346.819	532.824	3.873	4295.490
Income ratio (%)	6.274	1.586	0.980	12.800
Asset ratio (%)	20.233	15.856	0.000	100.000
Equal ratio (yen)	20938.690	6214.446	0.000	60500.000
Per capita ratio (yen)	20263.350	5107.440	0.000	42000.000
No. of collections (times/year)	8.473	1.806	0.000	12.000

Source Based on the Ministry of Health, Labour and Welfare, "National Health Insurance Operations Report."

5 Results of Estimations

5.1 Results of Estimations of the Adjustment of Finances and Insurance Contributions Payment Rate

Table 4 shows the results of the estimations from the estimation model from Formula (17). All the results of the estimations in this chapter were rejected in a Hausman test at the 1% level, so a fixed-effects model was adopted. In addition, in terms of the overall trend from the results of the estimations, the result for the fiscal year dummy was negatively significant, so it is assumed that the current year's payment rate is trending downward.

Table 4 Results of estimations by number of insured persons per habitable area

Current year's payment rate	Model 1		Model 2		Model 3		Model 4	
	All insurers		All insurers		Highly integrated insurers		Lowly integrated insurers	
	Coefficient	*t*-value	Coefficient	*t*-value	Coefficient	*t*-value	Coefficient	*t*-value
General affairs costs per insured person	0.0004	0.35	0.0004	0.40	0.0028	1.12	0.0017	0.75
State treasury expenditure per insured person (regular adjustment subsidies)	−0.00006	−1.42	−0.0008	−1.84*	−0.0007	−1.09	0.0017	1.63
Prefectural expenditure per insured person (special adjustment subsidies)	0.0011	3.41***	0.0011	3.31***	0.0000	0.00	0.0012	2.23**
Insurance-base stability per insured person (insurance tax reduction portion)	−0.0012	−0.64	−0.0025	−1.34	−0.0036	−1.09	0.0056	1.09
Insurance tax dummy	0.0025	0.52	0.0024	0.51	0.0066	0.97	−0.0002	−0.02
Carried-forward delinquent payment rate	0.0066	6.09***	0.0069	6.29***	0.0094	3.43***	0.0078	4.20***
Rate of loss from non-collection of carried-forward delinquent payments	0.0004	1.25	0.0004	1.12	0.0027	2.69***	0.0001	0.20
Income ratio	−0.0175	−6.76***	−0.0175	−6.75***	−0.0272	−4.16***	−0.0233	−4.22***
Income per insured person			−0.0025	−0.93	−0.0058	−0.91	0.0125	2.34**
Early-stage elderly rate			0.0293	4.09***	0.0138	1.38	0.0330	1.63
No. of insured persons per habitable area			−0.0118	−1.05	−0.0217	−0.78	−0.0230	−0.92
FY2008 dummy	−0.0037	−7.82***	−0.0030	−4.77***	−0.0043	−3.43***	−0.0042	−2.42**
FY2009 dummy	−0.0065	−15.09***	−0.0066	−12.99***	−0.0090	−9.05***	−0.0048	−3.91***
Constant term	−0.0407	−2.11**	0.0847	1.24	0.1646	0.80	−0.0511	−0.43
Modified R square	0.1191		0.4236		0.1483		0.3567	
F-Test, Wald test	F(1528, 2366) = 51.180***		F(1527, 2361) = 34.600***		F(388, 596) = 48.820***		F(359, 451) = 18.740***	
Hausman test	chi2(10) = 333.060***		chi2(13) = 99.120***		chi2(15) = 50.050***		chi2(13) = 36.550***	
No. of observations	3905		3902		998		868	

In the panel analysis, a fixed-effects model was adopted based on the Hausman Test

*, **, ***indicate that the null hypothesis was rejected and they are statistically significant results at the significance levels of 1, 5, and 10%, respectively

Below, each model is investigated in detail. In Models 1 and 2, the factors affecting the current year's payment rate will be analyzed, targeting all insurers. In Model 1, only the factors relating to insurers, namely the "finances factor," "insurance contributions factor," and the "carried-forward delinquent-payments factor" were used as the explanatory variables.

In Model 2, after controlling for the "environmental factors" relating to insured persons, we verified the effects of the factors relating to insurers, the "finances factor," the "insurance contributions factor," and the "carried-forward delinquent-payments factor" on the current year's payment rate.

With regard to the "finances factor," general affairs costs per insured person include the cost of measures for the collection of payments, but it was not seen to affect the payment rate in the results of the estimations. The insurance-base stability per insured person (insurance tax reduction portion) was not observed to affect the payment rate. However, prefecture expenditure per insured person (special adjustment subsidies) had a significantly positive effect on the current year's payment rate. It would seem that special adjustment subsidies demonstrate the function of adjusting finances to improving the payment rate. In Model 2 also, National Treasury expenditure per insured person (regular adjustment subsidies) was negatively significant, although its effect was weak.

With regard to the "insurance contributions factor," the insurance tax dummy was not significant. Although there are legal differences in insurance contributions and insurance tax, in the management by insurers, noticeable differences in terms of the effects on the current year's payment rate are not considered. Alternatively, only a few insurers adopt insurance tax and it might have been the case that it was not possible to detect a significant difference in the effects on the payment rate. Income-based contributions using the insurance contributions rate (tax rate) was significantly negative with regard to the current year's payment rate. Therefore, a hike in the insurance contributions rate (tax rate) was shown to invite the risk of a reduction in the payment rate.

With regard to the "carried-forward delinquent-payments factor," the payment rate was positively significant, but a significant result was not obtained for the rate of loss resulting from the non-collection of carried-forward delinquent payments. A rise in the payments rate for carried-forward delinquent payments reflects insurers' collection efforts, and may increase the awareness of payment among the insured persons. However, the fact that the rate of loss from the non-collection of carried-forward delinquent payments was not significant shows that insurers' processing of the deficit from delinquent payments does not affect the payment rate.

In Model 2, in addition to the explanatory variables, "environmental factors" such as income per insured person, the early-stage elderly rate, and number of insured persons per habitable area were also controlled. In this case, the same results as from Model 1 were obtained. The fact that there were no major changes in the results of the estimations even on considering the "environmental factors," which show the conditions of the insured persons, indicates that the current year's payment rate is affected mostly by factors concerning the insurers, rather than the insured persons.

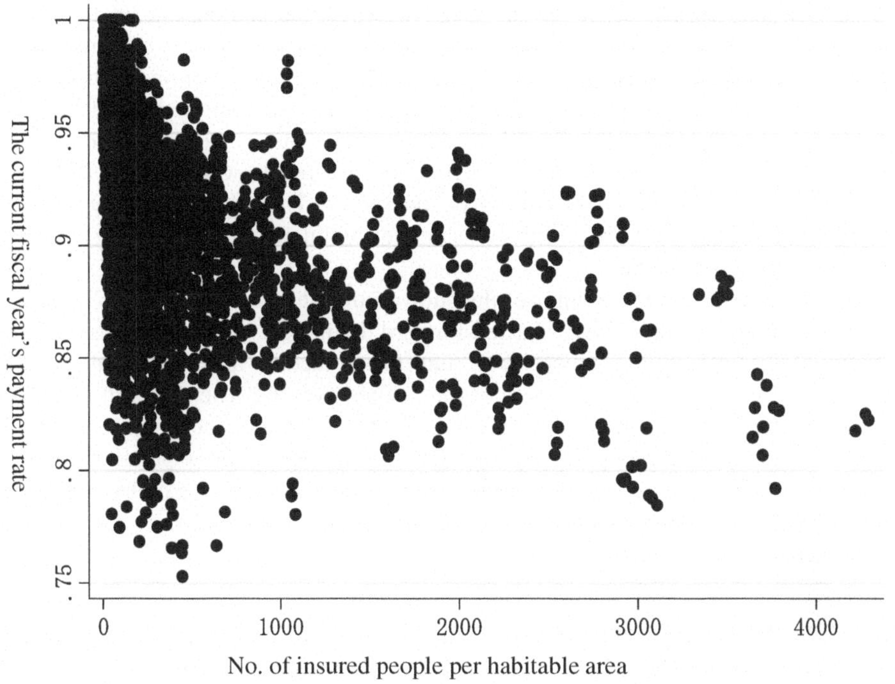

Fig. 4 The current fiscal year payment rate and number of insured persons per habitable area (fiscal 2010). *Source* Based on Ministry of Health, Labour and Welfare (2010), "Report on the Status of National Health Insurance Operations (Operations Annual Report)"

It is recognized that there are regional characteristics in the current year's payment rate.[21] In Figure 4, on observing the relation between the payment rate and number of insured persons per habitable area, we see that the higher the number of insured persons per habitable area, the lower the payment rate.

The extent of the population density of insured persons may affect the payment rate. Therefore, the quartile method was used for the number of insured persons per habitable area to divide the data, and estimations were carried out. Here, the 1st quartile are <low population-density insurers> and the 4th quartile are <high population-density insurers>. Table 4 shows these results. Model 3 is the result of estimations for the <high population-density insurers> and Model 4 for the <low population-density insurers>. Only those results that differed from the results of the estimations for all insurers are summarized below.

With regard to the "finances factor," prefecture expenditure per insured person (special adjustment subsidies) did not have a significant effect for <high

[21]For example, Tanaka (2005) and others have pointed to the existence of regional characteristics in payment rates.

population-density insurers>, but the result was positive and significant for <low population-density insurers>. Therefore, adjustment of finances by prefecture expenditure (special adjustment subsidies) is said to have the function of improving the current year's payment rate for insurers with low population density of insured persons. For the "carried-forward delinquent-payments factor," the rate of loss from the non-collection of carried-forward delinquent payments was positive and significant for <high population-density insurers>. This suggests that <high population-density insurers> actively conduct delinquency processing, which improves the payment rate.

To summarize the above, the results showed that the "finances factor," "insurance contributions factor," and "carried-forward delinquent-payments factor" affect the current year's non-payment rate, but these factors have different effects depending on the population density of the insured persons. Therefore, in terms of measures for the collection of National Health Insurance contributions, it is important to aim to improve the payment rate by considering the population density in terms of number of insured persons in the area and to conduct the collection work and to deal with the carried-forward delinquent payments and the deficit from delinquent payments accordingly.

5.2 Results of the Estimation of the Methods of Paying Insurance Contributions and the Payment Rate of Insurance Contributions

Table 5 shows the results of the estimations from the method of paying insurance contributions obtained from the estimation formula (18). Model 5 shows the results obtained from formula (4), which used all of the methods of paying insurance contributions (income-based contributions, assets-based contributions, equal contributions, and per capita-based contribution). From Models 6 to 11, the estimations were carried out by changing the combinations of the insurance contributions, based on income-based contributions. Model 6 is the result of three methods *A* (income-based contributions, assets-based contributions, and per capita-based contribution); Model 7 of three methods *B* (income-based contributions, equal contributions, and per capita-based contribution); Model 8 of two methods *A* (income-based contributions and assets-based contributions); Model 9 of two methods *B* (income-based contributions and equal contributions), Model 10 of two methods *C* (income-based contributions and per capita-based contribution), and Model 11 of only one method (income-based contributions).

In all these models, after controlling for factors relating to insurers, namely the finances factor, the carried-forward delinquent payments factor, and the environmental factors relating to insured persons, the effects of the "insurance contributions factor" were verified

Table 5 Results of estimations for the methods of paying insurance contributions

(1)						
Current year's payment rate	Model 5		Model 6		Model 7	
	Formula 4		Formula 3A		Formula 3B	
	Coefficient	*t*-value	Coefficient	*t*-value	Coefficient	*t*-value
No. of collections	0.0045	2.20**	0.0045	2.21**	0.0033	1.73*
Income ratio	−0.0152	−3.96***	−0.0148	−3.92***	−0.0142	−4.23***
Asset ratio	0.0040	1.99**	0.0043	2.19**		
Equal ratio	0.0023	0.54			0.0024	0.66
Per capita ratio	−0.0075	−1.60	−0.0067	−1.50	−0.0096	−2.29**
General affairs costs per insured person	0.0007	0.63	0.0007	0.65	0.0003	0.26
State treasury expenditure per insured person (regular adjustment subsidies)	−0.0008	−1.66*	−0.0008	−1.66*	−0.0009	−1.88*
Prefectural expenditure per insured person (special adjustment subsidies)	0.0012	3.28***	0.0011	3.28***	0.0011	3.37***
Insurance-base stability per insured person (insurance tax reduction portion)	0.0014	0.56	0.0016	0.64	0.0004	0.16
Insurance tax dummy	0.0011	0.21	0.0011	0.22	0.0023	0.49
Carried-forward delinquent payment rate	0.0063	5.25***	0.0063	5.28***	0.0070	6.41***
Carried-forward delinquent payments loss from non-collection rate	0.0003	0.93	0.0003	0.92	0.0004	1.10
Income per insured person	−0.0012	−0.40	−0.0011	−0.37	−0.0012	−0.44
Early-stage elderly rate	0.0297	4.01***	0.0296	4.00***	0.0277	3.83***
No. of insured persons per habitable area	−0.0100	−0.75	−0.0098	−0.74	−0.0105	−0.92
FY2008 dummy	−0.0027	−3.47***	−0.0027	−3.47***	−0.0029	−4.58***
FY2009 dummy	−0.0057	−9.52***	−0.0057	−9.51***	−0.0064	−12.46***

(continued)

Table 5 (continued)

(1)

Current year's payment rate	Model 5		Model 6		Model 7	
	Formula 4		Formula 3A		Formula 3B	
	Coefficient	*t*-value	Coefficient	*t*-value	Coefficient	*t*-value
Constant term	0.0562	0.69	0.0656	0.82	0.1010	1.37
Modified R square	0.4126		0.4137		0.4149	
F-Test, Wald test	F(1124,1628) = 32.840***		F(1124,1629) = 32.890***		F(1508,2319) = 34.480***	
Hausman test	chi2(17) = 74.690***		chi2(16) = 75.130***		chi2(16) = 99.410***	
No. of observations	2770		2770		3844	

(2)

Current year's payment rate	Model 8		Model 9		Model 10		Model 11	
	Formula 2A		Formula 2B		Formula 2C		Formula 1	
	Coefficient	*t*-value	Coefficient	*t*-value	Coefficient	*t*-value	Coefficient	*t*-value
No. of collections	0.0045	2.17**	0.0032	1.67*	0.0033	1.74*	0.0031	1.67*
Income ratio	−0.0181	−5.95***	−0.0178	−5.94***	−0.0132	−4.25***	−0.0176	−6.77***
Asset ratio	0.0044	2.26**						
Equal ratio			−0.0003	−0.08				
Per capita ratio					−0.0091	−2.52**		
General affairs costs per insured person	0.0007	0.64	0.0003	0.26	0.0004	0.42	0.0005	0.44
State treasury expenditure per insured person(regular adjustment subsidies)	−0.0008	−1.62	−0.0009	−1.83*	−0.0008	−1.83*	−0.0008	−1.79*
Prefectural expenditure per insured person (special adjustment subsidies)	0.0011	3.21***	0.0011	3.28***	0.0011	3.39***	0.0011	3.32***

(continued)

Table 5 (continued)

(2)								
Current year's payment rate	Model 8		Model 9		Model 10		Model 11	
	Formula 2A		Formula 2B		Formula 2C		Formula 1	
	Coefficient	*t*-value	Coefficient	*t*-value	Coefficient	*t*-value	Coefficient	*t*-value
Insurance-base stability per insured person (insurance tax reduction portion)	−0.0003	−0.14	−0.0020	−0.97	0.0004	0.17	−0.0025	−1.33
Insurance tax dummy	0.0010	0.20	0.0022	0.47	0.0024	0.50	0.0022	0.47
Carried-forward delinquent payment rate	0.0063	5.30***	0.0071	6.46***	0.0069	6.28***	0.0069	6.33***
Rate of loss from non-collection of carried-forward delinquent payments	0.0003	0.90	0.0003	1.07	0.0004	1.11	0.0004	1.11
Income per insured person	−0.0020	−0.67	−0.0021	−0.76	−0.0015	−0.55	−0.0026	−0.93
Early-stage elderly rate	0.0306	4.15***	0.0292	4.04***	0.0278	3.86***	0.0293	4.08***
No. of insured persons per habitable area	−0.0099	−0.75	−0.0107	−0.94	−0.0104	−0.92	−0.0114	−1.01
FY2008 dummy	−0.0027	−3.54***	−0.0030	−4.66***	−0.0029	−4.52***	−0.0030	−4.70***
FY2009 dummy	−0.0058	−9.81***	−0.0066	−12.79***	−0.0064	−12.42***	−0.0066	−12.91***
Constant term	0.0297	0.39	0.0695	0.96	0.1177	1.67*	0.0752	1.10
Modified *R* square	0.4167		0.4200		0.4216		0.4252	
F-Test, Wald test	*F*(1124,1632) = 32.890***		*F*(1509,2322) = 34.420***		*F*(1526,2350) = 34.650***		*F*(1527,2359) = 34.610***	
Hausman test	chi2(15) = 73.070***		chi2(15) = 94.460***		chi2(15) = 100.850***		chi2(14) = 96.850***	
No. of observations	2772		3847		3892		3901	

All the explained variables and explanatory variables are taken as logarithms

In the panel analysis, a fixed effects model was adopted based on the Hausman Test

*, **, ***indicate that the null hypothesis was rejected and that these are statistically significant results at the significance levels of 1, 5, and 10%, respectively

First, the insurance tax dummy was not significant. There are legal differences in insurance contributions and tax, but in the management by insurers, noticeable differences in terms of the effects on the current year's payment rate are not considered. Alternatively, a few insurers adopt insurance tax and it might have been the case that it was not possible to detect a significant difference in the effects on the payment rate.

Second, general affairs costs per insured person include the costs of measures for the collection of payments, but this did not seem to affect the payment rate in the results of the estimations.[22]

Third, it was shown that number of collections positively affects the current year's payment rate. According to the descriptive statistics in Table 3, the average annual number of collections is 8.473, and the payment rate can be raised by increasing the number of collections.

Fourth, the insurance contributions rate of income-based contributions affects the current year's payment rate both significantly and negatively. Therefore, it was shown that hiking the insurance contributions rate of income-based contributions involves the risk of reducing the payment rate.

Fifth, the insurance contributions rate of assets-based contributions significantly and positively affects the current year's payment rate, and it is considered that the insurance contributions rate of assets-based contributions promotes improvement in the payment rate. Assets-based contributions require payment of insurance contributions according to the fixed assets held by the insured person, and collection of payments from relatively wealthy insured persons may increase the payment rate.

Sixth, no significant result was obtained for equal insurance contributions in which a fixed amount is levied on the unit of a household, but per capita-based contributions, which are levied on individual insured persons, had a significantly negative effect on the current year's payment rate. Raising the insurance contributions rate of per capita-based contributions may reduce the payment rate. The burden for equal contributions is reduced when the number of household members increases, and compared to the per capita-based contributions, its effects on the payment rate are thought to be small.

Next, the results of the estimates of the control variables, other than the insurance contributions factor, are explained.

First is the finances factor. Insurance-base stability per insured person (insurance tax reduction portion) was not seen to affect the payment rate. It was shown that the payment rate does not improve even when insurance contributions are reduced for low-income insured persons.

However, prefecture expenditure per insured person (special adjustment subsidies) had a positive and significant effect on the current year's payment rate. It

[22]General affairs costs include the costs of measures for the collection of payments, but data on the cost of measures for the collection of payments could not be established and, therefore, we conclude that its effects on the payment rate could not be detected. Or, while one may suspect that effective measures for the collection of payments are not being carried out, it is not possible to confirm this because of data constraints.

seems that special adjustment subsidies demonstrate the function of adjusting finances to improve the payment rate. In addition, National Treasury expenditure per insured person (regular adjustment subsidies) had a negative and significant effect, although it was weak.

Second is the carried-forward delinquent-payments factor. The payment rate for carried-forward delinquent payments was positive and significant, but a noteworthy result was not obtained from the rate of loss as a result of non-collection of carried-forward delinquent payments. A rise in the payments rate for carried-forward delinquent payments reflects insurers' collection efforts. However, the fact that the rate of loss from non-collection of carried-forward delinquent payments was not significant shows that the processing of the deficit from delinquent payments does not affect the payment rate.

Third is the environmental factor. Income per insured person and number of insured persons per habitable area did not affect the payment rate, but the result showed that the early-stage elderly rate significantly improved the current year's payment rate. As many of the early-stage elderly pay National Health Insurance contributions as a deduction from their public pension, this may have a positive effect on the payment rate.

To summarize, after controlling for the finances factor, the carried-forward delinquent-payments factor, and the environmental factor, on verifying the effects of the insurance contributions factor, differences were observed in the effects on the current year's payment rate from combining the content of the methods of paying insurance contributions. Therefore, it is important when collecting insurance contributions to adopt responses that are effective for the payment rate, while considering the effects that the method of paying insurance contributions will have on the payment rate.

6 Conclusions

In this chapter, an analysis was conducted focusing on the adjustment of finances and the insurance contributions payment rate, and the method of paying insurance contributions and the insurance contributions payment rate. The results of the analysis are summarized as follows.

First, we focused on the reduction in the payment rate of insurance contributions as a factor causing National Health Insurance finances to weaken, and the effects of the system of adjusting finances were verified as factors affecting the payment rate.

The results of the analysis showed that while the adjustment of finances by special adjustment subsidies (prefectures) causes the current year's payment rate to increase, regular adjustment subsidies (national government) and insurance-base stability transferred funds (municipalities) do not have the effect of improving the current year's payment rate.

Therefore, in order to improve the payment rate and thereby increase the sustainability of the National Health Insurance finances, it is necessary to provide insurers with incentives to improve their payment rates in the form of special adjustment subsidies (prefectures), and not by imposing penalties like regular adjustment subsidies (national government) or granting subsidies such as insurance-base stability transferred funds (municipalities).

Here, a rise in the payments rate for carried-forward delinquent payments will cause the current year's payment rate to increase, so even if there are carried-forward delinquent payments, the steady collection of payments will contribute to an improvement in the current year's payment rate.

Special adjustment subsidies are one part of a prefecture's expenditure, and the findings suggest that the efforts on the prefectural units are vital for the improvement of insurers' payment rates. In fact, the National Health Insurance system is considering area expansion on the unit of prefectures and for joint payment collection, with the aim of implementing joint measures and setting payment rate targets. Progressing toward such wide-area measures for the collection of payments is an important task in terms of improving the sustainability of the National Health Insurance finances.

Next, the effects on the payment rate of the different methods of paying insurance contributions in the National Health Insurance system were verified. After controlling for the various factors, namely the finances factor, carried-forward delinquent-payments factor, and the environmental factor, the results of the empirical analysis by insurer clarified that the combination of the contents of the National Health Insurance contributions pay-as-you-go systems have different effects on the current year's payment rate. Specifically, it was clarified that the insurance contributions rate of income-based contributions causes the current year's payment rate to decline, that assets-based contributions have the effect of increasing the payment rate, and that equal contributions do not have any significant effect, but that per capita-based contributions cause the collection of insurance contributions to decline.

Therefore, when setting insurance contributions with the aim of improving the current year's payment rate, it is effective to investigate settings based on a consideration of the respective effects on the payment rate of income-based contributions, assets-based contributions, equal contributions, and per capita-based contributions.

In fact, the implementation of joint work on the unit of prefectures in order to improve financial sustainability is being considered for National Health Insurance operations. As part of this, the integration of two methods, income-based contributions and per capita-based contributions, is also being considered. If assets-based contributions and equal contributions are abolished and income from insurance contributions is maintained, it will be necessary to increase the insurance contributions rate of income-based contributions and insurance contributions from per capita-based contributions; thus, a reduction in the payment rate will be unavoidable.

Alternatively, other payment collection measures include projects targeting area expansion on the unit of prefectures. According to the results of the analysis, raising the number of collections increases the payment rate. It will be necessary to consider the fact that consolidating the system into these two methods will reduce the payment rate and, therefore, it will be necessary to implement effective measures for payment collection.

Chapter 8
Expanding the Scope and Improving the Efficiency of National Health Insurance Administrative Work

1 Introduction

Since the establishment of the National Health Insurance system in 1961, with municipalities as the main insurers, insurance benefit costs have been rapidly increasing as a result of factors such as the aging population, the increasing prevalence of lifestyle diseases, and advancements in medical services technologies. In contrast, insurance contributions (tax) income has been slumping and the government is facing a difficult financial situation.

According to the Ministry of Health, Labour and Welfare's "Report on the Status of National Health Insurance Operations (Operations Annual Report 2010)," insurance contributions (tax) income in fiscal 2010 National Health Insurance finances had declined 2.1% from the previous fiscal year (average decline of 0.6% for the previous three years). In contrast, insurance benefit costs had increased 3.2% on the previous fiscal year (an average increase of 0.8% for the previous three years).[1]

The severe state of National Health Insurance finances is evident from the size of the non-statutory funds transferred from the general accounts of municipalities. Essentially, if the National Health Insurance special accounting system functions properly, it should not be necessary to transfer non-statutory funds from general accounts. However, of the 764.7 billion yen funds (statutory portion + non-statutory portion) transferred from general accounts in fiscal 2010, more than half, at 397.9 billion yen, were non-statutory transferred funds. Further, the number of insurers receiving non-statutory transferred funds was 1212, which is 70.26% of the total number 1725.

[1]The calculations came from data on insurers, most of which were municipalities, in the Ministry of Health, Labour and Welfare's "Report on the Status of National Health Insurance Operations (Operations Annual Report 2010)" (including wide-area union and partial-affairs associations). The long-term care portion and the latter-stage elderly support funds portions were omitted. The same also applies to the analysis below.

Y. Adachi, *The Economics of Tax and Social Security in Japan*,
https://doi.org/10.1007/978-981-10-7176-8_8

Thus, to improve the sustainability of National Health Insurance finances, it will be essential to increase income and control expenditure. To increase income, it will be necessary to hike the National Health Insurance contributions (tax) or the insurance contributions (tax) payment rate. However, the payment rate for National Health Insurance contributions (tax) is trending downward, and in the current circumstances it will be difficult to hike National Health Insurance contributions (tax) to above their current level.[2] On the other hand, various viewpoints are being discussed regarding the measures that need to be implemented in order to reduce expenditure. One such measure would be to improve operational efficiency.

In recent years, since the start of the latter-stage elderly medical care system in fiscal 2008, there has also been investigation into area expansion that adopts operations management on the prefectural units as a possibility for the National Health Insurance system. Specifically, National Health Insurance operations management, which is the target of area expansion measures, comprises insurers' administrative work, measures to optimize medical services costs, measures for payment collection, and health-related operations.

Insurers' administrative work includes certification of insured persons and calculating the costs of expensive medical benefits, and measures to optimize medical services costs, including inspection of receipts and sending notifications of medical services costs. In addition, insurers are also responsible for campaigns that prevent, for example, duplicate consultations and so-called "convenience" consultations. There are other measures for payment collection such as conducting administrative work to improve the payment rate and to process delinquent payments, and health-related operations, including specific medical consultations and specific health guidance. It is highly likely that the efficiency of the above-described administrative work will improve if the area is expanded from the municipal unit to the prefectural unit. In fact, a number of prefectures have formulated policies to support area expansion in the National Health Insurance system.[3] Further, improving the efficiency of operational costs has also been cited as an important issue for area expansion in the National Health Insurance.

For example, Shiga Prefecture (2010) investigated the joint implementation of insurers' administrative work and measures for the optimization of medical services costs, measures for the collection of payments, and health-related operations as a specific measure that would expand the area of operations. The goal is to stabilize

---

[2]The National Health Insurance contributions (tax) payment rate (current year's portion) in fiscal 1991 was 94.16%; in fiscal 1996 it was 93.00%; in fiscal 2001 it was 90.87%; in fiscal 2006, 90.39%; in fiscal 2007, 90.49%; in fiscal 2008, 88.35%; in fiscal 2009, 88.10%; and since then it has continued to decline year by year. However, the drop from fiscal 2008 onwards can be partly attributed to the effects of the introduction of the latter-stage elderly medical care system.

[3]For example, in several prefectures, the establishment of an environment toward implementing projects on the unit of prefectures, such as for joint projects targeting the expanding medical care costs, has been discussed. Please refer to the Social Security Weekly Editing Bureau (2012a, b). The prefectures of Japan consist of 47 pref ectures. They form the first level of jurisdiction and administrative division of Japan. Th ey consist of 43 prefectures proper, two urban prefectures , one "circuit" or "territory" and one "metropolis".

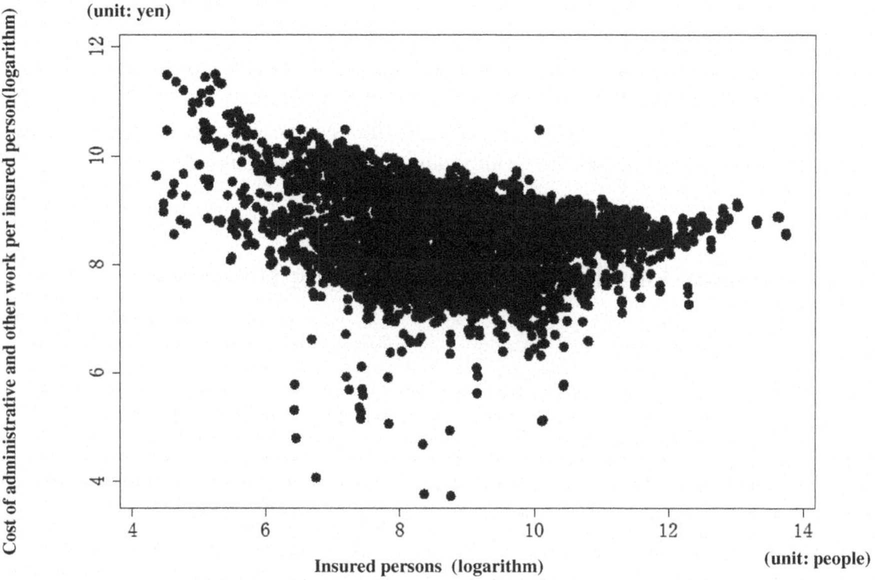

Fig. 1 Number of insured persons and per capita cost of administrative work. *Source* Based on the Ministry of Health, Labour and Welfare, "Report on the Status of National Health Insurance Operations (Operations Annual Report 2010)"

the National Health Insurance system by implementing such area expansion measures for financial management.

The objective of area expansion is to improve the cost efficiency of National Health Insurance operations, but an important question is whether economies of scale can be demonstrated for these operations. Figure 1 shows the relation between the number of insured persons and the costs of administrative work per capita (both are logarithms) for each insurer in fiscal 2010. As can be seen from Fig. 1, the tendency is for the cost of administrative work per capita to decline alongside an increase in the number of insured persons held by the insurers.

Further, insurers—most of which are municipalities—conduct National Health insurance operations, and as many municipalities are small, there are many small-scale insurers. If there are economies of scale for the number of insured persons relative to the cost of administrative work, then it will be possible to reduce operational costs by increasing the scale of the insurers (namely, increasing the number of insured persons they have).

Therefore, in this chapter, we shall look at whether or not economies of scale currently exist in the National Health Insurance system, investigate operational costs, and clarify whether or not increasing the number of insured persons would be effective in order to improve the efficiency of National Health Insurance operations.

The chapter is structured as follows. In Sect. 2, the existing research will be introduced and the position of this chapter indicated. In Sect. 3, an overview of the data used for the analysis will be presented, and the variables and estimation model will be described. In Sect. 4, the results of the estimations from the empirical analysis will be shown. Finally, in Sect. 5, the results will be summarized and conclusions and implications for policymaking will be discussed.

2 Positioning This Paper Among Existing Research Studies

With regard to the cost of administrative work (general affairs costs) in the National Health Insurance system, Kishida (2002) and Izumida (2003) clarified that there are economies of scale for the number of insured persons and the number of households, respectively.[4] Further, Yuda (2010) ascertained the management costs of National Health Insurance operations to be the total of general affairs costs, screening fees, contributions to joint-project health-related operational costs, and direct examination account contributions, and pointed to the existence of economies of scale for the number of insured persons.

Kishida (2002) used panel data for the seven Kinki prefectures (Shiga, Mie, Kyoto, Nara, Hyogo, Osaka, and Wakayama) over four years, from fiscal 1996 to 1999, while Izumida (2003) used panel data for the four years from fiscal 1995 to 1998 on municipal insurers nationwide, and Yuda (2010) used cross-sectional data from fiscal 2000 on municipal insurers nationwide.

This existing research indicated the existence of economies of scale for the cost of administrative work for the National Health Insurance program, and therefore we consider that it is possible to reduce the cost of administrative work by expanding the area of operations.

Even when simplifying this area to include only National Health Insurance operations, this category includes a diverse range of operations such as the issuance of insurance certificates, the examination of receipts, and the collection of insurance contributions. Each insurer carries out these operations separately; the effectiveness of area expansion has been discussed, as it is considered that costs could be reduced by conducting this administrative work collectively. Although National Health Insurance costs come under the category of special accounting, financial resources for the administrative work are also expenses from the statutory portion of the

[4]Suzuki (2001) analyzed the effects of subsidies in the National Health Insurance finances. Moreover, while not focusing on the National Health Insurance system, existing research that has verified economies of scale for the cost of administrative work (general affairs costs) in the public long-term care insurance system includes Yamauchi (2006) and Hirota and Yunoue (2009).

general accounts transferred fund. Moreover, National Health Insurance operations are conducted by insurers (most of which are municipalities) ranging in scale from small to large, so there may be differences in scale.

In this chapter, an analysis shall be conducted that considers the content of these operations, their targets, the financial resources that are based on the system, and the differences in scale. A summary of the differences between our study and the existing research follows.

First, as in the existing research, our focus is on the costs of administrative work (and the costs of management); however, here operations relating to administrative work will be extracted and the existence of economies of scale will be verified. The focus in this chapter is not only on expenditure items, but also on revenue items. The financial resources for the cost of administrative work include general accounts transferred funds. Therefore, in this chapter, improved efficiency for the cost of administrative work will be evaluated after controlling for general accounts.

Second, the analysis period for all of the existing research was the period up to fiscal 2007. However, the latter-stage elderly medical care system was introduced in fiscal 2008, which greatly transformed the National Health Insurance system. At that time, a new mechanism for the adjustment of finances relating to early-stage elderly and latter-stage elderly and joint projects was introduced. There is a discontinuity in terms of systems for the data up to fiscal 2007 and data from fiscal 2008 onwards, and the characteristics of the National Health Insurance system are considered to have changed based on this new system. Therefore, in this chapter, data from fiscal 2008 onwards is used.

Third, in order to evaluate economies of scale, it is necessary to consider municipal mergers. Since the first major municipal mergers in the Japanese Heisei period, area expansion has been conducted by means of the merging of municipalities. During the analysis period for this chapter, from fiscal 2008 to fiscal 2010, a number of municipalities were merged. Therefore, economies of scale in the National Health Insurance system will be evaluated after creating balanced panel data that take into consideration these municipal mergers and the controlling effects of area expansion.

Fourth, as economies of scale for National Health Insurance operations may vary depending on the scale, the analysis was carried out after dividing the data into the scale of insurers, according to the number of insured persons. In particular, if economies of scale are seen in small-scale insurers, we consider that improvement of the cost efficiency of administrative work could be achieved through area expansion, such as to the unit of prefectures.

This chapter differs from the existing research on the above four points. The analytical method used will be described in the next section.

3 Analytical Method

In this chapter, most of the data for analysis comes from the Ministry of Health, Labour and Welfare's "Report on the Status of National Health Insurance Operations (Operations Annual Report)."[5] The analysis period is from fiscal 2008 to fiscal 2010.[6] In this chapter, in addition to the estimations for each single year from fiscal 2008 to fiscal 2010, estimations are made from the panel data.

However, the total number of insurers in each fiscal year is different owing to the progress made so far in merging municipalities. Therefore, in order that the total number of insurers match the total in fiscal 2010, which is the final year of the analysis period, the number of insurers in fiscal 2008 and 2009 were adjusted to reflect the actual mergers of municipalities, and the three-year balanced panel data set was prepared.[7]

The above data were used to create the following variables. Here, data in "" are the names of the data items in the "Report on the Status of National Health Insurance Operations (Operations Annual Report)" while data in 【】 indicates the created variables. As this chapter focuses on the relationship between the cost of administrative work and economies of scale, 【the cost of administrative work per insured person】 is used for the explained variable and 【the number of insured persons】 for the scale-factor explanatory variable.

- Explained variable
  【Cost of administrative work per insured person】 = "general affairs costs"/ "number of insured persons"
- Explanatory variable (scale factor)
  【Number of insured persons】 = "number of insured persons"

Next, operations related to the National Health Insurance administrative work will be considered as the operations factor. As described above, National Health Insurance operations include administrative processing, the collection of insurance contributions, and the review of receipts. Therefore, the costs of employees actually

---

[5]In the "Report on the Status of National Health Insurance Operations (Operations Annual Report)," "Table 13 Report on the Status of National Health Insurance Operations (Operations Annual Report) Table A," "Table 14 Report on the Status of National Health Insurance Operations (Operations Annual Report) Table B (1)," and "Table 14 Report on the Status of National Health Insurance Operations (Operations Annual Report) Table B (2)" were used.

[6]Following the launch in fiscal 2008 of the latter-stage elderly medical care system, the latter-stage elderly aged 75 years and above and the early-stage elderly with a disability were withdrawn from the health insurance system and incorporated into the latter-stage elderly medical care system. Therefore, data on the persons in question differs in the "Report on the Status of National Health Insurance Operations (Operations Annual Report)" from before and after fiscal 2008. In this chapter, data from fiscal 2008 and onwards was used in consideration of the implementation of the latter-stage elderly medical care system.

[7]Number of insurers in fiscal 2008 was 1646 and in fiscal 2009 and fiscal 2010, it was 1587. When preparing the panel data, the number of insurers in each fiscal year was unified as 1587.

responsible for administrative processing; the current year's insurance contributions payment rate, and the carried-forward delinquent payments insurance contributions payment rate, reflecting the number of payment collections; and the inpatient and outpatient rates, which indicate the number of receipts reviewed, shall be used as the explanatory variables.

- Explanatory variable (operations factor)
  【Employee costs per insured person】 = "employee salary costs, etc."/"number of insured persons"
  【Current year's payment rate】 = "current year's collection amount"/("current year's settled amount"—"current year's whereabouts-unknown persons' settled amount")
  【Payments rate for carried-forward delinquent payments】 = "carried-forward delinquent-payments collection amount"/("carried-forward delinquent payments settled amount"—"carried-forward delinquent payments whereabouts-unknown persons' settled amount")
  【Inpatient rate】 = "hospitalization number of cases"/"number of insured persons"
  【Outpatient rate】 = "non-hospitalization number of cases"/"number of insured persons"

Further, in National Health Insurance operations, special accounting is not independent and employee costs for administrative work are covered by "transferred funds" from the general accounts of municipalities. Therefore, the statutory portion of transferred funds will be considered as the finances factor.

- Explanatory variable (finances factor)
  【transferred funds per insured person (statutory portion)】 = ("transferred funds"—"other" in "transferred funds")/"number of insured persons"

Here, the "(reprinted) long-term care portion" "(reprinted) latter-stage elderly support funds, etc., portions" are removed from the "transferred funds (statutory portion)" data because these portions are expended in finances for the public long-term care and latter-stage elderly medical care systems.

Based on the above, after controlling for the operations factors and the finances factor, we analyze the factors for economies of scale relating to the cost of administrative work. It is assumed that the fundamental estimation model is determined by the following log-linear cost function.[8] Here, μ is the error term.

[8]It was decided to use a logarithmic linear function in order to interpret the coefficients obtained from the estimations as elastic values. Izumida (2003) organizes the value as a costs function and the coefficient corresponding to cost elasticity.

$$\ln(y_{it}) = a_0 + a_1 \ln(H_{it}) + a_2(\ln(H_{it}))^2 + a_3 \ln(C_{it}) + a_4 \ln(S_{it}) + a_5 \ln(M_{it}) + a_6 \ln(Z_{it}) + \mu_{it} \quad (1)$$

The left-side explanatory variable y_{it} is 【cost of administrative work per insured person】. On the other hand, the right-side explanatory variable, H_{it}, shows the scale of the insured persons, and 【number of insured persons】 and its square were used. For C_{it}, 【employee costs per insured person】 was used as the costs of administrative work. As the operational factors relating to administrative work, operations for the collection of insurance contributions such as 【current year payment rate】 and 【payment rate for carried-forward delinquent payments】 were set as $S_{it.}$, and operations corresponding to the number of reviews of receipts, including 【inpatient rate】 and 【outpatient rate】. 【Transferred funds per insured person (statutory portion)】, as the revenue necessary for this administrative work, was set as Z_{it}. In addition, subscript i shows the insurers, and t shows each fiscal year. Table 1 presents the descriptive statistics of the variables.

4 Results of Estimations

Table 2 shows the results of the estimations by single fiscal year, with the cost of administrative work as the explained variable.

Model 1 indicates the results of the estimations for fiscal 2008, Model 2 for fiscal 2009, and Model 3 for fiscal 2010. In these results, 【employee costs per insured person】 were positively significant, while 【number of insured persons】 was negatively significant for the linear term and positively significant for the quadratic term.

In terms of economies of scale, it is clarified that the 【number of insured persons'】 linear term is negatively significant and the quadratic term is positively significant. Therefore, economies of scale relating to the number of insured persons are acting on the 【cost of administrative work per insured person】. Consequently, while 【employee costs per insured person】 is a factor causing the cost of administrative work to increase, if expansion of scale on the unit of the insurers increases the number of insured persons, the cost of administrative work can be reduced.

Next, financial resources for the costs of administrative work, the 【general accounts transferred funds per insured person (statutory portion)】 were found to have a positively significant effect. In other words, transferred funds from general accounts are a factor increasing the cost of administrative work per insured person.

Further, individual operations within the National Health Insurance program's scope of operations were verified. The results show that in operations involving collection of insurance contributions, neither the 【current year's payment rate】 nor the 【payments rate for carried-forward delinquent payments】 had a significant

Table 1 Descriptive statistics

Item name	No. of samples	Average	Standard deviation	Minimum value	Maximum value
Cost of administrative work per insured person	5169	6844.696	6058.020	0.000	98,470.930
Cost of benefits per insured person	5169	249,158.900	41,215.440	92,701.360	490,601.500
Money transferred per insured person (statutory amount)	5169	20,493.640	8611.405	3946.226	96,099.160
Money transferred per insured person (non-statutory amount)	5169	6246.039	11,152.050	0.000	237,932.600
Receipts-expenses balance per insured person	5169	12,926.340	24,730.620	−209,166.500	468,730.700
Employee costs per insured person	5169	5372.259	5232.949	0.000	83,138.270
Insurance contributions per insured person	5169	59,597.850	11,119.780	14,547.070	109,573.900
No. of insured persons per habitable area	5163	406.205	730.342	3.873	6703.529
Early-stage elderly rate	5169	0.324	0.061	0.080	0.561
Inpatient rate	5169	0.238	0.064	0.057	0.616
Outpatient rate	5169	7.371	0.829	3.736	12.033

effect. In the receipt-review operations, 【inpatient rate】 had a positively significant effect, but a significant result was not obtained for the 【outpatient rate】. Therefore, the effects of economies of scale were not observed in operations that involved the collection of insurance contributions; but in receipt-review operations, while the 【inpatient rate】 was a factor increasing the cost of administrative work, the results showed that the 【outpatient rate】 does not affect the cost of administrative work.

Table 3 shows the results of the estimations from panel data. Different results were obtained from the estimations by single fiscal year for the following results. The same results were obtained for economies of scale from the number of insured persons, financial resources for the administrative work from the general account transferred funds (statutory portion), and operations to collect insurance contributions, but the 【outpatient rate】, which is related to receipt-review operations, had a negatively significant result. A fixed effects model that considers individual characteristics was adopted for the panel analysis, as results at the 1% level were rejected in the Hausman test, and based on the individual characteristics of insurers and changes to the fiscal year, it was understood that the 【outpatient rate】 does not increase the cost of administrative work.

Table 2 Results of estimations of the cost of administrative work (Models 1–3)

Cost of administrative work per insured person	Model 1		Model 2		Model 3	
	FY2008		FY2009		FY2010	
	Coefficient	*t*-value	Coefficient	*t*-value	Coefficient	*t*-value
Employee costs per insured person	0.4480	39.56***	0.5169	45.48***	0.4329	41.03***
No. of insured persons	−0.3488	−4.69***	−0.3116	−4.29***	−0.5609	−8.75***
No. of insured persons 2	0.0141	3.51***	0.0129	3.29***	0.0250	7.17***
General accounts money transferred per insured person (statutory portion)	0.2642	8.22***	0.2033	6.79***	0.2315	8.10***
Current year's payment rate	−0.2483	−0.84	−0.3370	−1.18	0.1073	0.41
Carried-forward delinquent payments portion payment rate	0.0077	0.33	−0.0043	−0.18	0.0247	1.15
Inpatient rate	0.2704	5.60***	0.2612	5.41***	0.2601	5.85***
Outpatient rate	0.0392	0.40	0.0795	0.87	0.0814	0.94
Constant term	4.5404	7.70***	4.1393	7.33***	5.9815	11.38***
Modified R square	0.6778		0.7102		0.7059	
F-Test	F(8,1468) = 389.670***		F(8,1495) = 461.510***		F(8,1511) = 456.780***	
No. of observations	1477		1504		1520	

Remark 1 *, **, ***indicate that the null hypothesis was rejected and that these are statistically significant results at the significance levels of 1, 5, and 10%, respectively
Remark 2 In the panel analysis, a fixed effects model was adopted based on the Hausman Test

As mentioned above, many of the insurers in the National Health Insurance program are small-scale municipalities. It is considered that greater economies of scale can be expected for small-scale municipalities, but economies of scale are already being utilized in large-scale municipalities. Specifically, economies of scale differ depending on the scale of the insurer. Therefore, the quartile method was used for the prepared panel data and the estimations were carried out to clarify the features according to scale, in terms of the number of insured persons. Table 3 shows the results of the estimations. The 4th quartile indicates the large-scale insurers that have a significant number of insured persons, the 1st quartile shows the

Table 3 Results of estimations of the cost of administrative work (Models 4–7)

Cost of administrative work per insured person	Model 4		Model 5		Model 6		Model 7	
	Total no. of samples		Large-scale insurers		Medium-scale insurers		Small-scale insurers	
	Coefficient	*t*-value	Coefficient	*t*-value	Coefficient	*t*-value	Coefficient	*t*-value
Employee costs per insured person	0.2580	24.75***	0.3982	14.18***	0.3019	21.15***	0.1865	8.41***
No. of insured persons	−3.4151	−4.74***	−13.3241	−2.37**	−1.2638	−1.04	−7.3483	−3.87***
No. of insured persons 2	0.1497	3.37***	0.5843	2.19**	0.0605	0.85	0.4862	3.53***
General accounts money transferred per insured person (statutory portion)	0.0268	1.74*	0.0130	0.51	0.0036	0.18	0.0548	1.52
Current year's payment rate	0.3159	1.16	0.3766	0.78	0.0499	0.14	0.8012	1.40
Carried-forward delinquent payments rate	0.0075	0.53	0.0535	1.67*	0.0071	0.35	−0.0104	−0.43
Inpatient rate	0.0889	1.81*	0.1199	0.75	0.1124	1.62	0.1077	1.35
Outpatient rate	−0.4768	−3.80***	−0.9323	−3.18***	−0.3866	−2.28**	−0.4285	−1.72*
FY2008 dummy	−0.0532	−7.04***	−0.0467	−4.03***	−0.0805	−7.35***	−0.1105	−4.87***
FY2009 dummy	−0.0935	−15.15***	−0.0440	−4.41***	−0.1096	−13.03***	−0.1676	−9.84***
Constant term	25.8105	8.60***	82.7131	2.79***	13.4969	2.52**	35.4993	5.23***
Modified R square	0.329		0.3216		0.3784		0.3369	
F-Test	F(1540,2950) = 18.470***		F(418,807) = 14.420***		F(807,1498) = 20.990***		F(352,616) = 15.560***	
Hausman test	chi2(10) = 409.720***		chi2(8) = 104.660***		chi2(10) = 175.470***		chi2(11) = 135.760***	
No. of observations	4501		5163		2262		1105	

Remark 1 *, **, ***indicate that the null hypothesis was rejected and that these are statistically significant results at the significance levels of 1, 5, and 10%, respectively

Remark 2 In the panel analysis, a fixed effects model was adopted based on the Hausman Test

small-scale insurers that have few insured persons, and the 2nd and 3rd quartiles denote the medium-scale insurers.

From the results of the estimations, it was confirmed that 【employee costs per insured person】 was positively significant for all scales of insurers, and 【employee costs per insured person】 is a factor that increases the cost of administrative work. With regard to 【number of insured persons】, large-scale insurers and small-scale insurers were negative with the linear function and became positively significant with the quadratic function, which confirms that there are economies of scale. Therefore, the scale of the municipality does not necessarily affect economies of scale.

In the results for factors relating to administrative work, 【payments rate for carried-forward delinquent payments】 was a factor increasing the cost of administrative work. In the case of large-scale insurers, there were many delinquent payments of insurance contributions, which are considered to increase administrative costs. With regard to the receipt reviews, 【outpatient rate】 was negatively significant for all scales of insurers, indicating that receipt reviews do not necessarily increase the cost of administrative work.

5 Conclusion

The focus of this chapter was on economies of scale relating to the number of insured persons in National Health Insurance operations, and after controlling for general accounts transferred funds (statutory portion), an analysis was carried out which took the content of the administrative work into consideration.

As in the existing research, the results of the empirical analysis showed the presence of economies of scale relating to the number of insured persons for the cost of administrative work in National Health Insurance finances. In other words, it was clarified that by securing a certain number of insured persons, economies of scale can be demonstrated and that the cost of administrative work for National Health Insurance operations can be reduced.

Moreover, in this chapter, an analysis was conducted according to the scale of the insurers, specifically in terms of the number of insured persons, and it was confirmed that economies of scale are found both in regions where insurers have few insured persons and in regions where insurers have a large number of insured persons.

In addition, as employee costs is a factor that increases the cost of administrative work, economies of scale relating to the number of insured persons were considered for the cost of administrative work per insured person. After controlling for the financial resources of the general accounts transferred funds (statutory portion), it was shown that employee costs and the inpatient rate increase the cost of administrative work, but they also have economies of scale relating to the number of insured persons. Therefore, it was clarified that expanding the scale in terms of the unit of insurers and increasing the number of insured persons can reduce the cost of administrative work per insured person.

Based on the results of the analysis in this chapter, it was possible to confirm the existence of economies of scale relating to the number of insured persons. As has been investigated in recent years for National Health Insurance operations, which are mainly managed by municipalities, expanding the scale of the unit from municipalities to prefectures may lead to a reduction in the cost of administrative work.

Chapter 9
Expanding the Scope and Improving the Efficiency of Long-Term Care Insurance Operations

1 Introduction

1.1 Overview of Long-Term Care Finances

Since the beginning of the Heisei era in Japan, administrative and financial management by local governments has aimed to utilize scale and economies of scale through the merger of municipalities and area expansion. To reflect this, management of administrative districts and the allocation of administrative work have been restructured.[1]

In the context of the declining birth rate, small-scale municipalities that are highly dependent on the national government find it difficult to maintain the personnel and financial resources to deal with the complex administrative processing involved; therefore, there is a need to secure administrative districts of a certain scale and to conduct efficient operations. For those divisions in which finances have been tight since the system was first established, the formation of associations for certain aspects of administrative affairs (hereafter, partial-affairs associations) and wide-area unions has been actively recommended for long-term care. The number of municipalities conducting area expansion for long-term care insurance operations in 2000 was 408, but by 2003, this had increased to 502.[2]

---

[1]With regard to the mergers of municipalities, after the enactment of the Special Merger Law in 1999, following the strengthening of financial measures to support mergers in the Special Merger Law enacted in 1999, the number of municipal bodies declined from 3200 at the end of March 1999 to 1727 at the end of March 2010.

[2]According to the Ministry of Health, Labour and Welfare (2006) "Meeting of the Heads of the Departments Responsible for Long-term Care Insurance Nationwide", the breakdown of municipalities conducting insurance management over a wide area was 307 municipalities in wide-area unions, 183 municipalities in partial-affairs associations, and 12 municipalities conducting joint projects for the mutual stabilization of municipal finances.

Y. Adachi, *The Economics of Tax and Social Security in Japan*,
https://doi.org/10.1007/978-981-10-7176-8_9

Long-term care insurance finances are in a serious condition. Japan has moved decisively toward "socialization of care" for the frail elderly by initiating public, mandatory long-term care insurance (LTCI) on April 1, 2000. The long-term care insurance covers both institutional and community-based caregiving. Everyone age 40 and older pays premiums. Everyone age 65 and older is eligible for benefits based strictly on physical and mental disability, in six categories of need. Benefits are all services, with no cash allowance for family care, and are generous, covering 90 percent of need.

When the system was first established in fiscal 2000, the total costs of long-term care were 3.6 trillion yen, but by 2005, this had increased to 6.8 trillion yen, and by the time of implementation in 2010, long-term care costs had more than doubled to 7.9 trillion yen. Insurance contributions and national revenue support the total costs of long-term care. The average standard amount for first insured persons insurance contributions, which are used to pay for the rapidly increasing total costs of long-term care, are rising fast. On average, the standard amount of First insured persons' insurance contributions in the first period (2000–2002) were 2911 yen, but by the fourth period (2009–2011), the figure rose to 4160 yen.

The total costs of long-term care are composed of the costs of long-term care benefits (insurance benefit costs) and long-term care administrative work costs (general affairs costs). According to the Ministry of Health, Labour and Welfare's (2009) "Report on the Survey of Actual Conditions in Long-term Care Insurance," in terms of the national average, long-term care insurance operations, special accounting expenditure breakdown, and the costs of long-term care benefits constitute more than 90% of the total costs, while long-term care administrative work costs make up only a small percentage.

In this chapter, we focus on the area expansion measures that the Ministry of Health, Labour and Welfare first recommended when the system was first set up, and which it continues to advocate as a means of achieving efficiency and stability in long-term care finances. According to the Ministry of Health, Labour and Welfare's (2006) document "Meeting of the Heads of the Departments Responsible for Long-term Care Insurance Nationwide," the specific measures for area expansion are the creation of partial-affairs associations and wide-area unions. Table 1 indicates the specific content of long-term care insurance operations shown in the Osaka Prefecture (2012), "Report of the Study Group on the Area Expansion of Long-term Care Insurance in Osaka Prefecture." This chapter considers the allocation of operations in the event of area expansion for long-term care insurance operations either by means of a wide-area union on the unit of prefectures, or between municipalities.

Three advantages can be cited for the area expansion of long-term care insurance operations. The first of these is the opportunity to reduce management costs through joint projects. Second, the ability to respond flexibly to diverse needs through the joint management of long-term care services with the administrative district. Third is the opportunity to reduce risk by expanding the scale of insurers' finances. Conversely, the disadvantages present considerable problems, such as the fact that expansion requires adjustment of finances between insurers, it renders operations for the collection of insurance contributions more complicated, and it can be unclear who has responsibility.

Table 1 Specific content of long-term care insurance operations in a wide-area union

		Wide-area union	Municipalities
Costs of long-term care administrative and other work	Accounting work	– Establishment of special accounting • budget • revenue • expenditures – Cost burden, payment of national, government, and municipalities burden – Insurance contributions payments – Application for loans to the Fiscal Stability Fund, repayment of debt	Cost burden
	Work to set the insurance contributions	– Formulation of the long-term care insurance operations plan – Setting the insurance contributions, setting the insurance contributions rate for primary insured persons	* Cooperation for plan formulation (considering geographical conditions, the current state of the system to supply long-term care services, etc., to set optimal daily life zones, etc.)
	Work to collect the insurance contributions	– Supporting municipalities – Setting a long-term care insurance examination board	– Ordinary collection (assignment of payment-related administrative work to private individuals, agency administrative work for direct payments through life insurance implementation agencies) – Special collection (confirmation and notification of targeted persons, etc.) – Demands, processing delinquent payments
	Administering the certification of insured persons		– Administering the certification of insured persons, preparing ledgers, issuing insured persons certificates, etc.
	Necessary long-term care certification work		– Necessary long-term care (support) certification administrative work – Establishing long-term care certification review boards

(continued)

Table 1 (continued)

		Wide-area union	Municipalities
Long-term care benefits work	Insurance benefits work	Insurance benefits	Work related to accepting applications
	Education work	• Operations that contribute to the optimization of long-term care benefits, including measures toward improving the quality of care managers • Long-term care benefits expenses notification (information required by insured persons)	• Optimization of necessary long-term care certification • Optimization of housing repairs • Welfare-equipment purchasing and loan-related surveys • Matching with medical information (required medical information) • Work to contribute to the optimization of long-term care benefits, such as guidance, audits, etc.
	Inspection work	Care plan inspection, general inspection, utilization of benefit results	Care plan inspection, general inspection, utilization of benefit results
	Local support project work	Work to designate and guide operators	– Implementing local support projects – Establishing and managing comprehensive local support centers
	Work to maintain the long-term care services infrastructure	– Designating and guiding operators (partially subsidized)	– Designating and guiding operators (partially subsidized) (community-based services)

Source Based on Osaka Prefecture (2012), "Report of the Study Group on the Area Expansion of Long-term Care Insurance in Osaka Prefecture."

Area expansion may have different effects based on the type of long-term care service and the usage conditions by necessary long-term caregivers. When the long-term care insurance system was established, the number of first insured persons was 21.56 million. However, this had increased rapidly to 25.11 million by 2005 and to 29.10 million by 2010. Alongside this, the number of recipients has also been rising.

The operational costs for long-term care can be divided into number of recipients and per capita costs. Figure 1 shows the number of recipients and per capita costs by long-term care service.[3] Per capita costs declined temporarily around the time of

[3]Long-term care services include various services according to the level of necessary long-term care. If the level of necessary long-term care is low, home services such as day-care services and short-term admission services are used. As the level of necessary long-term care becomes higher, community-based services can be used, such as those that are provided even at night or early in the morning. In addition, in the event that it becomes difficult to continue long-term care at the person's home, they can be admitted to a facility.

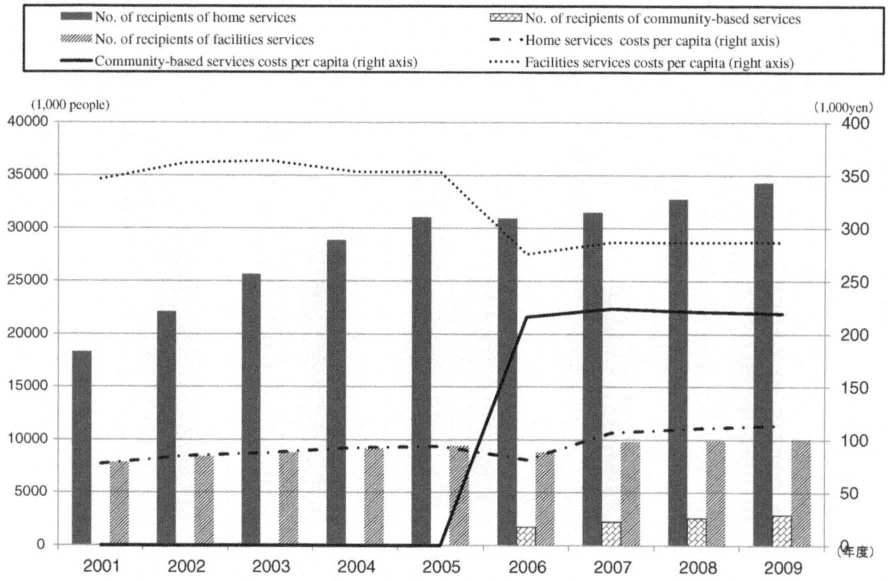

Fig. 1 Trends in the number of recipients and per capita costs by long-term care services. *Source* Based on the Ministry of Health, Labour and Welfare, "Report on the Survey of Actual Conditions in Long-term Care Insurance (Operations Annual Report 2010)." "Mild" indicates necessary long-term care at levels 1 and 2, and "serious" represents necessary long-term care at levels 4 and 5

the establishment of community-based services, but have continuously increased since the establishment of the system. Breaking down the number of recipients, the highest is for home services, with facilities services at approximately one quarter of this number. In per capita costs, facilities services costs are the highest, followed by community-based services costs, with home services costs being the lowest.

In other words, a feature of facilities services is that they have fewer recipients compared to home services, but a higher per capita cost. The opposite trend is seen for home services, which have a larger number of recipients, but for which the per capita costs are being kept low.

Figure 2 shows the trend in long-term care costs by the level of necessary long-term care. For necessary long-term care, serious long-term care costs are high. In this chapter, "serious" indicates necessary long-term care at levels 4 and 5.[4]

---

[4]The states of necessary long-term care are defined in the Nursing Care Insurance Law for the Elderly (Article 7). According to its "categories corresponding to the different levels of long-term care needed," persons at necessary support levels 1 and 2 are eligible for preventive benefits as requiring social support. Persons at necessary long-term care levels 1–5 are eligible for long-term care benefits. Necessary long-term care level 1 is a state requiring partial long-term care, necessary long-term care level 2 is a mild state requiring long-term care, necessary long-term care level 3 is a medium-level state requiring long-term care, necessary long-term care level 4 is a serious state requiring long-term care, and necessary long-term care level 5 is the most serious state, requiring

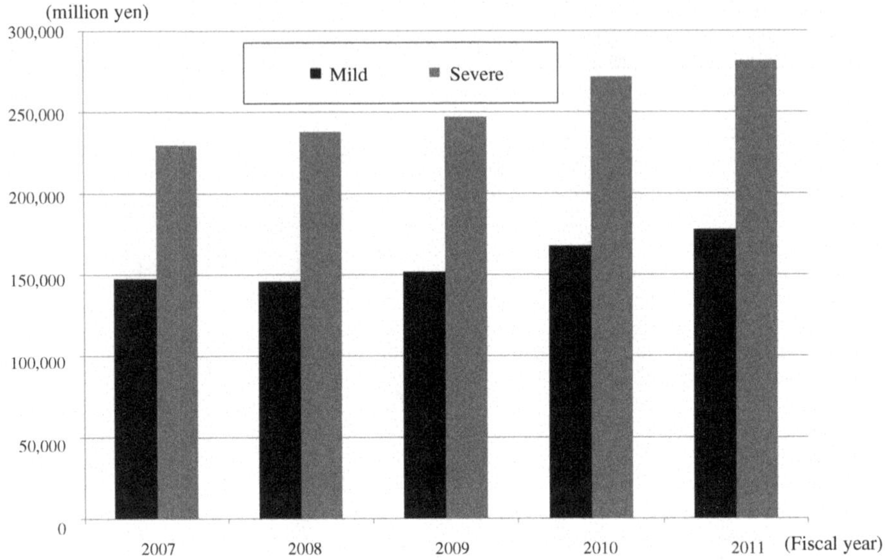

Fig. 2 Trends in long-term care costs by level of necessary long-term care *Source* Based on Ministry of Health, Labour and Welfare, "Report on the Survey of Actual Conditions in Long-term Care Insurance (Operations Annual Report 2010)." "Mild" indicates necessary long-term care at levels 1 and 2, and "serious" represents necessary long-term care at levels 4 and 5

The focus below will be on the provision of benefits-in-kind services within local governments' social security services, such as those relating to long-term care insurance benefits. For example, if there is even a single recipient within an administrative district, even if they are in a remote location, it is necessary to have a long-term care employee to provide the person with long-term care services. However, in long-term care services, even if the number of employees increases through area expansion, in the event that an insufficient number of users of these services can be secured, then area expansion will not necessarily result in economies of scale. Moreover, the breakdown of costs for benefits-in-kind services will be different depending on the type of service. Facilities services entail not only personnel costs for the providers of long-term care services but also fixed costs such as those associated with the maintenance and management of buildings in which the services are provided. Insurance benefit costs of home services and community-based services, which have variable costs, are basically dependent on the number of recipients.

long term care. In this chapter, with reference to the "categories corresponding to the different levels of necessary long-term care needed," the concepts of "mild" and "serious" were used. Further, in the event that a person at the necessary long-term care level 3 can move by their own efforts, it is considered that this is clearly different to the serious levels of levels 4 and 5 of necessary long-term care.

On the other hand, unlike long-term care services themselves, long-term care administrative work can be processed jointly and collectively. This is because the general affairs costs, which constitute the cost of administrative work, are fixed costs, so it is very likely that as the number of recipients eligible for long-term care increases, the more such per capita costs will decrease. Therefore, when evaluating whether there are economies of scale associated with area expansion, it is important to distinguish between long-term care services and long-term care administrative work, and to divide the services according to type.

1.2 Existing Research

A wide variety of discussions in the large body of existing research have focused on the economies of scale for local governments' administrative districts. There are studies on the incentives for area expansion and on trends in expenditure and the local allocation of tax following municipal mergers, as well as empirical analysis of the optimum scale for finances and verification of the effects on local public services.

As described in Yoshimura (1999), Hayashi (2002), Uemura and Washimi (2003), and Miyazaki (2006a), it is considered that there are certain economies of scale that have the effect of reducing local governments' expenses. Akai and Takemoto (2008) discussed the optimal scale of local government for this reduction to occur, and performed a simulation based on the estimated parameters.

Nishikawa (2002), Miyazaki (2006b), Hirota (2007), Miyazaki (2010), and Yamashita (2011) also discussed the incentives for area expansion and the merging of municipalities. However, these existing studies did not focus on long-term care services. Although these studies recommend area expansion in general, only a few of them discuss area expansion and financial scale in the field of long-term care insurance operations.

Kobayashi and Natori (2004) conducted a questionnaire survey targeting the mayor of major cities nationwide and the city council chairperson concerning wide area for long-term care insurance operations, and found that the greater the subjective achievement for the elderly health and welfare plan, the greater the approval toward area expansion for long-term care insurance operations.

With regard to that survey, Yamauchi (2008) noted that the questionnaire was conducted before the implementation of long-term care and that the model did not include population size and the area for each municipality. Yamauchi (2008) used data from fiscal 2001, the year after the implementation of long-term care; arranged the variables of population, area, and financial strength, and the demand factors and supply factors for long-term care services; and conducted estimations using a logit analysis. The results of these estimations showed that municipalities with a small population and a weak financial base were more positive about area expansion, while municipalities with a large area were cautious about area expansion.

The existing research has also discussed the efficiency of long-term care administrative work and verified that it is possible ensuring that administrative districts keep to a certain scale. However, the subject of analysis in the existing research was long-term care administrative work, and these studies did not consider long-term care services, which account for a significant portion of long-term care operational costs.

The insurers (mostly municipalities) conduct sectional accounting for long-term care services, using long-term care insurance special accounting. The general affairs costs, which correspond to the costs of long-term care administrative work, are covered through transfers from general accounts. The financial resources that are required in order to pay for the costs of long-term care benefits include insurance contributions, the National Treasury expenditure, prefecture expenditure, and general financial resources. In other words, the financial resources needed for the costs of long-term care administrative work and for long-term care benefits are different.

Yamauchi (2006) and Hirota and Yunoue (2008), whose approach to the problem was similar to ours in this chapter, verified that there are economies of scale for the costs of long-term care administrative work in long-term care insurance special accounting.[5] However, it would have been helpful if they had also focused on the large-scale expenses of the costs of long-term care benefits.

As explained in the previous section, long-term care operational costs include the costs of both long-term care administrative work and of long-term care benefits. In the event that the effects of area expansion are demonstrated, it became more beneficial to the costs of long-term care administrative work by economy of scale, because a feature of the costs of long-term care administrative work is that they are fixed costs. It is possible that the effects of the costs of long-term care benefits will vary depending on the type of long-term care service. There are three types of long-term care service—home services and community-based services, which have variable costs, and facilities services, which have fixed costs—and they clearly have different characteristics. Therefore, it is also necessary to consider that the effectiveness of area expansion will vary for each long-term care service. However, none of the existing studies have considered this perspective.

Therefore, in this chapter, the costs of long-term care administrative work and costs of long-term care benefits will be clearly differentiated; financial variables will be prepared based on the financial resources data of long-term care insurance special accounting, in which each operation is accounted for; and an empirical analysis will be conducted to investigate the economic effects of the area expansion of administrative districts by long-term care service.

[5]While they did not address long-term care insurance, with regard to the management of National Health Insurance, Kishida (2002) and Izumida (2003) clarified that economies of scale in terms of the number of employees engaged in administrative work have an effect on the general affairs costs.

This chapter is structured as follows. Section 2 provides an overview of the data used for empirical analysis and describes the model and the variables. Section 3 summarizes the results of the empirical analysis and reports the findings derived from the results. Section 4 summarizes the results of the analysis.

2 Analytical Method

2.1 Data

The main microdata used for analysis in this chapter come from the Ministry of Health, Labour and Welfare's insured data of "Report on the Status of Long-term Care Insurance Operations."[6] The analysis period is from fiscal 2007 to fiscal 2009. From the aforementioned report, data was collected for "number of insured persons aged 65 years to 74 years," "number of insured persons aged 75 years and above," "number of recipients (primary insured persons)," and "long-term care costs (primary insured persons)" by long-term care service, level of necessary long-term care, and by insurer. Items within quotation marks indicate the data used from this report.

However, owing to the progress made in municipal mergers, the total number of insurers is different in each fiscal year. Moreover, for the data based on the final fiscal year, there is a period during the analysis when both municipal mergers and area expansion were being carried out. There were also cases of insurers who withdrew from the wide-area union they belonged to because of a merger, and cases of insurers who did not merge and remained in a wide-area union.[7]

In order to extract the effects of area expansion on long-term care insurance operational costs, the main problem we address in this chapter, a balanced panel dataset was prepared with fiscal 2007 as the standard. Here, the data on newly merged insurers or those who formed a wide-area union in fiscal 2008 or fiscal 2009 were considered as new data, and the data on insurers that had disappeared at the same time were treated as missing values.

Using the above data, the variables shown below were prepared for each insurer.

[6]Specifically "Table 2<by insurers> the number of first insured persons," "Table 5<by insurers> number of recipients of at-home long-term care (preventive long-term care) services," "Table 6<by insurers>number of recipients of community-based long-term care (preventive long-term care) services," "Table 7<by insurers>number of recipients of facilities services," "Table 8-2<by insurers>insurance benefits long-term care benefits • preventative benefits for first insured persons (number of cases, number of units, costs amount, benefit costs)," and "Table 14<by insurers>long-term care insurance special accounting deductions Insurance operations account—(expenditure)—" were used (http://www.mhlw.go.jp/toukei/list/84-1.html :View date of February 5, 2018).

[7]The number of insurers in fiscal 2007 was 1662, in fiscal 2008 1646, and in fiscal 2009 and fiscal 2010 the number was 1587.

Number of primary insured persons = "number of insured persons aged 65 years to 74 years" + "number of insured persons aged 75 years and above"

Costs of long-term care administrative work per capita = "general affairs costs"/ "The number of primary insured persons"

The focus of this chapter is on economies of scale. A cost function in which average costs decrease according to scale is assumed, and the number of primary insured persons is used as the variable indicating scale.

Next, the variables shown below were prepared, taking into account that the total costs of long-term care are dependent on the composition of population of insurers and the areas of their region. For population composition, the latter-stage aging population rate was calculated from fiscal 2007 to fiscal 2009 from the Ministry of Health, Labour and Welfare's insured data from "Report on the Status of Long-term Care Insurance Operations" and it was set as the variable representing the aging population. For area, "habitable area" was extracted from fiscal 2007 to fiscal 2009 from the Ministry of Internal Affairs and Communications' municipality data from "Survey of Financial Conditions by Municipality."

Latter-stage elderly rate = "75 years and above insured persons"/("insured persons aged 65 years to 74 years" + "insured persons aged 75 years and above")

Habitable area per capita = "habitable area"/"The number of primary insured persons"

Further, from the Ministry of Health, Labour and Welfare's "Report on the Status of Long-term Care Insurance Operations," the data on per capita costs for each long-term care service was limited to the serious level of necessary long-term care and was prepared as shown below. The reason for limiting the analysis to the serious level in this chapter is that the total costs for those at this level are larger than at the mild level. Moreover, it is considered that the trends among those at the serious level of necessary long-term care will become an essential aspect of long-term care insurance finances in the future.

Home services costs per capita = "home services costs amount (primary insured persons)"/"number of recipients of home services (number of primary insured persons)"

Community-based services costs per capita = "community-based services costs amount (primary insured persons)"/"number of recipients of community-based services (number of primary insured persons)"

Facilities services costs per capita = "facilities services costs (primary insured persons)"/"number of recipients of facilities services (number of primary insured persons)"

Home services receipt rate = "number of recipients of home services (primary insured persons)"/"number of primary insured persons"

Community-based services receipt rate = "number of recipients of community-based services (primary insured persons)"/"number of primary insured persons"

Facilities services receipt rate = "number of recipients of facilities services (primary insured persons)"/"number of primary insured persons"

Finally, the method by which we prepared the control variables will be explained. Insurers' financial conditions affect the provision of long-term care services. In this chapter, in accordance with existing research, we used the "real income-to-expenditure ratio," as an indicator of the actual financial condition of insurers, and the "financial strength indicator," which expresses the reliance on national and prefectural government subsidies such as local subsidies. Further, as indicators of the finance implications of long-term care insurance operations special accounting, the variables shown below were prepared from the data on long-term care insurance operations special accounting, in the Ministry of Health, Labour and Welfare, "Report on the Status of Long-term Care Insurance Operations."

Long-term care insurance operations real income-to-expenditure ratio = ("revenue and expenditures discounted amount" - "fund transfer amount")/"revenue total"

Long-term care insurance operations financial strength indicator = "insurance benefit costs"/"expenditure total"

2.2 *Hypothesis*

The total costs of long-term care can be classified broadly as two types of costs: the costs of long-term care administrative work and the costs of long-term care benefits. These two types of operational costs have different qualities and are highly likely to be different even in an efficient administrative district. Therefore, assuming that the effects for both of these long-term care costs would vary depending on the type of expense, they were broken down into costs of long-term care administrative work and costs of long-term care benefits, and the effects of area expansion of the administrative district were verified.

First, with regard to the costs of long-term care administrative work, it is assumed that more or less the same administrative work is conducted regardless of the insurer and that area expansion will have the effect of keeping the costs of long-term care administrative work lower.

Second, with regard to the costs of long-term care benefits, when we assume a certain level of quality of long-term care services and the diversity of persons needing long-term care, it is possible to obtain responses tailored to the individual characteristics of those needing long-term care when providing long-term care services. Therefore, it is highly likely that area expansion will not always contribute toward reducing the costs of long-term care benefits.

However, as described above, the costs of long-term care benefits depend on the type of long-term care service, and there are cases whereby the variable-costs factor for the number of insured persons is large, and others whereby the fixed-costs factor is large. It would seem that in home services and community-based services with variable costs, if the number of insured persons increases, the costs of long-term care benefits will also rise. In contrast, as fixed costs are large for facilities services, it is considered that an increase in the number of insured persons will lead to a reduction in the costs of long-term care benefits per capita.

Therefore, from the above, the following hypothesis was established.

As long as the effects of the aging population are removed, the area expansion of the administrative districts of long-term care services will have different effects on the costs of long-term care administrative work and the costs of long-term care benefits.

To verify this hypothesis, variables representing area expansion, partial-affairs associations, and wide-area unions are used for the area expansion dummy, while habitable area per capita and the receipt rate are also used. The area expansion dummy, habitable area per capita, and the receipt rate are verified from an empirical analysis of the costs of both long-term care administrative work per capita and of long-term care benefits per capita, according to the long-term care service.

2.3 Model

In this chapter, it is assumed that the costs of long-term care administrative work and the costs of long-term care benefits are determined by the following linear function.[8] Here, μ is the error term.

$$\ln(y_{it}) = a_0 + a_1\ln(Z_{it}) + a_2D_{it} + a_3\ln(Z_{it})D_{\mathrm{it}} + a_4\ln(H_{it}) \\ + a_5\ln(K_{it}) + a_6\ln(M_{it}) + + a_7\ln(S_{it}) + a_8\ln(F_{it}) + \mu_{it}$$

The variable explained on the left-hand side y_{it} varies depending on the model. For each long-term care service, the costs of long-term care administrative work per capita, the costs of home services per capita, the costs of community-based services per capita, and the cost of facilities services per capita are set as the explained variable. On the other hand, the explanatory variables on the right-hand side are as follows.

The receipt rate of each of the long-term care services is shown by Z_{it}, and from the model, the home services receipt rate, the community-based services receipt rate, and the facilities services receipt rate were used.[9] The area expansion dummy is D_{it} in which insurers forming partial-affairs associations and wide-area unions are set as 1 and all others as 0. Further, H_{it} uses the number of first insured persons as the variable expressing scale.

For the regional factors, the latter-stage elderly rate is used for K_{1t}, and the habitable area per capita for M_{2t}. For the finance factors, the real

[8]It was decided to use a logarithmic linear function in order to interpret the coefficients obtained from the estimations as elastic values.

[9]In the subsequent actual estimations, the quadratic term of the receipt rate was considered.

income-to-expenditure ratio was used for S_{1t} and the financial strength indicator for F_{2t}. Subscript i shows insurers and t each fiscal year.

As regional factors affect the receipt rate and other explanatory variables, they were adopted as exogenous variables based on the results of the statistical verification by a Sargan test to determine whether they were determined exogenously.

The basic statistics for the above data are summarized in Table 1.

3 Results of Estimations

The results of the estimations are shown in Tables 2 and 3.[10]

3.1 Long-Term Care Administrative Work

After controlling for regional factors, including the latter-stage elderly rate and habitable area per capita, and insurers' finance factors such as the real income-to-expenditure ratio and the financial strength indicator, the relationship between the costs of long-term care administrative work and area expansion were verified (Table 4).

For the receipt rate for each long-term care service, different results were obtained for the costs of long-term care administrative work per capita by service. It was not significant for home services, but was positively significant for both the linear and quadratic functions for community-based services, and negatively significant for facilities services for both the linear and quadratic functions.

With regard to the area expansion dummy, this was negatively significant for home services and community-based services, but was not significant for facilities services. It was clarified that the cross term for the receipt rate and the expansion dummy for home services and community-based services had a negatively significant effect for both the linear and quadratic functions.

Here, in accordance with the estimated parameters, the theoretical values of the costs of long-term care administrative work were calculated based on the receipt rates of long-term care services. At this time, with regard to home services and community-based services with a negatively significant area expansion dummy, it was understood that the presence or absence of area expansion reduced the costs of long-term care administrative work per capita. On the other hand, for facilities services, in which the area expansion dummy was not significant, the effects of area

[10]When actually making the estimations, if the explained variables of the costs of long-term care administrative work per capita and the costs of long-term care benefits per capita were zero, these data were removed from the data used for the estimations.

Table 2 Basic statistics

Item	Definition	No. of samples	Average	Standard deviation	Minimum value	Maximum value
Per capita administrative work costs	General affairs costs/Number of insured persons	4880	8.524	5.533	0.017	95.599
Per capita home services costs	Home services costs (primary insured persons)/No. of recipients of home services (Number of insured persons)	4883	185.628	26.490	0.000	534.287
Per capita community-based services costs	Community-based services costs (primary insured persons)/No. of recipients of community-based services (Number of primary insured persons)	4548	243.505	80.842	0.000	2860.088
Per capita facilities services costs	Facilities services costs (primary insured persons)/No. of recipients of facilities services (Number of primaryinsured persons)	4892	298.518	56.859	0.000	3342.750
Home services receipt rate	No. of recipients of home services (primary insured persons)/Number of primary insured persons	4895	0.157	0.061	0.000	0.442
Community-based services receipt rate	No. of recipients of community-based services (primary insured persons)/ Number of primary insured persons	4895	0.021	0.018	0.000	0.287
Facilities services receipt rate	No. of recipients of facilities services (primary insured persons)/Number of primary insured persons	4895	0.243	0.075	0.000	0.852
Real revenue-to-expenditures ratio	(Revenue and expenditure discounted amount-fund transfer amount)/ revenue. total	4895	0.023	0.024	−0.180	0.195
Financial strength indicator	Insurance benefits/expenditures, total	4895	0.908	0.037	0.304	0.978
Number of No.1 insured persons	65–74 years insured persons + 75 years and above insured persons	4895	17313	38275	24	719624
Latter-stage elderly rate	75 years and above insured persons/(65–74 years insured persons + 75 years and above insured persons)	4895	0.509	0.068	0.295	0.719
Per capita inhabitable land area	Inhabitable land area/Number of No.1 insured persons	4892	0.013	0.024	0.000	0.255

Note The units are 1000 yen for each total long-term care services costs and each total long-term care services benefit costs; percentages for each receipt rate, the real income-to-expenditure ratio, and the latter-stage elderly rate; and km^2 for the area

Table 3 Results of estimations of the cost of administrative work (Models 1–3)

Per capita costs of long-term care administrative and other work	Home services		Community-based services		Facilities services	
	Model 1		Model 2		Model 3	
	Coefficient		Coefficient		Coefficient	
Home services receipt rate	0.074	1.03				
Home services receipt rate 2	−0.006	−0.41				
Community-based services receipt rate			0.248	4.85***		
Community-based services receipt rate 2			0.024	4.30***		
Facilities services receipt rate					−0.449	−2.75***
Facilities services receipt rate 2					−0.309	−5.54***
Area expansion dummy	−2.628	−2.99***	−2.132	−2.54**	1.668	1.27
Area expansion * Home services receipt rate	−2.531	−2.97***				
Area expansion * Home services receipt rate 2	−0.585	−2.97***				
Area expansion *Community-based services receipt rate			−2.142	−2.63**		
Area expansion *Community-based services receipt rate 2			−0.523	−2.78**		
Area expansion *Facilities services receipt rate					2.571	1.32
Area expansion *Facilities services receipt rate 2					0.912	1.28
Number of primary insured persons	−0.024	−3.03***	−0.002	−0.19	−0.020	−2.51**
Latter-stage elderly rate	0.688	10.4***	0.883	13.47***	0.176	2.39**
Per capita inhabitable land area	−0.044	−4.78***	−0.061	−6.78***	−0.074	−8.49***
Real revenue-to-expenditure ratio	−0.035	−5.82***	−0.046	−7.67***	−0.032	−5.30***
Financial strength indicator	−6.668	−36***	−8.576	−36.86***	−6.681	−36.61***
FY2008 dummy	0.001	0.04	−0.005	−0.29	0.006	0.33
FY2009 dummy	−0.001	−0.04	0.021	1.17	0.016	0.91

(continued)

Table 3 (continued)

Per capita costs of long-term care administrative and other work	Home services		Community-based services		Facilities services	
	Model 1		Model 2		Model 3	
	Coefficient		Coefficient		Coefficient	
Constant term	1.816	18.2***	1.853	14.46***	1.143	8.69***
Modified R square	0.267		0.2711		0.276	
Wald test	F(12,4607) = 141.280***		F(12,4289) = 132.950***		F(12,4614) = 146.610***	
AIC	6316.941		5523.32		6286.600	
No. of observations	4620		4302		4627	

Note 1 Data from 2007 to 2009 are panel data. Reports on individual effects have been omitted
Note 2 *** and **indicate a result that is statistically different to zero at the levels of 1 and 5%, respectively. Values in parentheses are t values
Note 3 The estimates were made by long-term care service

expansion on the costs of long-term care administrative work per capita were relatively small.

Therefore, for home services and community-based services, area expansion has the effect of reducing the costs of long-term care administrative work per capita. Moreover, with regard to home services, it was verified that demonstrating economies of scale by increasing the number of primary insured persons through area expansion can lower the costs of long-term care administrative work per capita. In this chapter, the number of primary insured persons represented economies of scale. From the results of the estimation, it had a negatively significant effect for home services and facilities services, but for community-based services the result obtained was not significant. In facilities services, the cost of administrative work per insured person are the so-called fixed costs, and if the number of primary insured persons eligible for long-term care increases, the cost of administrative work per insured person decreases.

3.2 Long-Term Care Benefits Operations

Next, the relationship between long-term care benefits operations and area expansion is considered. As previously mentioned, after controlling for the regional factors of the latter-stage elderly rate and the habitable area per capita, and insurers' finance factors for real income-to-expenditure ratio and the financial strength indicator, the effects on long-term care costs per capita were verified.

For the linear function and quadratic function of the receipt rates of long-term care services, the results were negatively significant for home services and community-based services, but a positively significant result was obtained for facilities services for both the linear and quadratic functions.

Table 4 Results of estimations of the cost of benefits operation (Models 4–7)

Per capita long-term care benefits operational costs	Home services		Community-based services		Facilities services	
	Model 4		Model 5		Model 6	
	Coefficient		Coefficient		Coefficient	
Home services receipt rate	−0.100	−4.74***				
Home services receipt rate 2	−0.040	−8.96***				
Rate of receipt of community-based services			−0.234	−8.44***		
Rate of receipt of community-based services 2			−0.025	−8.17***		
Facilities services receipt rate					0.170	6.72***
Facilities services receipt rate 2					0.060	6.93***
Area expansion dummy	−0.125	−0.49	0.511	0.88	0.283	1.39
Area expansion * home services receipt rate	−0.069	−0.28				
Area expansion * home services receipt rate 2	0.005	0.09				
Area expansion *Rate of receipt of community-based services			0.232	0.84		
Area expansion *Rate of receipt of community-based services 2			0.025	0.78		
Area expansion *Facilities services receipt rate					0.383	1.27
Area expansion *Facilities services receipt rate 2					0.124	1.13
Number of primary insured persons	0.001	0.64***	−0.010	−2.21**	0.003	2.58**
Latter-stage elderly rate	−0.103	−5.23***	−0.147	−4.16***	0.013	1.10
Per capita inhabitable land area	−0.040	−15***	0.041	8.39***	−0.012	−8.74***
Real balance ratio	0.002	1.34	0.009	2.88***	0.001	1.00

(continued)

Table 4 (continued)

Per capita long-term care benefits operational costs	Home services		Community-based services		Facilities services	
	Model 4		Model 5		Model 6	
	Coefficient		Coefficient		Coefficient	
Indicators of financial strength	0.719	13.14***	0.357	2.85***	0.035	1.23
FY2008 dummy	0.013	2.56**	0.028	3.06***	−0.005	−1.80
FY2009 dummy	0.031	5.84***	0.065	6.72***	0.015	5.43***
Constant term	4.955	167.7***	5.178	74.36***	5.735	281.16***
Modified R square	0.307		0.052			0.0694
Wald test	F					

(12,4620) = 171.580***F(12.4296) = 19.700***F(12,4627) = 28.750***AIC−4959.57211.8 −10987.950No. of observations463343094640*Note* The same as in Table 2

No significant result was obtained for the area expansion dummy for all the long-term care services. In addition, no significant result was obtained for any of the services for the cross terms between the receipt rate and the area expansion dummy.

Therefore, it was found that it is not possible to obtain cost-reduction effects for long-term benefits by means of area expansion; this indicates that it would be difficult to use area expansion to improve the efficiency of long-term care benefits operations.

As with the costs of long-term care administrative work, economies of scale for the costs of long-term care benefits were verified and the results showed a positively significant effect for home services and facilities services, but a negatively significant effect for community-based services.

4 Conclusion

In addition to the costs of long-term care administrative work, the focus in this chapter was on the costs of long-term care benefits, which constitute a large share of total costs.

From the results of the analysis, as in the existing research, it was clarified that in long-term care administrative work, area expansion can reduce the costs of long-term care. Examining the effects of area expansion, the results showed that it could improve the efficiency of home services and community-based services, but that it would be difficult to use it to improve the efficiency of facilities services. On the other hand, area expansion is not expected to improve the efficiency of long-term care benefits operations for any of the services.

Keeping long-term care operational costs as low as possible will be essential if we are to improve the efficiency of long-term care benefits operations. However, as area expansion is not expected to reduce the costs of long-term care benefits, it can be assumed that it will be necessary to improve the efficiency of long-term care benefits operations.

For the costs of long-term care administrative work, whose efficiency is expected to improve if area expansion is implemented, the immediate task would be to transform the operations system. This will include consolidating the provision of long-term care and converting to a system that uses cities as units in order to realize the aim: the provision of efficient long-term care services, including an approach for administrative districts in the future.

However, the costs of long-term care benefits depend not only on administrative districts, but also on improvements to the levels of necessary long-term care, the usage rates of long-term care services in regions with high and low population densities. This sort of real-world problem is not considered in this chapter and is an issue for future research.

Chapter 10
Guidelines for Policy Evaluation and Post-integration Reforms

In this book, we have investigated the present situation and the issues concerning tax and social security burden in the context of the advancement of The Comprehensive Reform, focusing in particular on the financial resources that will be needed to increase the sustainability of the social security system. This final chapter provides some guidelines regarding policy evaluation and post-integration reforms in relation to the tax and social security burdens.

Although The Comprehensive Reform is still at the implementation stage, we argue that it is necessary to think about the period after its implementation, and we explain this point of view as follows.

First, Japan's finances will likely worsen from 2024 fiscal onwards. Figure 4 in chapter 1 in the Prologue shows the trends in the ratio of national and local primary balance to nominal GDP according to the Cabinet Office, but as of July 2015, no forecasts have been provided for fiscal 2024 onwards.

However, even after fiscal 2024, the trends of declining birth rate and population aging are unlikely to stop, and expenses related to social security will continue to grow. Therefore, it becomes important for us to consider today what the future holds, in terms of finances from fiscal 2024 onwards.

Second, the strategy of the current Comprehensive Reform is to hike the consumption tax rate to 10% in April 2017, but there are no prospects, although policies leading to securing financial resources other than raising consumption tax are being studied. While not focusing solely on hiking the consumption tax rate, it is important to consider securing more than one financial resources in the future.

In this final chapter, we shall begin by summarizing the implications of each preceding chapter in terms of a policy evaluation of the tax and social security burdens. We shall then consider guidelines for the Post-The Comprehensive Reform.

Y. Adachi, *The Economics of Tax and Social Security in Japan*,
https://doi.org/10.1007/978-981-10-7176-8_10

1 A Policy Evaluation of the Tax and Social Security Burden

The Prologue described Japan's difficult financial conditions and the current state of its social security finances and noted that for future financial reconstruction, the approach of increasing the burden, reducing expenditure, and achieving economic growth are essential and, among them, the approaches taken for the burdens for tax and insurance contributions are particularly important. In addition, it is important to secure financial resources for social security based on the characteristic that the relationship between benefits and burden in social security services weakens in the order of self-payments, insurance contributions, and tax. Analyses were conducted from Chaps. 1–8 on each individual tax or social security burden.

In Chap. 1, estimations of the redistribution effects of income taxation and insurance contributions were made. Specifically, household microdata were used and the inequality scale was measured from income's present discounted value. In this analysis, the redistribution effect was evaluated while considering the effects on income of income taxation and insurance contributions in the lifecycle. The results of the analysis are summarized as follows.

First, a household's income distribution has an expanding trend when evaluated by present discounted value. Second, in contrast to income's expanding trend, income taxation has a positive redistribution effect causing income inequality to shrink. On the other hand, insurance contribution has a negative redistribution effect causing income inequality to expand. Third, when combined, income taxation and insurance contribution have a positive redistribution effect, but this effect has a downward trend. Therefore, it was shown that income inequality develops even after redistribution.

Furthermore, when considered by income group, the redistribution effect for the middle-income group is large, but declines for the low-income group. On estimating by generation group, the redistribution effect for the younger generation was relatively small in the 1960s, but expanded from the 1990s onwards.

Fourth, when assessed by income group and generation group, within the low-income group, income inequality was shown to be the widest among the younger generation, and the redistribution effects for the low-income group's income taxation and insurance contributions were both large for the middle-aged generation. Also, when we verified disparity by income group and by generation group for each decade, it was found that up to the 1990 s, it basically grew larger with each new decade and inequality expanded; but then from the 2000s onwards, inequality declined. While the redistribution effect of income taxation has been declining year by year in each group, the respective trends are different. Therefore, differences occur in the redistribution effects of income taxation and insurance contributions, and these effects vary by income group and generation group.

In Chap. 2, our focus shifted to indirect taxes, including consumption tax, which are considered a financial resource for social security in terms of The Comprehensive Reform. With regard to consumption tax, the problem of regressivity has been noted for the rate of tax burden on household income, with the rate becoming higher as income becomes lower. Therefore, by measuring the burden of individual indirect tax and consumption tax on households, we measured the indirect tax burden structure, including for individual indirect tax.

The results of the analysis can be summarized as follows. First, the low-income group's indirect tax burden rate is relatively high. The 1st quantile indirect tax burden rate is approximately three times larger than that of the *X* quantile. From this, it is recognized that indirect tax is regressive as a whole, including individual indirect tax.

Second, the weight of regressivity is larger for consumption tax than individual indirect tax. In particular, the indirect tax burden rate for consumption tax on the category of "food" is extremely high and its regressivity is relatively high. Therefore, it is necessary to consider some sort of measures to reduce the burden on the low-income group caused by the major regressivity of the consumption tax on "food." For "transport and communications" also, the burden from individual indirect tax is higher than from consumption tax. This is a factor of the burden of individual indirect tax, such as the volatile oil tax.

Third, the effects of a hike in consumption tax rate on households' indirect tax burden rate were considered. A number of policy patterns were estimated and it was found that the more regressivity grows the more the tax is increased. A hike in the consumption tax rate has a negative redistribution effect on the income groups, even if policies are adopted to alleviate the regressivity. This is because a reduced tax rate and zero tax are of benefit not only to the low-income group, but the high-income group as well. Therefore, even in the income redistribution policy, we need to focus on policies according to the target rather than focusing on the tax reduction rate.

In Chap. 3, the effects that income tax deduction and the tax rate have on tax revenues were presented quantitatively. In recent years, the labor force has reduced owing to the declining birth rate, and promoting the employment of women has become an important issue in the context of the concerns that a labor shortage may result in an economic recession. Alongside these changes to social conditions, there have been calls to review the spousal deduction system, which is considered to restrict the participation of married women in the labor market. Japan's finances are in a difficult condition and when reforming the tax deduction and tax rates, it is necessary to consider the kind of effects these reforms will have on labor supply and how tax revenues will change. Therefore, microdata from the Ministry of Internal Affairs and Communications' "National Survey of Family Income and Expenditure" were used to empirically verify the effects of spousal deduction on the participation of married women in the labor market by household income and age group.

First, with regard to the spousal deduction amount for all income groups, the results showed that it had a statistically negative effect on the supply of married women as labor in the high-income group, but the opposite effect on the supply of married women as labor in the low-income group. Therefore, it was clarified that the effect of spousal deduction in terms of suppressing the labor supply of married women does not necessarily occur in all households as this effect was not seen in the low-income group, and so its effects differ depending on the income group.

Second, regardless of age, spouse deduction has a negative effect on the labor supply of married women. However, within the age groups, it was found that this effect of suppressing the employment of married women is stronger in the younger age group than in the middle-aged and elderly groups. Therefore, while spousal deduction suppresses the supply of married women as labor in all the age groups, from the fact that within the groups this effect is stronger in the case of younger women, it could be seen that the extent of the suppression of employment differs according to age.

Third, with regard to income and age, it was found that in the high-income group, the effect of suppressing the employment of married women was detected in all the age groups. Nevertheless, in the low-income group, regardless of the age of the married woman, it was clarified that even if there is spousal deduction, it does not suppress the supply of married women in the labor force.

From the above results, we consider that spousal deductions are not a desirable system because of their impact on the labor supply of married women. The government has made efforts to strengthen the social infrastructure required to support the activities of women in society, by aiming to create a gender-equal society, and through the activities of the Council on Economic and Fiscal Policy. However, in view of this new perspective on the impact of spousal deduction on the participation of women in the labor force, we believe that the government should consider abolishing it. However, the effect of spousal deduction, that of suppressing the supply of married women to the labor market, is limited to the high-income group and is not seen in the low-income group. Thus, it was clarified that it does not affect all income groups in the same way. From this finding, we know that the loss of tax revenue from the effects of spousal deduction on the labor supply only occurs in the high-income group. Therefore, it is necessary to understand that spousal deduction is just one factor, and is not the main factor underlying women's employment adjustment.

Although self-payments and insurance contributions pay for the growing social security services, these financial resources are insufficient and so it is necessary to depend on "public revenue." Under the principle of social insurance scheme, it would be preferable to pursue a balance between benefits and burdens so that the relationship between these is made clear and the shortfall in financial resources from self-payments and insurance contribution is offset. However, social security benefits have hit a ceiling, and the low level of the payment rate is one of the factors underlying this.

In Chap. 4, we conducted analysis of the social security burden in the medical care insurance system. Specifically, in Sect. 1 we examined the National Health Insurance system and in Sect. 2, the latter-stage elderly medical care system. In addition to showing the regional disparity between the insurance contributions determined by the insurers, the relationship between medical care benefits and the burden of insurance contributions was clarified.

In Sect. 1 on the National Health Insurance system, after clarifying the breakdown of the benefits by means of a factor analysis of the costs of medical-services benefits, we investigated the regional disparity in insurance contributions and the relationship between benefits and burdens in terms of the costs of medical care benefits and insurance contributions. The results can be summarized as follows.

First, for the unit per insured person, it was established that regional disparity occurs for both the costs of medical care benefits and insurance contributions; but, when comparing the two, the disparity is higher for insurance contributions than for the costs of medical care benefits.

Compared to the coefficient of variation of the insurance contributions calculated amount, which is determined only by the prescribed calculation method, the coefficient of variation of the insurance contributions settled amount, in which tax reductions and exemptions targeting low-income earners are conducted, is high. This suggests that tax reductions and exemptions are causing the regional disparity in insurance contributions to widen.

Second, based on the trends with regard to the unit of insurers in recent years, the regional disparity in the costs of medical care benefits and insurance contributions was verified for the unit of municipalities. It was found that regional disparity could be reduced further for the unit of prefectures than the unit of municipalities, showing that the area expansion policy involving a shift to the unit of prefectures, which is being implemented as part of The Comprehensive Reform, could reduce the disparity.

Third, on verifying the relationship between the costs of medical care benefits and insurance contributions, as there was a negative correlation, whether by prefecture or by insurer, the results indicated that there is no relationship between the benefits and burdens.

Finally, analyses were conducted for the insurance contributions calculated amount, which is calculated only from insurance contributions and the insurance contributions settled amount that takes into consideration tax reductions and exemptions. In terms of its relationship to the costs of medical care benefits, it was found that the insurance contributions settled amount has a stronger negative correlation than the insurance contributions calculated amount, and so it is possible that tax reductions and exemptions cause the relationship between the benefits and burdens of the medical care benefits and insurance contributions to collapse. Therefore, these findings suggest that tax reductions and exemptions in insurance contributions not only cause the regional disparity to widen, they also further weaken the relationship between the benefits and burdens of both medical care benefits and insurance contributions.

In Sect. 2, the aim was to examine the burdens on the older generation and the younger generation in the context of the expected increase in medical services costs alongside the aging population; for this we took into account the latter-stage elderly medical care system that was established in 2008. First, a factor analysis was conducted on the breakdown of latter-stage elderly medical care benefits in order to clarify the actual conditions of medical care for the elderly aged 75 years and above. Next, disparities in insurance contributions were investigated.

As in the National Health Insurance system, each insurer also decides the insurance contributions in the latter-stage elderly medical care system, so the possibility of regional disparity occurring is high. In this chapter, after clarifying the regional disparity for the disparity using the coefficient of variation as the indicator, we examined how the insurance contributions burden is set for medical care benefits, while aiming to reduce the disparity.

First, in latter-stage elderly medical care, it was found that 90% of the costs of medical care benefits are for hospitalization, outpatient, and drug dispensing, and each of their respective coefficients of variation was small, indicating that regional disparity is also small. It was found that insurance premiums between insurers are larger than regional disparity in medical benefits compared to regions. Insurance premium disparity between insurers is expanding in the adjusted insurance premium amount, in comparing the adjusted insurance premium amount with calculated insurance premium amount. In other words, it can be seen that both tax reductions and exemptions broaden the interregional disparity of premiums while this effect varies depending on the reduction rate. Finally, a positive correlation was seen for the costs of medical care benefits and insurance contributions, but the result indicated that this correlation was weakened by tax reductions and exemptions.

From the above, we understand that while regional disparity is being reduced for medical care costs, most of which are for hospitalization, non-hospitalization, and drug dispensing, the regional disparity in insurance contributions is considerable. Moreover, tax reductions and exemptions, which aim to reduce disparity between areas within prefectures, actually widen the regional disparity in insurance contributions between them, and this effect varies depending on the reduction rate.

In addition, while a correlation was seen between the burden of insurance contributions and the benefits of medical care benefits, the implementation of tax reductions and exemptions weakens this correlation, so it was verified that the correlation relation between the burden of insurance contributions in accordance with the medical services benefits is reduced by tax reductions and exemptions.

Therefore, a point in common between the National Health Insurance system and the latter-stage elderly medical care insurance system is that disparities occur for insurance contributions that exceed the regional disparity for the costs of medical care benefits. Additionally, it was shown that tax reductions and exemptions in these insurance contributions systems not only cause regional disparity to expand, they also weaken the relationship between the benefits and burdens of medical care benefits and insurance contributions still further.

In Chap. 5, insurance contributions for the long-term care system, which was established in fiscal 2005, were analyzed. Since the establishment of this system, it has been forecast that the costs of benefits will rapidly increase due to the aging population and the associated demands this will place on long-term care, and the design of this insurance contributions system has been the subject of debate. Against this backdrop, as in Chap. 4, long-term care was also analyzed from the perspective of the relationship between benefits and burdens and regional disparity.

Further, with reference to the systems in foreign countries, Germany that started long-term care and South Korea that designed such a system in recent years, an analysis was also conducted of the policies to reduce insurance contributions for lowering the provision of benefits and securing financial resources.

The results of the estimations clarified that reducing benefits by abolishing services for necessary long-term care for people at level 2 and below, and securing financial resources, for which an increasing amount is required, for the number of insured persons aged 30 years and above, are policies that will contribute greatly to reducing long-term care insurance contributions.

In fact, if long-term care is provided as in the Korean or German system, it will not only secure funding for the increase in the number of insured persons but also abolishment of long-term care services, prevention services, and services requiring long-term care levels 2 and below, we can suppress benefits. On accumulating the effects of these measures, it actually becomes possible to reduce long-term care insurance contributions by more than 50%. However, increasing the number of insured persons causes regional disparity in long-term care insurance contributions to expand. On the other hand, hiking the self-payment ratio reduces regional disparity, although its effect in terms of reducing insurance contributions is relatively small.

Therefore, while it can be confirmed that to a certain extent aiming to optimize the benefits and burdens has the effect of reducing long-term care insurance contributions, it is necessary to also investigate and ascertain how this will affect regional disparity in long-term care insurance contributions.

In Chap. 6, the focus was on the payment rate of insurance contributions in the National Health Insurance system, where low payment rates are a particular problem, compared to the rates in the tax system and other social security systems. Specifically, the insurance contributions payment rate in the national insurance system was analyzed first in relation to the adjustment of finances, and second from its relation to the method of paying insurance contributions.

The results of the first analysis showed that the adjustment of finances from the special adjustment subsidies (prefecture) has the effect of raising the current year's payment rate, but regular adjustment subsidies (national government) and insurance-base stability transferred funds (municipalities) do not have this effect.

Therefore, in order to raise the payment rate to improve the sustainability of National Health Insurance finances, rather than imposing penalties, such as regular adjustment subsidies (national government), or granting subsidies, including insurance-base stability transferred funds (municipalities), it is necessary to provide incentives for insurers to raise their payment rates, through the introduction of measures such as special adjustment subsidies (prefecture).

Special adjustment subsidies form part of the prefectural expenditure, a fact which suggests that measures on the unit of prefectures are essential to improving insurers' payment rates. In fact, area expansion to the unit of prefectures is being considered for the National Health Insurance system, and the aim is to implement joint efforts for the collection of payments and to set targets for the payment rates. Advancing these types of wide-area measures for the collection of payments would be an important step towards improving the sustainability of National Health Insurance finances.

In the second analysis, the effects on the payment rate of the different methods of paying insurance contributions in the National Health Insurance system were verified. As empirical analysis results in controlling finances factors, delinquent payments carried-forward factor, and environmental factors, it clarified that the influence on the current year's storage rate differs depending on the combination and ratio of pay-as-you-go systems for National Health Insurance premium. Specifically, it was demonstrated that the insurance contributions rate of income-based contributions reduces the current year's payment rate, but asset-based contributions have the effect of increasing the payment rate; while equal contributions do not have a significant effect on payments, but per capita-based contributions reduce the collection of insurance contributions.

In Chap. 7, the focus was on economies of scale relating to the number of insured persons in National Health Insurance operations, and after controlling for transferred funds (statutory portion) in general accounts, an analysis was conducted which took the content of the administrative work into consideration.

As in the existing research, the results of this empirical analysis showed that there are economies of scale relating to the number of insured persons for the costs of administrative work in the National Health Insurance finances. In other words, it was clarified that economies of scale can be demonstrated when the insurers secure a certain number of insured persons, which makes it possible to limit the costs of administrative work in National Health Insurance operations.

Furthermore, in the same chapter, an analysis was conducted by dividing insurers into different scales based on the number of insured persons. It was found that economies of scale can be recognized in both types of region—in regions whose insurers have a small number of insured persons and in regions with insurers with a large number of insured people.

In addition, while employee costs are a factor causing the cost of administrative work to increase, economies of scale relating to the number of insured persons were seen to exist for the cost of administrative work per insured person. After controlling for the financial resources of general account transferred funds (statutory portion), it was found that while employee costs and the inpatient rate increase the cost of administrative work, economies of scale relating to the number of insured persons exist. Therefore, it was clarified that it is possible to reduce the cost of administrative work per insured person by increasing the number of insured persons through expanding scale on the unit of the insurer.

The results of the analysis in this chapter confirmed the existence of economies of scale relating to the number of insured persons. Municipalities mainly conduct National Health Insurance operations, but as has been shown by measures implemented in recent years, it may be possible to control the cost of administrative work by expanding the scale from the unit of the municipality to that of the prefecture.

In addition to the costs of long-term care administrative work, the focus in Chap. 8 was on the cost of long-term care benefits operations, which constitute a large share of total costs.

The results of this analysis clarified that as has also been shown by the results of the existing research, in long-term care administrative work, long-term care costs can be reduced through area expansion. When we examined the effects of area expansion, our results showed that it is possible to aim to improve the efficiency of home services and community-based services, but that it is difficult to improve the efficiency of facilities services. On the other hand, the results indicated that for long-term care benefits operations, area expansion is not expected to lead to improvements in efficiency by area expansion for any of the services.

Improving the efficiency of long-term care benefits operations will be essential if long-term care operational costs are to be reduced, but as it is not expected that area expansion will lead to a reduction in those costs, to reduce it will instead be necessary to improve the efficiency of long-term care benefits operations themselves.

For the costs of long-term care administrative work—where it is expected that area expansion will lead to improvements in efficiency—it is necessary to reexamine the management system with the aim of achieving efficient business improvement; this would include consolidating the provision of long-term care and converting to the unit of the city, as well as the provision of efficient long-term care services, including an approach for administrative districts in the future.

However, the costs of long-term care benefits depend not only on administrative districts but also on improvements to the levels of necessary long-term care, the usage rates of long-term care services and the population densities. This real-world problem was not fully considered in this chapter, but can be considered a topic for future research.

2 Guidelines for the Period Post "The Comprehensive Reform of Social Security and Tax"

Based on the results of the economic analyses of the tax and social security burden conducted in this book, what will be the situation after the implementation of The Comprehensive Reform? We will consider this next, in the following order: income tax, indirect tax, and the social security burden.

2.1 Income Tax

First, it is income tax. As a result of continuing tax cuts on income tax as an economic measure, income tax revenue has declined. Compared to other developed countries, the percentage of the national government's total tax revenue from income tax is low in Japan. On the other hand, income inequality is expanding, so it is desirable to strengthen the income redistribution function of income tax.

In order for income tax to be restored as the fundamental tax among national taxes, first it will be necessary to reform income deductions. It will be essential to consider not only the approach to spousal deduction, which is neutral in terms of ways of working, but also for large-scale deductions on income from salary, insurance contributions, and for public pensions. Furthermore, there is a need to search for other areas requiring reform, with nothing being off limits.

For deductions on income from salary, it is required to reexamine what specific expenditure deductions is deductible to be related expenses to business. Each type of income deduction has a negative income redistribution effect, so switching to tax deductions should be considered. Moreover, in conjunction with the declining birth rate and the aging population, social insurance contributions are expected to increase in the future. Social insurance contribution deductions are full-amount deductions. It is a major factor underlying the loss of tax revenues from income tax. Therefore, for example, setting an upper limit for insurance contribution deductions should be considered.

It is also important to verify public pensions deductions from the relationship with social insurance premium contribution deductions. That is, it is necessary to clarify whether the public pensions deductions lead to correct income inequality between the elderly generation and between generations. The public pension system is a system that carries forward income inequality during the working period to the retirement period. Social insurance contribution deductions are a deduction for all, leading to income tax revenue loss at the contributions stage and even at the benefits stage. Therefore, tax exemptions in the form of public pension deduction are an excessively favorable treatment for public pensions.

Changing the tax rate could be a difficult political process in the real world. Therefore, the income redistribution function of income tax and the ability to procure tax revenue should be strengthened by changing the taxation income brackets.

2.2 *Indirect Tax*

Second, it is indirect tax including consumption tax. Consumption tax will also play a particularly important role in the future as a financial resource for social security. The consumption tax rate is scheduled to be raised to 10% in April 2019, but even if there is a primary balance surplus in fiscal 2020 and in Japan's finances from fiscal 2024 onwards, even a tax rate of 10% will be insufficient to cover its finances. It will be necessary to consider a schedule for raising the consumption tax rate in the period after The Comprehensive Reform.

Also, with regard to reductions in the tax rate, while such a reduction is scheduled to be introduced for food, it is preferable to introduce these in as narrow a range as possible. The reason for this is that reduced tax rates not only make the tax system more complex, they also become a new vested interest and cause a loss in tax revenues. The target efficiency of reductions in tax rates is poor and they have hardly any effect as an income redistribution policy. Therefore, rather than aiming for income redistribution by reducing the tax rate, it is necessary to convert to a policy for social security benefits that is highly efficient in terms of who it targets.

2.3 Social Security Burden

Within the social security burden, let us first consider self-payments. In principle, the medical care insurance burden is 30%, and the elderly have a low self-payment ratio. In principle, the long-term care insurance burden is 10%. However, even among the elderly, the household economic conditions are varied, and some elderly persons have many financial assets. Therefore, there are limits to measuring a household's ability to pay solely from income, and a measurement that includes assets is required. Raising the self-payment ratio is appropriate for households that have a certain level of income and assets.

Changing the self-payment ratio according to the household's financial conditions signifies leaving behind the benefit principle of taxation and incorporating the ability-to-pay principle. However, both medical care insurance and long-term care insurance are facing tight financial conditions, so the partial incorporation of the ability-to-pay principle is a reform worth considering. Increasing the transparency of how the conditions are ascertained is also a prerequisite to achieving a fair allocation of the burden.

Next, we shall discuss insurance contributions. The relation between the burden and the receipt of social security services is stronger for insurance contributions than for consumption tax. Therefore, merely hiking the consumption tax rate should not be considered as the burden for the receipt of social security services; instead, first insurance contributions should be considered.

That said, a problem here is households' ability to bear (pay) the burden. In particular, for households that pay a fixed-amount insurance contribution, the burden of insurance contribution as a percentage of income becomes regressive. Further, in households that pay a fixed-rate insurance contribution, since insurance contributions do not have a minimum tax limit like income tax, the burden from the contribution feels heavier for such households. For these reasons, there are also certain limitations to raising insurance contributions.

Therefore, tax reductions and exemptions for insurance contribution must depart from the principle of social security that prioritizes the relationship between benefits and burdens. While it is essential to show consideration for low-income earners, it would seem important to reconsider the relationship between social security benefits and burdens.

A certain level of regional disparity is unavoidable in the regional insurances of National Health Insurance contributions and long-term care insurance contributions. From the balance of benefits and burden, the higher the benefits, the higher the premium. However, the National Health Insurance system is not a complete regional insurance, and the burden on the general taxpayer from non-statutory transfers has the effect of reducing the National Health Insurance contributions.

This creates a problem of fairness in terms of the burdens placed on subscribers to the National Health Insurance system and the general taxpayer.

To solve this fairness problem for the National Health Insurance system, it will be necessary to reintegrate the chaotic medical care insurance system into regional insurance, such as long-term care. Although the current concrete policy is prefectural units has been to strengthen the system's financial foundation, it is essential to design a place to serve as the final landing point for the medical care insurance system.

3 Conclusion

In this chapter, using the results of the analysis in each chapter of this book, we have provided a summary of the policy evaluations of the tax and social security burdens. Furthermore, we have included guidelines for the period after The Comprehensive Reform. Ideally, the period after The Comprehensive Reform should be planned for while the current series of integrated reforms are being implemented. Despite this, it would seem that the focus of the current financial management is on advancing the present series of reforms without having established a vision for the future.

Not only is the question of securing financial resources a major issue for social security; there is also the issue of limiting benefits. This point goes beyond the scope of this book, but whether or not benefits are efficient can is directly related to the burden size. Restricting benefits tends to have a negative image, but providing a targeted benefits system that is highly efficient is not the same as curtailing necessary benefits. Naturally, necessary benefits will be provided to households that need them, and it is essential to distinguish between benefits that are necessary and those that are unnecessary, and improve the system's efficiency.

Improving the efficiency of social security benefits will help to build a system of social security services that households can feel satisfied with, while also being satisfied with the tax and social security burden that is placed on them. Improving this sense of satisfaction will in turn lead to improvements in the collection rate and the payment rate. The creation of a system of efficient benefits and a sense of satisfaction with regard to the burden is the vision required for the period that will come after The Comprehensive Reform.

Erratum to: The Economics of Tax and Social Security in Japan

Erratum to:
Y. Adachi, *The Economics of Tax and Social Security in Japan*, https://doi.org/10.1007/978-981-10-7176-8

After publication of the book, it was brought to author's attention that in Page 127 of Chapter 5, Table 2 has been resized for better reading, and at the book end in References, the author name "Hirota, Keiro. 2007" has been corrected as "Hirota, Haruaki. 2007" so that the reference should read as: "Hirota, Haruaki. 2007. Verification of municipalities' selection behavior and merger factors. *Planning Administration* 30 (4): 75–81." The erratum book has been updated with the changes.

The updated online version of this book can be found at
https://doi.org/10.1007/978-981-10-7176-8_5
https://doi.org/10.1007/978-981-10-7176-8

Y. Adachi, *The Economics of Tax and Social Security in Japan*,
https://doi.org/10.1007/978-981-10-7176-8_11

References

Abe, Aya. 2000. The effects of the regressivity of insurance contribution son the level of income inequality between generations. *Quarterly Journal of the National Institute of Population and Social Security Research* 36: 67–80.

Abe, Aya. 2001. Amending the system of insurance contributions exemptions in the national pension: non-subscription and non-payment and the effects on regressivity. *Journal of the Japan Center for Economic Research* 43: 134–154.

Abe, Yukiko, and Fumio Otake. 1995. The tax system and the social security system and the labor-supply behavior of part-time workers. *Quarterly Journal of the National Institute of Population and Social Security Research* 31 (2): 120–134.

Adachi, Y., T. Uemura, and Y. Saitoh. 2017. Measuring the burden of indirect taxation including consumption tax in Japan by income group. *Public Finance and Management* 17 (3)

Adachi, Yoshimi. 2015. *The economics of financial resources and benefits in health and medical care and long-term care*. Osaka: Osaka University Press.

Adachi, Yoshimi, and Uemura, Toshiyuki. 2013a. The adjustment of finances and the insurance contributions payment rate in the National Health Insurance system. *Journal of Life-economics Research* 37: 15–26.

Adachi, Yoshimi, and Uemura, Toshiyuki. 2013b. Economies of scale in the National Health Insurance: an empirical analysis for the costs of administrative work and the costs of benefits operations. *Local Finances* 52: 210–223.

Adachi, Yoshimi, and Uemura, Toshiyuki. 2013c. The effects of community-based services on the long-term care costs for residential and facilities services. *Journal of the Board of Audit of Japan* 47: 139–153.

Adachi, Yoshimi, and Uemura, Toshiyuki. 2013d. Improving efficiency for the cost of administrative work in "The National Health Insurance". *Journal of Life-economics Research* 38: 1–9.

Akai, Nobuo, and Takemoto, Toru. 2008. An empirical analysis of approaches for efficient administrative districts and the allocation of administrative work—A verification of the cost reduction effects of restricting the administrative districts. In *Local finances in the era of decentralization*, ed. Kaizuka Hiroaki, 231–272. Tokyo: Chuokeiza-sha, Inc.

André, D., J. Loughrey, C. O'Donoghue, and D. Verwerft. 2010. How regressive are indirect taxes? A microsimulation analysis for five European countries. *Journal of Policy Analysis and Management* 29 (2): 326–350.

Chernick, H., and A. Recshovsky. 1997. Who pays the gasoline tax? *National Tax Journal* 50 (2): 233–259.

Y. Adachi, *The Economics of Tax and Social Security in Japan*,
https://doi.org/10.1007/978-981-10-7176-8

Davies, J., F. St-Hilaire, and J. Whalley. 1991. Some calculations of lifetime tax incidence. *The American Economic Review* 74 (4): 633–649.

DeCicca, P., and L. McLeod. 2008. Cigarette taxes and older adult smoking: Evidence from recent large tax increase. *Journal of Health Economics* 27 (4): 918–929.

Decoster, A., J. Loughrey, C. O'Donoghue, and D. Verwerft. 2010. How regressive are indirect taxes? A microsimulation analysis for five European countries. *Journal of Policy Analysis and Management* 29 (2): 326–350.

Fukawa, Tetsuo. 2006. Changes to households and income distribution. In *Japan's income distribution: the expansion of disparity and the role of policy*, ed. Oshio Takashi, Tajika Eiji, and Fukawa Tetsuo. Tokyo: University of Tokyo Press.

Fukui, Tadashi, and Yasushi, Iwamoto. 2007. Policy Options for financing the future health and long-term care costs in Japan. In *Fiscal policy and management in East Asia*, ed. Takatoshi Ito, and Andrew Rose, 415–442. Chicago: University of Chicago Press.

Fullerton, D., and D. Rogers. 1991. Lifetime versus annual perspectives on tax incidence. *From National Tax Journal* XLIV(3): 277–287.

Go, S.D., M. Kearney, S. Robinson, and K. Thierfelder. 2005. An analysis of south africa's value added tax. *World Bank Policy Research Working Paper* 3671.

Gronau, R. 1973. The intrafamily allocation of time: The value of the housewives' time. *American Economic Review* 63 (4): 634–651.

Gronau, R. 1977. Leisure, home production and work—The theory of the allocation of time revisited. *Journal of Political Economy* 85 (6): 1099–1123.

Gunderson, M. 1977. Logit estimates of labor force participation based on census cross-tabulations. *Canadian Journal of Economics* 10 (3): 453–461.

Hashimoto, Yasuyuki. 2002. Consumption tax's tax on profit and its countermeasures. *Tax Research* 18 (2).

Hashimoto, Yasuyuki. 2009. *An applied general equilibrium analysis of Japan's finances*. Kasugai: Seibunsha Co. Ltd.

Hashimoto, Yasuyuki, Hiroaki Hayashi, and Naosumi Atoda. 1991. The aging of the population and the tax and pension systems: and analysis of the effects of system reforms from cohort data. *Economic Research* 42 (4): 330–340.

Hayashi, H., and K. Hashimoto. 1993. The effective rates of indirect taxes in Japan. *The Journal of Yokkaichi University* 5 (2): 1–10. (in Japanese).

Hayashi, Hiroaki, and Hashimoto, Yasuyuki. 1993. Estimations of the effective tax rate of indirect tax by consumption item: trends from 1953 to 1990. *Yokkaichi University Collection of Papers* 52, 1–10.

Hayashi, Masayoshi. 2002. A local government minimum efficiency scale: economies of scale and crowding effects in the supply of local public services. *Financial Review* 61, 59–89.

Heckman, J. 1974. Shadow prices, market, wages, and labor supply. *Econometrica* 42 (4): 679–694.

Hidaka, Masahiro. 2011. Estimations of Japan's tax expenditure. *Osaka Gakuin University Collection of Economic Papers* 25, 17–66.

Higuchi, Mio, and Hira Hayami. 1984. A comparison of the labor supply of women in Japan and the United States. *Mita Business Review* 27 (5): 30–50.

Hirota, H., and H. Yunoue. 2008. Does broader-based local government affect expenditure on public long-term care insurance? The case of Japan. *Economic Bulletin* 18 (11): 1–20.

Hirota, Haruaki. 2007. Verification of municipalities' selection behavior and merger factors. *Planning Administration* 30 (4): 75–81.

Ichida Y, K. Kondo, H. Hirai, T. Hanibuchi, G. Yoshikawa, and C. Murata. 2009. Social capital, income inequality and self-rated health in Chita Peninsula, Japan: A multilevel analysis of older people in 25 communities. *Social Science & Medicine* 69, 317–326.

Iwamoto, Y., S. Ozaki, and Y. Maekawa. 1995. The divergence of the household savings trends between "Family Income and Expenditure Survey" and "National Accounts" part 1. *Financial Review* 35: 51–82. (in Japanese).

Iwamoto, Y., S. Ozaki, and Y. Maekawa. 1996. The divergence of the household savings trends between 'Family Income and Expenditure Survey' and 'National Accounts' part 2. *Financial Review* 37: 82–112. (in Japanese).

Iwamoto, Yasushi, Ozaki, Satoshi, and Maekawa, Yuki. 1995. Regarding the divergence between the trends in household savings rates in the "Family Income and Expenditure Survey" and "National Accounts Statistics" (1): Investigating the differences in concepts and the bias in the questionnaires. *Financial Review* 35, 51–82.

Iwamoto, Yasushi, Ozaki, Satoshi, and Maekawa, Yuki. 1996. Regarding the divergence between the trends in household savings rates in the "Family Income and Expenditure Survey" and "National Accounts Statistics" (2): The consistency of the micro data and the macro data. *Financial Review* 37, 82–112.

Izumida, Shigyo. 2003. *The scale of insurers in the national health system. Reforms of the medical care system and the function of insurers*, 121–136. Tokyo: Toyo Keizai, Inc.

Kawaguchi, Aki. 2002. Is the Douglas-Arisawa Law effective? *Japan Labor Review* 44 (4), 18–21.

Kawaguchi, Yawarii, and Ii, Masako. 2010. A study of the current state of social security and life protection in low income households. *Japanese Journal of Health Economic and Policy* 22, 91–108.

Kawakami, Ken, Kobayashi, Ryo, and Hashimoto, Hideki (eds). 2006. *Social disparity and health.* Tohyo: University of Tokyo Press.

Keeley, M.C., P.K. Robins, R.G. Spiegelman, and R.W. West. 1978. The estimation of labor supply models using experimental data. *The American Economic Review* 68 (5): 873–887.

Kikuchi, Jun. 2008. The sustainability of facilities-based services and long-term care. *Quarterly Journal of the National Institute of Population and Social Security Research* 43 (4): 365–379.

Kikuchi, Jun, Tajika, Eiji, and Yui, Ishiji. 2005. The current situation and the sustainability of long-term care insurance. In *Intergenerational disparity in medical care and long-term care*, 147–166.

King, Mervyn. 1974. Taxation and the cost of capital. *Review of Economic Studies* 41: 21–35.

Kishida, Kensaku. 2002. The costs of administrative work and economies of scale in the National Health Insurance system: An analysis of National Health Insurance in the 7 prefectures of Kinki using panel data. *Journal of the Japan Center for Economic Research* 45, 246–261.

Kitamura, Yukinobu, and Miyazaki, Tsuyoshi. 2012. An evaluation of income inequality and tax's income redistribution function: 1984 to 2004. *Economic Research* 67, 56–69.

Kobayashi, Yoshiaki, and Natori, Ryota. 2004. *Decentralization and welfare for the elderly—The development process of local autonomy.* Tokyo: Keio University Press, Inc.

Komamura, Kohei. 2001. Empirical analysis of the non-payment of insurance contributions. In *A comprehensive policy for the post-welfare state*, ed. Maruo Naomi, Masura Masakao, Yoshida Masahiko, and Iijima Ohna, 107–120. Tokyo: Minerva Publishing.

Komamura, Kohei, and Yamada, Atsuhiro. 2007. The grounds for compulsory subscription to the pension system—An empirical analysis of non-payment and non-subscription to the national pension. *Journal of the Board of Audit of Japan* 35: 31-49.

Komatsu, Hidekazu. 2008. How are regional differences in elderly medical-services costs reflected in insurance contributions and analysis of regular adjustment subsidies in the latter-stage elderly medical care system. *The Kyoto University Economic Review* 182, 71–81.

Kondo, Katsunori. 2005. *Health disparity society: What disturbs the mind?* Tokyo: Igaku-Shoin Ltd.

Lyon, Andrew B., and Robert M. Schwab. 1995. Consumption taxes in a life-cycle framework: Are sin taxes regressive? *The Review of Economics and Statistics* 77 (3): 389–406.

Maekawa, Satoko. 2004. Changes in benefits and burdens by generation due to social security reforms. *Financial Review* 72, 5–19.

Maruyama, Katsura, and Komamura, Kohei. 2005. The problem of the hollowing-out of the national pension and the approach for the pension system. In *Designing a new system for the social security system*, 223–250.

Masuda, Masaki. 2008. Considerations from a comparison of long-term care in Japan, Germany, and South Korea. In *Long-term care around the World*, 189–207.

Mathur, Aparna, and Adele C. Morris. 2014. Distributional Effects of a Carbon Tax in Broader U.S. Fiscal Reform. *Energy Policy* 66: 326–334.

Mirrlees, J, S. Adam, T. Besley, R. Blundell, S. Bond, R. Chote, M. Gammie, P. Johnson, G. Myles, and J. Poterba. 2010. Dimensions of tax design. In *The Mirrlees review*. Oxford: Oxford University Press for Institute for Fiscal Studies.

Mirrlees, J, S. Adam, T. Besley, R. Blundell, S. Bond, R. Chote, M. Gammie, P. Johnson, G. Myles, and J. Poterba. 2011. Tax by design. In *The Mirrlees review*. OXford: Oxford University Press for Institute for Fiscal Studies.

Miyazaki, Tsuyoshi. 2006a. The effects of the reduction in expenditure from the mergers of municipalities—Detecting the merger trend variables. *Finance Research* 2: 145–160.

Miyazaki, Tsuyoshi. 2006b. Establishment of legal merger councils by efficient municipalities—In relation to the 1999 Special Mergers Law. *Journal of the Japan Center for Economic Research* 54: 20–38.

Miyazaki, Tsuyoshi. 2010. The effects of local allocation tax reforms on the mergers of municipalities—A review of phase corrections and the reduction in local allocation tax. *Journal of the Japan Center for Economic Research* 63: 79–99.

Mochizuki, Masamutsi, Nomura, Yasushi, and Fukae, Keiji. 2010. *An empirical analysis of income tax: Aiming to revitalize fundamental tax*. Tokyo: Nihon Keizai Hyouronsha Ltd.

Morinobu, Shigeki, and Satoko Maekawa. 2001. Macro estimations of Japan's income tax base. *Financial Review* 57: 103–122.

Murasawa, T., M. Yuda, and Y. Iwamoto. 2005. A trade-off between efficiency and equity in adopting differential rates to the consumption tax. *The Economic Analysis* 176: 19–41. (in Japanese).

Murasawa, Tomohiro, Yuda, Michio, and Iwamoto, Yasushi. 2005. The trade-off between efficiency and fairness from the application of the reduced consumption tax rate. *Economic Analysis* 76: 19–41.

Nagase, Nobuko. 1997. The labor supply of married women: estimations of short-term and long-term labor functions. *Economic Analysis (Hitotsubashi University)* 49: 49–58.

Nakajima, Kunio, and Uemura, Toshiyuki. 2006. The effects of pension reforms from 1973 to 2004 on household consumption and savings plans. *Life Economics Research* 24: 15–24.

Nishikawa, Masashi. 2002. Reducing expenditure through the mergers of municipalities and changes to the structure of municipalities. *Journal of the Board of Audit of Japan* 39: 37–56.

Office of Financial History, Ministry of Finance. 1977. *The Financial history of Showa: From the end of the War to reconciliation*: V*ol. 8 Tax (2) tax administration*. Tokyo: Toyo Keizai, Inc.

Office of Financial History, Ministry of Finance. 1990. *The financial history of Showa: Showa 27 to 48: Vol. 6 tax*. Tokyo: Toyo Keizai, Inc.

Office of Financial History, Ministry of Finance (eds.). 1982a. *The financial history of Showa: From the end of the War to reconciliation: Vol. 7 Tax (1)*. Tokyo: Toyo Keizai, Inc.

Office of Financial History, Ministry of Finance (eds.). 1982b. *The Financial history of Showa: From the end of the War to reconciliation: Vol. 8Tax (2) tax Administration*. Tokyo: Toyo Keizai, Inc.

Office of Financial History, Ministry of Finance (ed.). 1982c. *The financial history of Showa: From the end of the War to reconciliation: Vol. 8 material (2)*. Tokyo: Toyo Keizai Inc.

Office of Financial History, Ministry of Finance (ed.). 1997a. The financial history of Showa: Showa 27 to 48: Vol. 6 tax. Tokyo: Toyo Keizai Inc.

Office of Financial History, Ministry of Finance (ed.). 1997b. *The financial history of Showa: Showa 27 to 48: Vol. 15 material (3) tax and government bonds*. Tokyo: Toyo Keizai, Inc.

Ogura, Masatari, and Chiba, Tomotaro. 1991. The burden of insurance contributions in Japan as seen from the viewpoint of fairness. *Financial Review* 19: 7–53.

Ohara, Miki. 2001. Is the housewife a symbol of the wealthy family? The effects of taxation on the employment of wives and income inequality. *Japan Labor Review* 493: 15-29

Ohno, Taro, Nakazawa, Masahiko, Miyoshi, Koyo, Matsuo, Kohei, Matsuda, Kazuya, Kataoka, Takuya, Takamizawa, Yuichi, Hachisuka, Kei, Masuda, Tomoko. 2013. Households' budget distribution: A comparison of the "National Survey of Family Income and Expenditure. "Family Income and Expenditure Survey," and the "Comprehensive Survey of Living Conditions," PRI Discussion Paper Series.

Oishi, Akiko. 2003. The labor supply of married women and the tax and social security systems. *Quarterly Journal of the National Institute of Population and Social Security Research* 39 (3): 286–300.

Oishi, Akiko. 2006. Trends and problems in income inequality. In *Research on economic disparity: Understanding Japan's distribution structure*, ed. Kaizuka Hiroaki. Tokyo: Chuokeiza-sha, Inc.

Okamoto, Minoru. 1988. A quantitative analysis of the labor supply of housewives in Japan. *Aoyama Journal of International Studies* 10: 73–91.

Oshio, Takashi. 2004. Trends in income inequality in the 1990s. *Quarterly Journal of the National Institute of Population and Social Security Research* 40 (3): 277–285.

Oshio, Takashi. 2009. The redistribution effects of social security and the tax system. In *An analysis of the effects of financial resources for social security*, ed. National Institute of Population and Social Security Research. Tokyo: University of Tokyo Press.

Oshio, Takashi. 2010. *An analysis of the redistribution of welfare: questioning its fairness and efficiency*. Nihon Hyouronsha.

Oshio, Takashi, and Kunio Urakawa. 2008. Trends in the creation of poverty in the first half of the 2000s and the redistribution policy. *Quarterly Journal of the National Institute of Population and Social Security Research* 44 (3): 278–289.

Oshio, Takashi, Tajika, Eiji, and Fukawa, Tetsuo. 2006. *Japan's income distribution: the expansion of disparity and the role of policy*. Tokyo: University of Tokyo Press.

Oshio, T., and M. Kobayashi. 2009. Income inequality, area-level poverty, perceived aversion to inequality, and self-rated health in Japan. *Social Science & Medicine* 69: 317–326.

Otake, Fumio. 1994. Income and asset distribution in the 1980s. *Quarterly Journal of Economics* 45 (5): 385–402.

Otake, Fumio. 2005. *Japan's inequality: the illusion and the future of a disparity society*. Tokyo: Nikkei Inc.

Poterba, J.M. 1991. *Is the gasoline tax regressive?* NBER Working Paper No. 3578.

Rogers, D.L. 1994. Distributional effects of corrective taxation: Assessing lifetime incidence from cross sectional data. *National Tax Association-Tax Institute of America* 87: 192–202.

Rosen, S., and F. Welch. 1971. Labor supply and income redistribution. *Review of Economics and Statistics August*, 278–282.

Saito, Yuri, and Uemura, Toshiyuki. 2011. The burden of indirect tax by income group. *Journal of the Board of Audit of Japan* 44: 27–40.

Saitoh, Y., and T. Uemura. 2011. Indirect tax burden of income groups in Japan. *The Journal of the Board of Audit* 44: 27–40. (in Japanese).

Shiga Prefecture. 2010. *Shiga Prefecture support policy for National Health Insurance area expansion, etc.*

Shikata, Masato, Murakami, Masatoshi, Komamura, Kohei, and Inagaki, Seiichi. 2010. An analysis of decision making on non-payments, exemptions, deferments, and additional payments of national pension insurance contributions. *RCSS Discussion Paper Series* 105: 1–18.

Shikata, Masato, Satoshiro Tanaka, and Yui Otsu. 2012. Analysis of non-payment of National Health Insurance contributions. *Japanese Journal of Health Economic and Policy* 23 (2): 120–145.

Shimada, Haruo, and Sakai, Yukio. 1980. An analysis of the labor force structure and employment behavior—A cross sectional analysis of households' employment behavior from individual questionnaires. *Economic Analysis* 79: 81–88.

Shirohase, Sawako. 2002. Japan's income inequality and elderly households—From the viewpoint of an international comparison. *Japan Labor Review* 500: 72–85.

Social Security Weekly Editing Bureau. 2012b. Clarification of the role and the responsibilities of the prefecture and municipalities for area expansion: a movement toward the unit of the prefecture for National Health Insurance (second half). *Social Security Weekly* 2670: 28–33.

Social Security Weekly Editing Bureau. 2012a. Can finances be stabilized by expanding the shared burden of medical-services costs? A movement toward a unit of prefectures for National Health Insurance (first part). *Social Security Weekly* 2669: 28–33.

Subramanian.V., and I. Kawachi. 2004. Income inequlity and health: What have we learned so far? *Epidemiologic Reviews* 26: 78–91.

Summers, L.H. 1981. Taxation and corporate investment: A q-theory approach. *Brooking Papers on Economic Activity*, 321–334.

Suzuki, Kazuyuji. 2001. *Capital investment and the financial markets: Information asymmetry and uncertainty*. Tokyo: University of Tokyo Press.

Suzuki, Wataru. 2001. An empirical analysis of the consistency of purpose and incentives in the National Health Insurance subsidies system. *Life Economic Research* 16: 91–103.

Suzuki, Wataru, and Zhou, Yanfei. 2001. An economic analysis of national pension non-subscribers. *Journal of the Japan Center for Economic Research* 42: 44–60.

Suzuki, Wataru, Masushima, Minoru, Shiroshi, Kosuke, and Morishige, Akihiro. 2012. The benefits and burdens by generation through social security. *ESRI Discussion Paper Series* 281: 1–51.

Suzuki, Yoshimitsu. 2011. Estimations of profit tax in consumption tax. *Journal of the Board of Audit of Japan* 43: 45–56.

Tajika, Eiji, and Jun Kikuchi. 2003. The development of long-term care insurance finances: Factors for increasing at-home long-term care benefits. *Quarterly Journal of the National Institute of Population and Social Security Research* 39 (2): 174–188.

Tajika, Eiji, and Kikuchi, Jun. 2004. Estimations of the total cost of long-term care insurance and the benefits to burden ratio by age group. *Financial Review* 74: 147–163.

Tajika, Eiji, and Yuji Yui. 1999. The aging population and the National Health Insurance and long-term care insurance: From a financial viewpoint. *Quarterly Journal of the National Institute of Population and Social Security Research* 35 (2): 128–140.

Tajika, Eiji, and Yui, Yuji. 2001. What happened in the first year following the introduction of long-term care insurance? A case study of three municipal health insurance associations in eastern Hokkaido. *Health Insurance* 55: 40–47.

Tajika, Eiji, and Yui, Yuji. 2003. Issues for long-term care insurance as seen from Okinawa, Kenporen. *Health Insurance* 9: 52–61.

Takayama, Noriyuki, and Arita, Fumiko. 1992. The actual situation in households in which both spouses work and the selection of employment by wives. *Journal of the Japan Center for Economic Research* 22: 19–45.

Takayama, Noriyuki, and Shiraishi, Kosuke. 2010. Levels of the consumption tax burden in Japanese households. *Hitotsubashi University Economic Research Institute Intergenerational Research Organization Discussion Paper CIS-PIE DP*, vol. 491.

Tanaka, Hideaki. 2010. The burden of tax and social insurance contributions and the structure of social security benefits: toward the integrated reform of the tax system and the social security system. *Hitotsubashi University Economic Research Institute Intergenerational Research Organization Discussion Paper*, CIS-PIE DP, vol. 481.

Tanaka, Satoshi. 2005. The current status of and problems with the National Health Insurance system. *National Diet Library: Survey and Information* 488: 1–11.

Tanaka, Satoshiro, Shikata, Masato, and Komamura, Kohei. 2013. An analysis of the tax and social security burden on the elderly: using individual questionnaire data from the "National Survey of Family Income and Expenditure. *Financial Review* 115: 117–133.

Tanaka, Satoshiro, Shikata, Masato, and Otsu, Yui. 2011. An analysis of the non-payment and willingness to pay National Health Insurance contributions. *RISS Discussion Paper Series 2* 6: 1–22.

Uemura, T. 2006. Household indirect tax burden and the future of consumption tax in Japan. *The Journal of the Board of Audit,* 33: 11–29. (in Japanese).

Uemura, Toshiyuki. 2004. Corporate income tax and corporate investment by industry: A reconsideration—tax-adjusted Q and cash flow. *Comprehensive Tax System Research*, 20–42.

Uemura, Toshiyuki. 2006. The future of household's indirect tax burden and consumption tax: Trends in the effective tax rate from the Goods and Services Tax (GST) era to the consumption tax era. *Journal of the Board of Audit of Japan* 33: 11–29.

Uemura, Toshiyuki. 2008. Estimations of tax expenditure in income tax: from the viewpoint of financial transparency. *Journal of the Board of Audit of Japan* 38: 11–24.

Uemura, Toshiyuki. 2009. *The economics of the public pension and financial resources*. Tokyo: Nikkei Publishing Inc.

Uemura, Toshiyuki. 2012a. An empirical analysis from a factor analysis of the tax revenue structure of income tax: calculations of the loss in tax revenue from income deductions and increases to revenue from changes to the tax rate. *APIR Discussion Paper Series*, 24.

Uemura, Toshiyuki. 2012. An empirical analysis from a factor analysis of tax-revenue deductions for income: Calculations of the loss of tax revenue from income deductions and increases to revenue from changes to the tax rate. *Economics Studies (Journal of Kwansei Gakuin University)* 66 (2): 119–135.

Uemura, Toshiyuki. 2013. *Is it really necessary to increase consumption tax?*. Tokyo: Kobunsha Co., Ltd.

Uemura, Toshiyuki. 2014a. The effects of income tax deductions and tax rate on tax revenues. *Tax Research* 30: 16–25.

Uemura, Toshiyuki. 2014. The effects of income tax and individual resident tax deductions on tax revenues. *Economics Studies* 68 (3): 319–332.

Uemura, Toshiyuki. 2015. The direction of and prospects for social security reforms and financial reconstruction. *Social Security Weekly* 69 (2807): 60–65.

Uemura, Toshiyuki. 2015b. Employment and pension income taxation. In *The transformation of employment and the public pension*, ed. Nishimura Jun, 21–41. Tokyo: Toyo Keizai, Inc.

Uemura, Toshiyuki, and Adachi, Yoshimi. 2015. *An economic analysis of the tax and social security burden*. Tokyo: Nihon Keizai Hyouronsha Ltd.

Uemura, Toshiyuki, and Washimi, Hidemori. 2003. The state of the establishment of merger councils and local allocation tax. *Journal of the Board of Audit of Japan* 28: 85–99.

Urakawa, Kunio. 2012. Factors behind the lack of important knowledge on the public medical care insurance system (special feature: the socio-economic factors behind health disparity. *Medical Care and Society* 22: 41–55.

Van Soest, A. 1995. Structural models of family labor supply. *Journal of Human Resources* 30: 63–88.

Wilkinson, R.G. 1992. Income distribution and life expectancy. *British Medical Journal* 304: 165–168.

Wilkinson, R.G., and E.K. Pickett. 2006. Income inequality and health: A review and explanation of the evidence. *Social Science & Medicine* 62: 1768–1784.

Yamada, Takeshi. 1998. A study of National Health Insurance and local finances investigating the general affairs costs and the economies of scale in the National Health Insurance. *Institute for Economic and Financial Research*, 17–31.

Yamashita, Koji. 2011. An empirical analysis of the financial behavior of merging organizations—A policy evaluation of the Special Mergers Law. *Journal of the Japan Center for Economic Research* 65: 43–64.

Yamauchi, Yasuhiro. 2006. Administrative work costs and economies of scale for public long-term care insurance—An analysis using panel data on nationwide insurers. *Journal of the Japan Center for Economic Research* 55: 99–110.

Yamauchi, Yasuhiro. 2008. Incentives for area expansion for social security finances—Preliminary considerations from data on nationwide long-term care insurers. *International Public Policy Research* 12 (2): 127–143.

Yoshimura, Hiroshi. 1999. *The optimal urban scale and the mergers of municipalities*. Tokyo: Toyo Keizai, Inc.

Yuda, Michio. 2006. A quantitative analysis of non-subscribers to the national pension and the National Health Insurance. *Economic Research* 57 (4): 344–357.

Yuda, Michio. 2010. The effects of the problems in the National Health Insurance system on national health finances: A preliminary analysis. *Chukyo University School of Economics Review* 21: 1–15.

Index

Y. Adachi, *The Economics of Tax and Social Security in Japan*,
https://doi.org/10.1007/978-981-10-7176-8

The manufacturer's authorised representative in the EU is Springer Nature Customer Service Centre GmbH, Europaplatz 3, 69115 Heidelberg, Germany. If you have any concerns regarding our products, please contact ProductSafety@springernature.com

Printed and bound by CPI Group (UK) Ltd, Croydon, CR0 4YY
30/09/2026
02225449-0009